A YEAR OF

Hands-on
Science

SCHOLASTIC

A YEAR OF
Hands-on
Science

by Lynne Kepler

NEW YORK • TORONTO • LONDON • AUCKLAND • SYDNEY
MEXICO CITY • NEW DELHI • HONG KONG • BUENOS AIRES

Teaching *Resources*

ACKNOWLEDGMENTS

I am grateful to all those individuals who, in sharing their expertise, talents, and time, helped to make this book. I would like to especially acknowledge the following individuals:

* Joan Novelli, editor, who collaborated with me on this book from the very beginning. I truly appreciate her guidance, her thoughtfulness, and her creativity. She made this book fun and untiring. I hope we can do it again!

* Terry Cooper, editor-in-chief, and Deborah Schecter, senior editor, Scholastic Professional Books, who supported this project from the start and are committed to helping primary teachers teach science.

* Jackie Swensen, designer, for helping to turn a massive manuscript into the friendly, elegant pages of this book.

* Lauren Leon, copy editor, for her creative abilities. She always seems to be able to "see" what I am writing about.

* Mary Faulk, elementary librarian, who took time to help find some great, science-related children's books.

* My family, Doug, Jake, Ty, and Muir. They encouraged me throughout this project by always wondering, asking questions, and reminding me to look at the world around us.

Edited by Joan Novelli
Cover design by Vincent Ceci and Jaime Lucero
Cover illustration by Jane Conteh-Morgan
Back cover photo by John C. Evans
Interior design by Solutions by Design, Inc.
Interior illustrations by James Graham Hale

ISBN-13: 978-0-545-07475-9
ISBN-10: 0-545-07475-4

CONTENTS

From the Author

I remember doing very little science in school—from the time I was an elementary student right through high school. Even as I entered college as an elementary education major I was unaware of the role science played in my life or that of my future students. But a couple of college courses in reading and language arts (yes, that's right) let me experience for myself the important role hands-on experiences play in a child's conceptual development. Children's enthusiasm for activities like comparing pets, collecting and sorting leaves in the schoolyard, and observing guppies in the classroom aquarium poured over into the rest of their school day. They graphed their pets' weights, wrote about the leaves, and read about fish. The science of the world around them linked language, math, even social skills in meaningful ways.

Young children have an innate sense of wonder; they are born to explore, ask questions, and find out—just what science is all about. Providing a classroom that is rich with hands-on science is only natural. Science experiences are exciting and meaningful, and give children a reason to learn in every subject area. Most importantly, the knowledge, skills, and attitudes that children gain while *doing* science will help them in *using* science to understand the world around them—a lifelong benefit that will help them make personal choices that will affect their everyday lives and their world.

—L.K.

CHAPTER 1

Science Leads The Way

Knowledge without love will not stick.
But if love comes first, knowledge is sure to follow.
—John Burroughs, naturalist

Think about what your students love—and it's easy to see how powerful hands-on science can be in the classroom. Children come to school with a love for doing science: playing in puddles, watching bugs, blowing bubbles, bouncing balls, digging in dirt—all connections to key science concepts and bridges to learning across the curriculum. When we see the world through children's eyes and develop classroom experiences around their interests and curiosities, knowledge *is* sure to follow—knowledge that will help to form a foundation for understanding and an appreciation for their world.

What about the equipment? What happens if the experiments don't go as planned? Won't it make a mess? As you browse through the activities in this book, you'll see that science at the primary level doesn't mean expensive tools and setups. What sparks meaningful science experiences for young children is right there in the world around them—weather, plants, animals, water, and soil, each a source of fascinating explorations and an inspiration to learn. Even unexpected results invite discovery. Kids learn how to refine investigations. They may even find themselves going in some new directions.

Messy? Maybe (though nothing a little newspaper can't contain). But when you hear the hum of students' excitement as they explore, discover, and want to learn more, you'll be convinced that this is the way students learn best.

The National Science Education Standards support this hands-on, inquiry-based approach to science education. The standards, developed by the National Research Council, part of the National Academy of Sciences, are a set of criteria intended to guide the quality of science teaching and learning. According to the standards, "Americans are increasingly confronted with questions in their public and personal lives for which scientific information and ways of thinking are necessary for informed decision making. A common question at the supermarket symbolizes this aspect of science literacy: 'Paper or plastic?' Perhaps most important, the personal fulfillment and excitement offered by science are benefits to be shared by everyone." It is crucial that we set the goal of providing science experiences for all of our children so that they all may grow up knowing how to make sense of, appreciate, and enjoy their world.

Though the standards do not mandate a curriculum, they are compatible with most states' objectives for science education and reflect an approach that a growing number of educators embrace. What this means is that, in many cases, the standards will support the active learning already happening in classrooms. To guide educators in helping students achieve scientific literacy, the standards offer recommendations for content, teaching, assessment, and professional development. A look at each area, plus ways this book supports the standards' goals, follows.

Scientific Literacy

Scientific literacy means that a person can ask and find or determine answers to questions derived from curiosity about everyday experiences.

—from The National Science Education Standards

Content

The standards outline eight essential science content areas that all students should understand. For grades K–4 these areas are:

1 **science as inquiry:** abilities necessary to do scientific inquiry; understanding about scientific inquiry

2 **physical science:** properties of objects and materials; position or motion of objects; light, heat, electricity, and magnetism

3 **life science:** characteristics of organisms; life cycles of organisms; organisms and environment

4 **earth and space science:** properties of Earth materials; objects in the sky

5 **science and technology:** abilities to distinguish between natural objects and objects made by humans; abilities of technological design; understanding about science and technology

6 **science in personal and social perspectives:** health; characteristics and changes in populations; types of resources; changes in environments; science and technology in local challenges

7 **history and nature of science:** science as a human endeavor

8 **unifying concepts and processes:** order and organization; evidence, models, and explanation; change, constancy, and measurement; evolution and equilibrium; form and function

As you use this book, you'll recognize components of the content standards woven into activities, though you may not necessarily see the same language. For example, an activity may not ask you to introduce "characteristics of organisms." But in Chapter 3 students do discover characteristics of organisms as they explore patterns on butterflies' wings and compare butterflies to themselves. Other chapters revisit this content standard as children look at bears, birds, and the human heart—even decomposers like worms and fungi. The content standard "properties of objects and materials" is supported throughout as children make observations (the soil has rocks in it) and use tools such as rulers, metersticks, and thermometers to measure size, weight, shape, color, temperature, and so on.

Other content standards are introduced and revisited throughout the book to reinforce and enrich students' understandings. The matrix on page 23 summarizes key concepts introduced in each chapter for four of the eight science content areas (life, earth, physical, and technology), with the remaining four integrated throughout. As an additional planning and organizing tool, the "Science Concepts and Skills" sections in each chapter list primary content standards covered in each theme.

Science and Teaching Methods

How you teach science in your classroom will have a major impact on the content, processes, and attitudes students acquire. "Effective teachers of science create an environment where they and their students work together as active learners."

(From The National Science Education Standards.) Guidelines for developing an effective science program follow.

Learning science is an active process. Students should have many hands-on learning experiences. These kinds of concrete experiences with manipulatives need to come before more abstract lessons. This idea is familiar to many teachers as a natural extension of Piaget's developmental stages.

A major portion of science instruction is inquiry-based. Inquiry involves "making observations, posing questions, examining books and other sources of information, planning investigations, reviewing what is already known in light of experimental evidence, proposing answers and explanations, and communicating the results." (From The National Science Education Standards.) For example, activities in Chapter 10 will have children exploring puddles, wondering why the puddles shrink, reading related children's literature, measuring puddles to validate what they see happening—*This puddle was 18 inches across this morning. Now it is 15 inches. It is shrinking.*—and recording results in a science journal. Teachers are encouraged to teach basic concepts within the context of inquiry and investigation.

Students have opportunities to apply science knowledge and to make connections between their everyday lives and what they learned. By integrating themes that children are interested in, you can develop an environment that encourages questions and promotes understanding. (By the way, if you ask children to list the topics they are interested in learning about, you'll discover that many of these topics are science-oriented!)

Teachers build on students' prior understandings, revisiting concepts and giving them opportunities to rethink misconceptions. The seasons, the water cycle, the changing appearance of the moon: These topics, as well as others, are not easily understood by children. In fact, many adults continue to hold misconceptions about why we have phases of the moon or what causes the changing seasons. In "Revisiting Science Concepts" *(Science and Children,* November/December 1994), G. Robert Moore writes, "By revisiting science topics, we are recognizing that students grow physically and mentally both within the year and from one year to the next...one activity or unit is not enough to ensure full conceptual understanding; students need a chance to modify and clarify their understandings over time."

Integrate science with other subjects. When you coordinate science with other subjects in the elementary grades, such as language arts and math, students see connections between the subjects—more closely representing the world they encounter daily. The result? Enhanced student achievement.

Assessment

One of the most exciting parts of teaching is observing how children think and learn. As a teacher you are well aware of the need for assessment. The National Science Education Standards stress that teachers who teach science need to "provide students with an opportunity to demonstrate their understanding and skill in doing science." The standards then state that "teachers use many strategies to gather and interpret the large amount of information about student understanding of science that is present in thoughtful instructional activities."

Traditionally, the emphasis has been placed on the memorization of facts and terminology rather than on the understanding of broad concepts and processes. But hands-on science experiences invite a more varied approach to assessment. Just as we provide a variety of learning experiences, it is essential that we include various forms of assessment, giving all students an opportunity to demonstrate what they have learned. As they participate in and observe activities, teachers can assess students' learning as it is happening.

In their book *Active Assessment for Active Science* (Heinemann, 1994), George E. Hein and Sabral Price state, "It's time for new assessment in science education. To do science, children must interact with the physical world—drop objects, observe butterfly larvae, measure length and speed, plant seeds and watch the seedlings sprout, build electric circuits and test them—and they must participate in the world of ideas—design experiments, test theories, hypothesize, predict, discuss, and argue. The only way to assess the rich and varied experiences that constitute doing science is to devise ways for the actions and their products to become part of assessment. If the assessment of science is limited to passive responses, we will never fully understand what our students know. Assessing science through paper-and-pencil tests is akin to assessing a basketball player's skills by giving a written test. We may find out what someone knows about basketball, but we won't know how well that person plays the game." (Page 12.)

Hein and Price's book describes a variety of ideas for collecting information regarding students' understanding of concepts and their ability to use science. Following is a sampling of assessment strategies you'll want to consider and plan for when teaching science. As you use *A Year of Hands-on Science,* you'll find many of these suggestions woven into the activities. Keep a list of these and other strategies handy to remind you of all the ways students share assessment information with you every day, and for times you want to incorporate additional assessment tools.

* brainstorming

* concept maps

* demonstrations

* diagrams and drawings

* discussions with individuals or groups of students

* journal entries

* photographs of students doing activities

* prediction activities

* products created by students

Note: This book includes 22 reproducible science journal pages, at least one for each theme. They will provide you with important assessment information, and serve as records for tracking progress throughout the year.

As you prepare your curriculum, plan on when and how you will be assessing your students. Make sure assessments match the goals you have set. For example, in Discover Butterflies, Activity 1 (see Chapter 3, page 32), students build homes for their caterpillars and then watch as the butterflies emerge. Assessment for this activity might look at several areas: how individual students contribute to the group, how well each group follows the directions, and how much detail students use in recording observations in their journals. Following are some questions to guide your journal assessment.

* Can students explain their predictions?

* Do estimates improve in accuracy?

* Do students show increased use of detail in recording observations? Does their language become richer and more detailed?

* As children's process skills develop, do they add to their descriptions by using both nontraditional and traditional measuring devices? (For example, early observations of temperature might be general: hot, cold, whereas later observations might include degrees, wind direction, etc.)

* Do students reflect an understanding of the way key concepts connect their world? For example, does a child recognize that, like butterflies, people experience changes in life, too?

Try to use a variety of assessment techniques for each theme you teach. This will allow students several opportunities to demonstrate what they have learned and will accentuate their strengths rather than their weaknesses.

Finally, while you give students opportunities to reflect on what they have learned, consider giving yourself the same opportunity. Keep your own science journal. Make notes about each activity. Were students able to follow directions? What are they most excited about? If an experiment didn't go as planned, what unexpected discoveries did you and your students make? What changes do you want to make next time? You can refer back to these notes to apply what you have learned, improve instruction, and plan future lessons and themes.

Professional Development

The National Science Education Standards for professional development include learning science, learning to teach science, and learning to learn. "The overarching concept of learning to teach science as with the student learning is that of articulating questions, pursuing answers to those questions, interpreting information gathered, proposing applications, and fitting the new learning into the larger picture of science teaching." (From the National Science Education Standards.) So in order to be an effective teacher of science, you, just like your students, need to be an active learner. Let your questions and those of your students guide the science you teach. Then learn together by doing!

Science Connects the Curriculum

As you prepare to teach great science in your primary classroom, you might be thinking about its impact on the other subjects in your curriculum. Now more than ever before, the strategy of theme teaching and integrating subjects is receiving attention as a way to accomplish the goals already discussed in this chapter. The National Standards encourage teachers to coordinate the subjects they teach in order to enhance student achievement and to maximize use of time for student learning. When children are involved in hands-on science activities, they are developing many skills shared by all areas of the elementary curriculum. (The chart on page 18 lists and describes these skills.)

Here's how science connects with the other curriculum areas you are teaching.

SCIENCE AND LANGUAGE ARTS

Following directions, recording data, organizing facts, recognizing cause and effect relationships, summarizing new information, sequencing ideas, and recognizing main ideas.... You'll recognize these as reading skills, but they are also important science skills. Giving children opportunities to apply these skills in reading and hands-on science activities enhances achievement in both subjects as a result.

Science also provides the concrete (and high-interest) experiences that invite children to read and write with purpose and meaning. Journal entries, illustrations, story problems, diagrams, lists, poems, songs, and maps are just some of the kinds of writing that science activities can inspire. Writing can be an individual or a collaborative effort. Writing allows students to communicate their observations and thoughts, enhancing language development and strengthening understanding of key concepts in the process. And as an added bonus, their writing provides you with assessment material:

* Do students use detail in their writing?

* Does their writing reflect understanding of key concepts?

* Do students explain their reasoning?

Students' reading abilities are further enhanced by wonderful children's books with science connections. These books help students to further explore science concepts, both on their own and in a group, and to build on their reading and science strengths in the process. In "Science Trade Books and the Educational Market," Alfred A. Bortz writes, "Trade books speak the language of science in individual ways. They are written for finders and are thus invaluable resources for teachers who want to involve their students in finding out" (*Appraisal,* Spring 1988). Whether a book is fictional, like Jim Arnosky's *Every Autumn Comes the Bear,* or nonfictional, like Franklyn Branley's *The Moon Seems to Change,* using literature in conjunction with hands-on science activities promotes a love of science and books that can last a lifetime.

SCIENCE AND MATH

Science and math are a natural fit in the elementary classroom. The standards recommend that "the science program should be coordinated with the mathematics programs to enhance student use and understanding of mathematics in the study of science and to improve student understanding of mathematics overall." When your students are involved in doing science, they will also be using math skills in a meaningful way. In their book *Math and Science for Young Children,* Rosalind Charlesworth and Karen Lind state, "Math and science are interrelated in that the basic math concepts of comparing, classifying, and measuring are basic process skills of science. That is, basic math concepts are needed in order to solve problems in science. The other science process skills (observing, communicating, inferring, hypothesizing, and defining and controlling variables) are equally important for solving problems in both science and mathematics."

For example, let's say your students are learning about pumpkins. Children might begin by observing pumpkins closely and describing shape, color, and texture and then holding the pumpkins to compare how heavy each feels, ranking them by weight. They can then use scales to find the actual weights of the pumpkins, comparing the information they collect to their original ordering. Students can compare pumpkin size and weight, and determine if there is any relationship between size and weight. All this without even going inside the pumpkin—where just as many math and science connections await.

As you prepare to use the ideas presented in this book, always remember and be guided by the fact that young children have a natural love of science, and get ready for the desire for knowledge that will follow!

Process Skills

SKILL	DESCRIPTION
observing	using the senses to notice details and enhance understanding
comparing	identifying similarities and differences helps children construct meaning
classifying	sorting and grouping objects according to some specified characteristic or system; encourages attention to detail and creative problem solving
communicating	exchanging information in some form, such as speaking, drawing, writing, and making graphs
measuring	finding out the size or the extent of something
inferring	making an assumption based on reasoning
predicting	telling what may happen in the future, based on prior experiences or observations
collecting data	gathering information from observing, questioning, and reading
recording data	organizing collected information in some format like a graph, table, chart, or paragraph
interpreting	using the information collected to draw a conclusion
making models	making representations of objects with different materials

PROFESSIONAL RESOURCES

Active Assessment for Active Science: A Guide for Elementary School Teachers by George E. Hein and Sabral Price (Heinemann, 1994). An excellent and practical source for teachers who want to implement authentic assessment in their science curriculum.

A Head Start on Science: Encouraging a Sense of Wonder edited by William C. Ritz (NSTA Press, 2007). A resource replete with engaging lessons that support developmentally appropriate practice in the early childhood classroom.

Appraisal This periodical features reviews by scientists and children's librarians of fiction and nonfiction for grades K–12 in every issue. For information, contact Appraisal, Longfellow Hall, 13 Appian Way, Cambridge, MA 02138.

Math and Science for Young Children by Rosalind Charlesworth and Karen Lind (Cengage Delmar, 2006 [5th edition]). Weaves in child-development theory and classroom examples with the knowledge and skills needed to teach these subjects. A handy resource for primary teachers interested in knowing how their students learn.

National Science Education Standards by the National Committee on Science Education Standards and Assessment National Research Council (National Academies Press, 1996). Veteran educators and new teachers alike will consider this book to be a helpful guide. Use it to inform and enhance curriculum development.

TECHNOLOGY CONNECTIONS

Learningscience.org
(www.learningscience.org/index.htm)
Want to find the best online resources out there? Utilize this site, a collaborative project of the Central Bucks School District of Pennsylvania, the teachers of the Central Bucks School District, The College of Education at Temple University, and George Mehler Ed.D. Don't miss the site's Science Education Hall of Fame with hotlinks to some of the best science sites on the Web.

Mid-Continent Research for Education and Learning (McREL)
(www.mcrel.org/)
McREL is a nationally recognized nonprofit organization that has compiled and evaluated national and state standards—and proposed what teachers should provide for their students to become proficient in science, among other curriculum areas. To learn more about the science topics and benchmarks within each standard, visit the Web site. Or, read *Content Knowledge: A Compendium of Standards and Benchmarks for K–12 Education* (4th edition), Mid-Continent Research for Education and Learning, 2006.

National Academy of Sciences (NAS)
(www.nap.edu)
Through the auspices of the National Academies Press, the National Academy of Science publishes hundreds of science-related reports, books, and teaching resources per year. (Many of which are available for free download in Adobe PDF format.)

National Science Teachers Association (NSTA)
(www.nsta.org/pd/)
This site provides teachers with quick links to a myriad of NSTA professional development opportunities and classroom resources. In the publications section of the site, you can peruse the archives of NSTA's professional journals. (More than a dozen articles in Science & Children address assessment.) And, don't miss the site's Learning Center and the Web Seminars—offering online learning tools to help you teach key content more effectively. You'll want to bookmark this site.

CHAPTER 2

Using This Book

This book contains 18 themed teaching units, two themes per chapter, organized seasonally around the traditional school year. September starts off the year with the themes Discover Butterflies and Moon Watch. Why? September is the time for caterpillars, making this a natural time for students to learn about the changes in butterflies, and in themselves, as they grow. The September full moon is spectacular. Introduce a moon unit now, and students will enjoy looking for patterns in the moon's appearance throughout the year.

You'll find natural connections like these in each month's themes, with plenty of hands-on science activities that correspond to what children are already observing in their world. Although they are presented seasonally, you can use the material in any order—whatever best meets your needs.

Here's an overview of what you'll find in each chapter, plus tips on using journals, a science concept chart to copy and post, a supplies checklist, and ideas for webbing with students.

Chapter Openers

Each chapter opens with a mini table of contents, listing the themes and the pages on which you'll find them. On the next page you'll find Highlights of the Month, including dates, reminders, and seasonal suggestions to note on your class calendar, plus suggestions for planning ahead.

Next, the reproducible Science at Home newsletter is designed to:

* introduce the themes and activities for the month;

* enhance communication between school and home;

* promote parents' involvement in what their children are learning in school; and

* serve as a planning tool for the teacher.

As you prepare to start a new chapter, review the newsletter and adapt it to meet your needs. Jot down requests for theme-related materials and note special events or reminders in the space provided before copying. You could even invite a couple of children each time to add theme-related illustrations.

You might want to attach a note to the first newsletter, explaining the theme approach, what parents will find in the newsletter each month, and how they can use the information to support their child's learning. Both children and their families will look forward to each month's newsletter to discover what's in store!

Theme Organization

Each theme follows a similar format to make it easy to find what you're looking for as you teach. First you'll find an introduction that connects each theme to children's everyday lives, followed by: Science Concepts and Skills; Science Dictionary; Science on Display; several complete science activities; Book Breaks; Curriculum Connections; a reproducible Science Journal page; at least one other reproducible; and resources for children and teachers, including book and technology recommendations. More detail on each section follows.

Science Concepts and Skills

Typically, each theme explores one or two concepts through the suggested activities. This chart lets you see at a glance how the concepts developed in each chapter connect with the National Science Standards. Note that there are four broad areas under which the concepts are grouped: physical science, life science, earth/space science, and science/technology.

Science Concepts and Skills

CHAPTER	PHYSICAL	LIFE	EARTH/SPACE	TECHNOLOGY
SEPTEMBER **Discover Butterflies** **Moon Watch**		characteristics of organisms; life cycles	moon as an object in the night sky; patterns of moon's appearance	
OCTOBER **Falling Leaves** **Degrees of Weather**	recognizing observable properties; grouping by properties	life cycles	patterns in weather over time; describing weather in measurable terms	using tools to enhance observation
NOVEMBER **Harvest Time** **Bears in Winter**	recognizing observable properties	plants as food; basic needs of animals	recognizing characteristics of the seasons	
DECEMBER **Ice and Snow** **For the Birds**	changes in the state of matter	basic needs of animals		using tools to enhance observation
JANUARY **The Night Sky** **Push and Pull**	position and motion can be changed by push and pull		stars as objects in the night sky	inventing tools to solve problems
FEBRUARY **In the Shadows** **Healthy Hearts**	light travels in straight lines	basic needs of humans		using tools to measure
MARCH **Windy Weather** **Flying Things**	motion		changes in weather	inventions; using tools to measure
APRIL **Rain Comes and Goes** **Seeds and Soil**	recognizing observable properties	basic needs of plants	changes in weather; recognizing components of the Earth's surface	using tools to measure
MAY **Animals at Home** **Sun Power**		basic needs of animals; characteristics of organisms	the sun as an object in the sky appears to move in same pattern	using tools to measure

Each theme's activities also engage students in using a range of process skills, including observing, comparing, classifying, communicating, inferring, predicting, making models, measuring, collecting and recording data, and interpreting. For easy reference in lesson planning, you might want to reproduce and post the annotated list of process skills that appears on page 18. You may also want to add this list to your personal teaching journal.

Science Dictionary

A large clip (like the kind used to close snack bags) and a piece of cardboard make a handy portable clipboard for the class science dictionary.

Words that are significant to the concepts in each theme are defined in easy-to-understand language. You may want to let students do the activities, explore the concepts, and describe their experiences **before** you define the words for them. This will greatly enhance their understanding of the words and the concepts.

You might want to do more with science vocabulary by having students create a chart-size dictionary. First, create a blank book with pages labeled *A* through *Z*. As new words are introduced, add them to the dictionary, letting students write in and illustrate the definitions. Also include words that aren't listed in this book but that your students discover themselves! See the science dictionary on pages 297–302, for a complete list of science words from each chapter in alphabetical order for easy reference.

Science on Display

Each theme includes how-tos for a theme-related, interactive science display that you and your students can create together. This center doesn't have to be a large area, just someplace where students can explore the special display and other materials, read and write about science, and share their discoveries with classmates. Let students be in charge of finding books that are related to each topic and can become a part of the center.

Activities

Following an introduction to each activity, you'll find a list of materials. In most cases, the materials are inexpensive—often free—and easy to find. You'll probably have quite a few of them

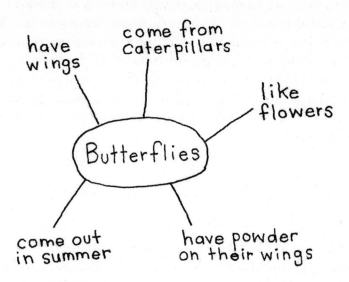

You might want to use webs as a strategy for introducing activities, writing the theme in the center and what children know in the space outside. After the activities, web what students have learned and what they still want to know. Use three different colors to distinguish one step from the next.

available already. (See Stock Up for Science, page 26.) In some cases they're used for more than one activity, saving you setup time (and the cost of additional materials). As you prepare to send out the reproducible parent newsletter each month, check to see if there are materials you'll need that month that parents might be willing to donate, like newspapers, boxes, birdseed. In some cases you may also want to request parent participation in the activities. Note these things in the Wish List section of the newsletter before copying.

Most of the activities begin by asking students to make predictions and share what they know about the topic. This gives students a chance to activate their prior knowledge about a topic and gives you a chance to find out what they already know.

Many activities are designed for small groups of two to three students. Often these groups come together at the end of the activity to share and reflect on their discoveries. Feel free to change the grouping to best suit your situation. What is most important is that students have time, space, and materials to do the activities.

Book Break

Take time out to read the great children's literature recommended in the Book Breaks sprinkled throughout each chapter. Suggested titles often connect with specific activities and include a brief description of the book and discussion or follow-up activities.

Curriculum Connections

Because science has natural links to other subject areas, you'll probably find yourself making connections as you teach each theme. To facilitate this interdisciplinary approach, each theme offers a variety of cross-curricular activities. From reproducible poems and folktales to math, art, movement, and dramatic arts activities, these pages give children opportunities to build on skills in other subject areas, as well as to continue to develop understanding of key concepts introduced in the theme.

Stock Up for Science

While each activity comes with its own list of materials, you might want to stock your classroom with some general supplies. Here's a list of these general supplies, most of them free or low-cost. Consider sending the list home with a note, requesting that parents donate what they can.

* newspapers (for keeping work areas clean)
* reclosable plastic bags in assorted sizes
* jars
* plastic one-liter bottles
* used manila file folders (for making patterns)
* plastic cups
* paper towels
* paper plates
* glue sticks

* markers
* construction paper
* tape
* chart paper
* butcher paper
* craft sticks
* thermometers
* hand lenses

Reproducibles

Each theme includes a set of reproducibles designed to help students record and reflect on observations and discoveries made as a result of the activities. The Science Journal page, featured in each theme, helps students form a cumulative record of experiences throughout the school year that invites them to look back and reflect on observations and make connections from month to month. (See Setting Up Science Journals, right.) A three-ring binder makes a handy journal. Students can create dividers for each theme and easily add paper for additional entries, supplementing the reproducible journal pages with their own notes about various topics, questions they may still have, pictures they make or find in magazines, poems, and other items that apply.

Other reproducibles are for use with specific activities and in some cases are designed for families, offering suggestions for reinforcing the concepts at home.

Setting Up Science Journals

Each theme includes a reproducible Science Journal page. Have students set aside a pocket notebook or section in a three-ring binder for these pages. Or they can create their own journals by folding a 12-by-18-inch sheet of construction paper in half, storing the pages inside, and then binding them together at the end of each theme or each month. Encourage students to revisit key concepts by taking time to look back through their journal pages. This is a good opportunity for evaluation, too. Does the amount of detail in observations grow as the year progresses? Do students' remarks reflect understanding of concepts? Do they explain their reasoning? Do they explain their predictions? (For more information on journals and assessment, see page 36.)

Resources

At the end of each theme you'll find an annotated listing of theme-related resources for children and teachers, including details and descriptions for using children's literature, professional books, and technology in the classroom.

Within the technology resources presented, there are recommended Web site addresses (Uniform Resource Locators [URLs]) that you can use to build children's background knowledge, support and extend lessons and instruction, and supplement your own professional development. The URLs in this book represent an assemblage of Web sites with stamina—first-rate organizations that will likely maintain their site for many years to come. You may find though that a few of the URLs you visit will have moved. Others will have shut down. So, before inviting students to visit a site, take a few minutes to visit a Web site. Make sure the site is up and running, content-appropriate, and a valuable addition to classroom instruction.

Note: Evaluate what your computer can handle before you begin a computer-supported endeavor. If you're not sure how to proceed, ask a tech-savvy teacher or librarian to help you determine whether the computer you're using has what it takes to handle large volumes of data and multiple forms of media (graphics, sound, video). If the computer isn't up to tackling those state-of-the-art tasks, you may need to upgrade its memory or lobby for its replacement . . . and reschedule that virtual field trip.

A final note before you turn to Chapter 3 and the first two themes, Discover Butterflies and Moon Watch: Remember, this book is for you and your students. Make it your own by adding your own observations, reflections, and notes about the experiences and discoveries in your classroom. And if your students are really into a theme, by all means, let this be your cue to extend the unit.

CHAPTER 3

September

Highlights *of the* Month

Mark these dates, events, and activities on your calendar to help plan and supplement this month's themes.

* Early September is a good time to look for monarch butterflies.

* This month's full moon is the Harvest Moon, long ago named for the extra amount of light the moon provided farmers to harvest their crops.

* The autumnal equinox usually falls around September 23. (Check your calendar for the exact date and write it in.) On this day there are equal amounts of light and dark due to the angle of the Earth's axis and the alignment of the sun.

* If your students get school pictures taken this month, ask for copies of each child for use with activities in later months.

* Gather seeds for planting butterfly gardens in the spring. Milkweed, asters, and cosmos all attract butterflies.

* Look for signs of fall.

* September 26 is Johnny Appleseed's birthday. Have an apple-tasting party with green, yellow, and red apples. Take a survey. Which is students' favorite?

Planning Ahead

You may want to order butterfly larva ahead of time to ensure that you have butterflies for the activities here. (Let the company know when you need them and they'll be shipped accordingly.) When ordering, be sure to ask if the caterpillars will be shipped with the food they need. Expect caterpillars to be $1/4$ inch or less in length when they arrive.

Ordering Information

Insect Lore, P.O. Box 1535, Shafter, CA 93263; (800) LIVE-BUG; insectlore.com; Painted Lady caterpillars.

The Butterfly Place, P.O. Box 1541, 120 Tyngsboro Rd., Westford, MA 01886; (508) 392-0955; butterflyplace-ma.com. Painted Lady caterpillars, also chrysalids of different butterfly species, including monarchs, during certain months.

SCIENCE AT HOME

Date _____

This month we are starting two new science themes.

1. Discover Butterflies

Your child will watch a caterpillar turn into a butterfly and will participate in activities to better understand life cycles. Learning about metamorphosis gives children a chance to make connections to ways they grow and change, too! You can help your child learn more about the concept of life cycles by keeping a journal together. Record changes in your child, such as growth. From time to time, look back on the journal to reinforce the idea of change.

2. Moon Watch

Like many children, your child may wonder why the moon seems to change shape. As we investigate the moon this month, we will be keeping a Moon Watch calendar in class. Each night, one child will bring home a Moon Ticket to fill in with a picture of the moon for that night. (You will receive more information about this.) To strengthen your child's understandings, take time to notice the moon together. How does it seem to change?

Wish List

Do you have materials you can donate for our science explorations? For this month's activities, we need:

_____

_____

_____

Reminders _____

_____

_____

Discover Butterflies

The monarch butterfly is a sign that summer is coming to a close and another school year is here. Children often build bug boxes on their own for monarch caterpillars and chrysalids, and share them at school during the first couple of weeks of September. While studying monarchs or other butterflies, students can also learn more about themselves and their classmates.

 Science Dictionary

butterfly the adult stage of this colorful, winged insect

caterpillar the larval or wormlike stage of a butterfly or moth

chrysalis the hard shell covering the pupa

habitat the place where a plant or animal lives

larva the second stage of metamorphosis, when the insect is wormlike and wingless

metamorphosis the changes that happen during a lifetime

pupa the third stage of metamorphosis, when the larva is changing into the adult insect inside a hard shell or cocoon, also called a chrysalis

Science Concepts and Skills

Concepts: Students will develop an understanding of the characteristics and the life cycles of organisms.

Process Skills: observing, classifying, comparing, communicating, measuring, predicting

Science on Display

Pull your butterfly activities together with this interactive display. First, attach a butterfly net to a bulletin board (see illustration). Use the net to "collect" butterflies that students make in the following activity.

OUR BUTTERFLY QUESTIONS

1 Let students brainstorm what they already know about butterflies. List their ideas on a piece of chart paper.

2 Have the group observe real butterflies or pictures of butterflies. What do students notice about butterflies? Encourage them to observe the patterns and designs found on butterflies' wings.

3 Invite each student to cut out and decorate a butterfly (see butterfly pattern reproducible, page 41).

4 Have students write a question they have about butterflies on the back of one of the butterfly's wings.

5 Ask students to fold the butterflies in half and then place them in the bulletin board butterfly net. Use students' questions to help guide your theme study. During the unit, give students an opportunity to pursue answers to their questions through activities and resources. By the end of the unit, make sure students have had a chance to record responses to their questions on the other wing of their butterflies.

6 Place a desk or two near the bulletin board for related displays during this theme study.

ACTIVITY 1 ∿∿∿∿∿∿∿∿∿∿∿∿∿∿∿∿∿∿∿∿∿∿∿∿∿∿∿∿

Caterpillars in the Classroom

In this activity, students work in groups to make a home away from home for their classroom caterpillars, then observe as their caterpillars metamorphose into butterflies. You'll want to have students keep their journals handy so that they can record daily observations in pictures and words.

Materials (for each group of three or four students)

* ✳ caterpillar (ideally, one per group)
* ✳ two 1-liter plastic soda bottles (one must be clear)
* ✳ piece of cheesecloth (6 by 6 inches; a piece of old panty hose works equally well)
* ✳ tape
* ✳ chart paper

Note: Before the activity, cut off the top of one of the bottles and remove the bottom of the other bottle for each group (see illustration). To easily remove the bottoms, soak bottles in a sink filled with warm water for five to ten minutes. You should then be able to just pull off the bottoms. Punch 10 to 12 holes in the bottoms. These become the lids for students' caterpillar containers. Have children add blank pages to their science journals for this activity.

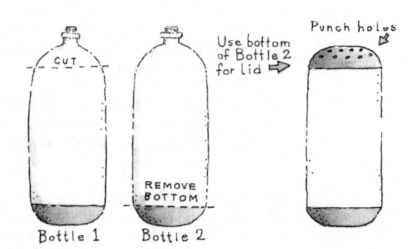

1 Explain that students will be using the liter bottles to make butterfly habitats. Introduce the word *habitat* (see Science Dictionary, page 32), then discuss what the caterpillars need to live. Mention that each kind of caterpillar has special food needs. For example, monarch caterpillars feed only on plants in the milkweed family. Therefore, if you are keeping monarch caterpillars, you will need to put fresh milkweed leaves in the containers. (If you order caterpillars from a science supply company, make sure they will be shipped with the right food.)

List caterpillars' needs on chart paper and post at your science center or display area.

BOOK BREAK

As a springboard to Activity 1, share *Monarch Butterflies* by Gail Gibbons (see Resources, page 42), or another nonfiction book about butterflies to provide students with background information on the changes from egg to butterfly.

2 Have students gather their materials and then follow these steps to prepare the lid, cutting a piece of cheesecloth to fit inside the lid and taping it in place. (This will give the caterpillars a place to attach themselves and will keep tiny caterpillars from crawling through the holes in the lid—but still let air in.)

3 Have students prepare their caterpillar habitats, adding food and a couple of twigs to the truncated liter bottle. Students may also like to add flowers and leaves to their mini-environments. Once the caterpillars are safely inside, place the lids on the bottles.

4 Let each group personalize its caterpillar home with stickers, the caterpillar's name, and so on.

5 Have students observe their caterpillars daily, recording the date, time, and what they see in their journals. (Students will use this information to make books in Activity 3.) Take time to introduce words from the Science Dictionary (see page 32) as they correspond to new stages students observe.

6 After the caterpillars have formed chrysalids, have students carefully remove the milkweed or other food source. (Leaving it in may result in a lot of fuzzy mold!) Of course, if a chrysalis is hanging from a stem or twig, leave that in the container. Some of the chrysalids may be hanging from the cheesecloth. In this case, have students remove the food source and replace the lid carefully so as not to disturb them. Again, have students note the day and time of their observations.

7 Once the butterflies have emerged, give them a few hours to dry their wings and then set them free! (see Science Celebration, below). Have students refer to their journals to calculate the time it took for the caterpillars to become butterflies.

Science Celebration

Plan a simple celebration for setting butterflies free. Some suggestions follow.

✽ Invite parents or another class to witness the release.

✽ Take "family photos" of children with their butterflies. (A parent volunteer might be willing to snap a photo of each student or of each group.)

✽ Invite students to read aloud poems or stories about butterflies, then release their butterflies after the readings.

ACTIVITY 2 ～～～～～～～～～～～～～～～～～～～～～～～～～～～～～～～～

Butterfly Buddies

Students compare themselves with their butterflies.

～～～～～～～～～～～～～～～～～～～～～～～～～～～～～～～～～～～～

Materials

❋ Butterfly Buddies Science Journal page (see page 40)

～～～～～～～～～～～～～～～～～～～～～～～～～～～～～～～～～～～～

1 Divide the class into pairs. Ask these butterfly buddies to think of some ways that they are like butterflies. (For example, they are both living things, they are both symmetrical in some ways, they both get bigger as they grow.)

2 Now have butterfly buddies think of ways that they are different from butterflies, such as: wings/no wings, six legs/two legs, hatches from an egg/born alive.

3 Introduce the Butterfly Buddies Journal page. Have students work with their buddies to complete this page.

4 Bring students together to share their ideas with the whole group. List ideas on a chart showing the ways students are alike and different from the butterflies.

Tips for Setting Up Science Journals

Each theme in Chapters 3 through 12 includes a reproducible journal page designed to help students reflect on what they are learning. You might have students keep a separate three-ring notebook to hold these pages. Provide a hole-punch at your science or writing center so that students can add each journal page to their notebooks. Students can also add blank paper for recording additional observations during a theme study. Or have students fold a 12-by-18-inch sheet of construction paper in half to create a folder for their journal pages. At the conclusion of each theme or each month, have students punch holes and bind these folders together with string or paper fasteners. (For more ideas on how to use the Science Journal pages, see page 27.)

ACTIVITY 3 ～～～～～～～～～～～～～～～～～～～～～

Watch Us Grow

The changes from egg to caterpillar to chrysalis to butterfly are dramatic—as are the changes from child to adult.

1 Invite each student to bring in a picture of him- or herself as an infant or toddler. Ask them to keep the photos hidden from their classmates. Explain that the photographs will be part of a guessing game.

2 On the day of the activity, hold up each student's photograph, one at a time, to see if classmates can identify the student. Discuss how students have changed since they were babies. In what ways have they stayed the same? What characteristics do infants have in common? What are some differences?

3 Compare changes students have undergone with changes they observed in their butterflies. Consider having students make a picture time line of these changes, using their journal notes as reference. Brainstorm ways to depict students' changes over time, then have them work in groups to try out some of the ideas.

COMMUNITY HELPERS

Butterfly Garden

Invite parents or grandparents with an interest in gardening to take students on a walk around the school grounds, looking for plants that attract butterflies, such as milkweed or cosmos. Have students gather seeds if they can for planting a spring butterfly garden (if not, you can order some from a seed catalog). Save the seeds and invite volunteers back in the spring for planting. Have students plant seeds in containers they can take home, too. Conclude by writing a class story about the project. Make copies and send the story and plants home together.

Curriculum Connections

LANGUAGE ARTS
Two Books in One

Students make life-cycle books to show what they've learned about their butterflies and about themselves. This is a good time to review the Science Dictionary words (see page 32). If you've copied these words on a chart, remind students to refer to it for help with word choice and spelling.

Materials

✳ white butcher paper (one 8-by-16-inch piece per child)

✳ old manila folders (or other heavy paper) precut into 3-by-3-inch squares (two per child)

1. Have students fold the paper in half lengthwise.

2. Demonstrate how to fold the paper into four equal sections, as shown. Assist students in doing the same with their papers (or prefold students' papers).

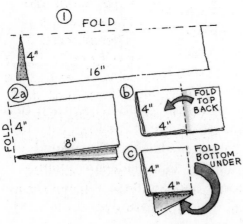

3. Have students glue manila folder squares inside the two end sections of their folder paper, making sure to glue both sides of the end section to the heavy paper.

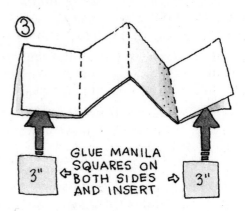

GLUE MANILA SQUARES ON BOTH SIDES AND INSERT

4. On one side of their books, have students write about and/or illustrate the stages in their butterflies' lives (egg, caterpillar/larva, chrysalis/pupa, butterfly/adult), recording the dates that correspond to each stage. Remind students to refer to their journals for this information.

5. Next, have students flip the book upside down, then over. On this side, have students write about stages in their own lives. They can include the photos they brought in for Activity 3—or copies of them. (If you make copies, let students color them in!) Each square should show a picture from a stage in their lives and the year of that stage.

6. Invite students to share their books with classmates at the science or reading area.

MATH
Symmetry

Take time to discuss the concept of symmetry, then invite children to look at their butterflies and find examples of symmetry (in the wing and leg structure, wing design, etc.). Have students write about or draw what they see in their journals. Then ask: Where else in nature can we find symmetry? Leaves, insects, winged maple tree seeds (also called samara) are all examples. Finally, ask students how their bodies are symmetrical.

Follow up by having students create their own symmetrical designs by folding paper in half and cutting out designs on the fold. Before they unfold the papers, ask students to draw pictures of how they think their unfolded designs will look. Have students unfold their cutouts and compare.

SCIENCE
Habitats

Monarch butterflies will only lay their eggs on milkweed. What happens when people mow down milkweed? This is a good opportunity to discuss the effect of loss of habitat on butterflies and other creatures. Pose a problem for students to solve. Ask: What do you think a town should do if an area marked for mowing is a place where milkweed grows and butterflies breed? Discuss all suggestions. From here, students might like to investigate endangered butterflies and how people are working to protect them.

MOVEMENT
The Dance of the Butterflies

Have children recall the different ways their caterpillars and butterflies moved throughout the different stages of the life cycle. Play a selection of classical music such as the "Dance of the Sugar Plum Fairy" from the *Nutcracker* ballet. As you describe the steps involved in the butterfly metamorphosis, invite children to move (first like caterpillars and then like butterflies) in time to the music as they act out the process.

Name ______________________________

THEME: Discover Butterflies

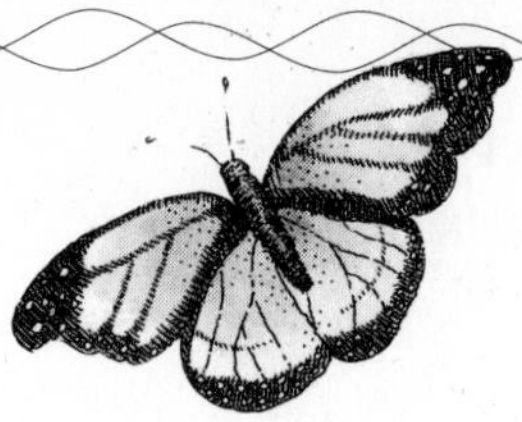

Butterfly Buddies

My buddy's name ______________________________

Our butterfly's name (kind) ______________________________

Ways we are the same as our butterfly

____

____

Ways we are different from our butterfly

____

____

Ways my buddy and I are the same

____

____

Ways my buddy and I are different

____

____

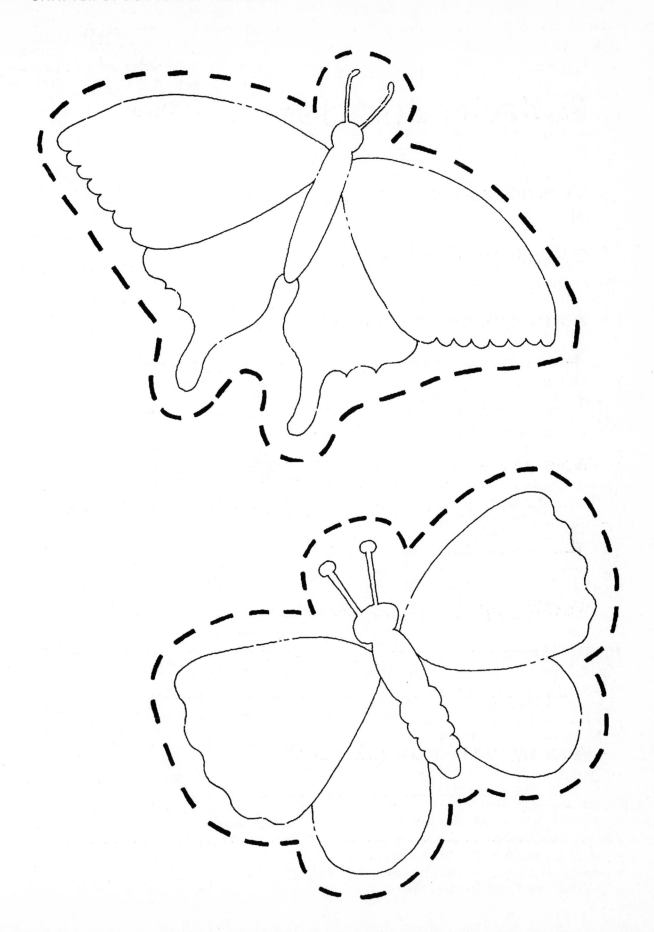

RESOURCES

FOR CHILDREN

DK Readers: Born to Be a Butterfly (Dorling Kindersley, 2000). This easy-reader book with engaging visuals shares information about a caterpillar's transformation into a Red Admiral butterfly. Nonfiction.

Bugs by Nancy Winslow Parker and Joan Richards Wright (Greenwillow, 1987). This book makes factual information about insects fun. Includes illustrated descriptions of different kinds of metamorphosis. Nonfiction.

"The First Butterflies" from *Keepers of the Animals* by Michael J. Caduto and Joseph Bruchac (Fulcrum Publishing, 1991). This Native American folktale explains how the Great Spirit combined all things in nature to make the world's first butterflies. Fiction.

From Caterpillar to Butterfly (Let's-Read-and-Find-Out Science, Stage 1) by Deborah Heiligman (HarperTrophy, 1996) Inviting text and watercolor illustration guides students through each remarkable stage of a Painted Lady butterfly's life. Nonfiction.

Monarch Butterflies by Gail Gibbons (Holiday House, 1989). Here's everything you need to know about your monarchs, including how to care for them. Nonfiction.

The Very Hungry Caterpillar by Eric Carle (HarperCollins, 1969). The title character in this brightly illustrated classic nibbles his way through a medley of foods before metamorphosing into a butterfly. Fiction.

FOR TEACHERS

Butterfly Activity Book by Patricia J. Wynne (Dover, 2007). Forty reproducible puzzles help children build background knowledge and increase their overall understanding of butterfly anatomy and life cycles.

Butterflies and Moths: A Golden Guide by Robert T. Mitchell and Herbert S. Zim. (Golden Press, 1962). A field guide illustrating North American butterflies and moths. Includes information about caterpillar food sources.

Exploring Science in Early Childhood Education by Karen K. Lind (CENGAGE Delmar Learning; 4th edition, 2004). Offers strategies and activities that support different types of learning—and connect with national standards in science and mathematics.

Grow a Butterfly Garden by Wendy Potter-Springer (Storey Publishing, Bulletin A-114). This handy reference lists plants and the butterflies they attract. Take it along when you look for seeds for your butterfly garden (see Community Helpers, page 37).

Mini-Book of the Week by Maria Fleming (Scholastic, 2005). Promote literacy with easy-to-read reproducible books on fiction and nonfiction topics, including the butterfly life cycle.

TECHNOLOGY CONNECTIONS

The Butterfly King directed by Lee Larcheveque (Imago Productions, 2005). This DVD with a run time of just 23 minutes amply provides children with extraordinary close-up views of Monarch butterflies. A winning way to kick off or conclude a unit on the life cycle of butterflies.

The Butterfly Place and Insect Lore (www.butterflyplace-ma.com and www.insectlore.com)
Two teacher-tested sources from which you can obtain raise-your-own-butterfly kits. The kits include everything you need to house, feed, and order live larva.

Children's Butterfly Site (http://bsi.montana.edu/web/kidsbutterfly)
This site, made available in part by the Big Sky Institute at Montana State University, includes answers to FAQs about butterflies and moths, links to other Web resources, and a must-see photo gallery of butterflies from all over the world.

Reading Rainbow: Bugs by Nancy Winslow Parker (Greenwillow, 1987). GPN Educational Media (http://shopgpn.com/stores/1/RR_BookLists.cfm)
This episode of Reading Rainbow invites the whole class to enjoy a read-aloud of the text and then join LeVar on a sightseeing tour of the insects at Cincinnati Zoo's Insect World. This episode, with a run time of 30 minutes, is available as a DVD and as part of a CD-ROM. For more information visit GPN Educational Media's Web site, where you can search for favorite books by title, author, and illustrator.

Moon Watch

Young children are naturally drawn to the moon. From the time they can talk, many will ask questions about this natural night-light: Can I touch the moon? Why does it shine? How does it change shape? Why can we sometimes see the moon during the day? Though the moon is at its brightest when children are not in school, there are still many activities you can do during daylight hours to enhance your students' understanding of the moon.

Science Concepts and Skills

Concepts: Students will develop their understanding of the moon as an object in the sky, and will notice differences between how the moon looks at night and how it appears when it can be seen during the day. Students will also recognize that the moon's shape seems to change in a pattern over a monthlong period.

Process Skills: observing, predicting, comparing, communicating

S c i e n c e   D i c t i o n a r y

crater a bowl-shaped dent or hole made when something like a meteoroid crashes into a surface

moon huge ball of rock; the closest planetary body to our planet

moon phases new, waxing crescent, first quarter, waxing gibbous, full moon, waning gibbous, last quarter, waning crescent (about every 29 days the moon passes through all its phases); the phase or appearance of the moon depends on how much of the sunlit half of the moon we are able to see from Earth; if you look closely at the moon during the various phases (excluding a full moon), you will probably see the part of the moon that is in Earth's shadow

New   Crescent   Quarter   Gibbous   Full   Gibbous   Quarter   Crescent

relief the changes or ups and downs in a surface

Science on Display

Use dark blue or black butcher paper to create a background border strip about four inches high that will wrap the walls of your science area, at a level students can reach. (Students will complete this border in Activity 3: How Does the Moon Change?) Display a sign that says MOON WATCH. Have students add some foil stars or glitter paint to the border to create a sparkly night sky background for the moon border.

ACTIVITY 1

Make a Moon Diary

Start your study of the moon by having students create moon diaries for recording questions and observations about the moon. This is a good time to introduce words in the Science Dictionary (see page 44), including the names of the moon's phases. Copy the names of the phases on a chart, along with simple illustrations of the moon's phases, and display for easy reference.

Materials

* Moon Diary Science Journal page (see page 53)
* extra paper (optional)
* stapler (optional)
* paper fasteners (optional)

BOOK BREAK

Share *Moon Man* (Delacorte Press, 1991), Tomi Ungerer's lively tale of what happened when the moon caught a ride on a comet to pay a visit to Earth. This story also follows the moon through its phases. Near the end of the story, ask students to predict what phase the moon will be in when the scientist sends it back up to space in a capsule (the third, or crescent, when it would be small enough to fit).

1 Make a class set of the reproducible Moon Diary. Invite students to write questions they have about the moon in the space provided at the bottom. If you want students to observe the moon over more than one month, make extra copies of the reproducible, punch holes, and staple or bind with paper fasteners. Students can also add plain paper to their diaries for additional notes.

2 Have students write in the names of the phases pictured on their diary pages. Remind them to use the chart as a reference. Have students save the diaries for use in Activity 3.

CHAPTER 3: SCIENCE JOURNAL PAGE   53

Name _____

THEME: Moon Watch

Moon Diary

Sunday	Monday	Tuesday	Wednesday	Thursday	Friday	Saturday

ACTIVITY 2 ~~~~~~

Portrait of a Moon

Here's a chance for students to creatively express what they know about the moon and for you to gather valuable information about your students' level of knowledge.

Materials (for each student)

* white crayon
* sheet of white watercolor paper
* paintbrush
* black paint (watercolor or tempera will work)
* cups for water
* newspaper to protect work area

1   Invite students to use white crayon to draw pictures of the moon. Explain that for this activity students need to fill in their moon shapes completely with the crayon.

2   After students complete their drawings, ask them to paint over the entire paper with black paint.

3   Allow paintings to dry, then let students sit in a "full moon" circle and share their portraits. How do they compare? Does the real moon look the same every night?

4   Display the moon portraits in the classroom. As students learn more about the moon, encourage them to label the phase of the moon they illustrated.

ACTIVITY 3 ~~~~~~

How Does the Moon Change?

This activity helps students discover the predictable pattern of the moon's phases. Lead into it by asking students why they think the moon seems to change. Some may think that the moon grows and shrinks, while others may wonder where the old moon goes when the new moon comes. It is difficult for

Note: Try to start this activity around the time of the new moon. Check a calendar or an almanac for the date.

children to understand why we see phases of the moon, so it's important to introduce this concept early and to revisit it throughout the school year.

Materials

* Moon Diaries (see Activity 1)
* class set of Parent Page/Moon Ticket (see page 54)
* pencils or crayons

1   Have children take out the Moon Diaries they made in Activity 1. Students will use this page to record their observations of the moon.

2   Ask students to fill in the dates on their calendars, starting with the day you hand out the calendars. (Students will not necessarily begin with the first day of the month—the calendar may include parts of two months.)

3   Assign each child a night to be in charge of recording what the moon looks like. Have students circle their nights on their calendars. (You might want to assign two students per night in case of absences.) On their assigned nights, students will take home a moon ticket and parent letter. Students will record their observations on the calendars and on the moon ticket. The next day, they'll paste the completed moon ticket in place on the Science on Display border (see page 44). Classmates can then copy the moon phase drawing in the appropriate space on their own calendars.

4   By the time students fill in the boxes for each night, they should see the moon returning to where it started in the first box. (This will also be apparent from the moon tickets displayed on the border strip.) Counting these days will reveal that it takes the moon about 29 days to complete the cycle of phases.

5   At the end of the cycle, bring students together to look at the moon phase border. Discuss how the moon changed. Can students predict what the moon will look like tomorrow night? Can they guess how many days will pass until the next full moon?

6   Plan on making this activity a part of students' science experiences throughout the year. Over time, students will

begin to recognize the pattern of the moon phases. Add to your moon border, too, wrapping it around the room as students gather additional data.

Note: Explain that the new moon is invisible at night when it is dark. However, they may be able to see the outline in the evening. You might want to keep a calendar on hand to inform students of any special circumstances like this and to let them know the times of the moonrise on their assigned nights. Explain that other factors might prevent them from seeing the moon on their assigned nights. The view might be obscured by tall buildings where they live, it might be a cloudy night, and so on. If this happens, just have students bring the moon ticket back to class the next day and complete the information based on the calendar or almanac.

ACTIVITY 4 ~~~~~~~~~~~~~~~~~~~~~~~~~~~~~~

Moon Face

BOOK BREAK
Read aloud Allan Fowler's *So That's How the Moon Changes Shape* (see Resources, page 55). Follow up by inviting students to tell what they learned about the phases of the moon. Make a list and post it. You might also refer students to their Moon Diaries. Do they now know the answers to any of the questions they wrote down?

As students observe the moon, they may naturally question the dark spots they see. There is a misconception that shadows on craters are what create the light and dark spots on the moon. Help children understand what really causes the light and dark spots by explaining that the moon, like the Earth, has relief. There are highlands (like mountains) and basin areas (like valleys). If possible, have a relief map on hand to share. Explain that the light and dark areas are a result of the different kinds of rock that make up the moon. The dark areas we see are smooth, dark lava rock. Areas untouched by lava (highlands) are the bright areas we see. Because the moon is so far away, try the following activity to help students understand more about the moon's surface.

Materials

 * dough (see recipe, page 49)
 * marbles, pebbles, BB's
 * newspaper to protect work surfaces

1 Ask students to cover their work spaces with newspaper. Give each child a ball of dough to form into a pancake about ¼ inch thick.

DOUGH RECIPE

Ingredients:

  2 cups flour

  1 cup salt

  1 cup water

Directions:

Mix the flour and salt together, then slowly add the water. Knead the dough until it is smooth and firm, not sticky.

Note: If you prefer, you can use dry sand or flour in place of the dough. This will result in larger craters when children drop the marbles, however, the dough will harden, allowing children to save their moon surfaces and share them with their families.

2 Have students drop marbles and BB's from different heights onto their dough pancakes and observe the different impressions left by the objects.

3 When students are finished making the craters, ask them to gently run their fingers over the surface of the clay. How does it feel? Compare the surface of the dough with the surface of the moon. Explain that the moon's surface is covered with craters like these, formed by meteoroids striking the surface of the moon. From their own observations, can they draw any conclusions about the relationship between the size of what they drop and the size of the craters?

4 Let the dough air-dry. Students may leave craters naturally colored or paint them.

Tip

To give students a closer look at the impact of meteorites, try videotaping the drop. Use the slow-motion function on the video recorder if it has one. Play back the tape so that students can see what happens when the meteorites hit. Ask them to predict what the impact would be like if they dropped the objects from a greater distance. Closer? What if they use bigger objects? Smaller? Lighter? Heavier? Allow time for testing some of the predictions.

MOON MUNCHIES

Offer each child a large, round sugar cookie. Tell children that it takes 13 nights for a full moon to recede (or grow smaller) until it reaches the point at which no moon is visible to us. As you count from 1 to 13, have the children begin nibbling their cookies into smaller and smaller crescent-shaped configurations representing the various phases of the moon, until, by number 13, the moon cookies have disappeared. Ask children: How is the real moon like your cookies? How is it different? (Unlike their cookie moons, the real moon does not actually vanish.)

Curriculum Connections

LANGUAGE ARTS
Moon Stories to Share

Instead of displaying students' moon portraits around the room, compile them into a class book. On the back or at the bottom of each moon portrait, have students write or dictate a description of the moon. Create a title page for the book, calling it "Our Moon," or let students brainstorm a title for the book. On the inside of the cover, write a note to students' families, encouraging them to read the book together. Laminate pages for durability, hole-punch near the top and bottom of the left margin, then clip together with two metal O-rings. Schedule the book to go home with all students so they can share their work with their families.

MATH
Playing with Patterns

As students become familiar with the phases of the moon, challenge them to find other examples of patterns in their world. Clothing, floor tiles, and brickwork on buildings are just some of the places they might look. Follow up by inviting students to create their own patterns using pictures they cut out of magazines. Have students cut out and paste one "cycle" in their patterns—for example: car, car, person—then trade papers to see if others can continue the patterns.

To make a moon-shaped book, cut pages in the shape of one of the phases, have students paste in their pictures (trimming if necessary), and bind.

SOCIAL STUDIES
Native American Moons

 Hundreds of years ago, Native Americans gave the moons of the year names, each based on a season's weather or natural events. Share these moon names with students and talk about how they might have gotten their names. Follow up by inviting students to come up with their own names for the moons.

Note: The names given to moons varied by region. For example, the Snow Moon in New England is called Opening Buds Moon in the Gulf of Mexico. The information provided here is from Twelve Moons of the Year *by Hal Borland (G.K. Hall, 1985), a collection of nature essays.*

January
Wolf Moon (The month of January is a time when the "fangs of winter" bite and the wind howls.)

February
Snow Moon (Snowdrifts are at their deepest at this time of the year.)

March
Worm Moon (As the ground thaws, worms make their way back up to the surface.)

April
Pink Moon (This is in reference to the first flowers of spring.)

May
Flower Moon (A continuation of April's reference to flowers that are blossoming. Also a time for planting seeds.)

June
Hot Moon (The first heat of summer; also summer solstice occurs.)

July
Buck Moon (The reference to this moon is unclear, but the dry heat of summer may make this a good time to dry meats.)

August
Green Corn Moon (Sweet corn is ripening.)

September
Harvest Moon (This name came from the full moon, which provides farmers with extra daylight for harvesting crops; probably not a Native American term, but it stuck.)

October
Hunter's Moon (The moonlight provides light for hunting.)

November
Beaver Moon (A prime time for hunting beaver, the pelts of which were a major source of trade. Also, like the wise beaver, this was a time for preparing for winter.)

December
Cold Moon (The longest nights of the year occur now; time of winter solstice.)

A STORY TO SHARE

Moon's Little Sister

This is a retelling of a North American story about the moon. Read it aloud to students, then invite them to share their own stories about why the moon does not shine so brightly. You can also reproduce the story for students to add to their moon journals and to share at home.

Did you know that once the moon shone more brightly than the sun? What happened? Well, being as friendly as he was, the Moon decided to have all of his friends over for a feast one day. Stars came from all around and soon Moon's house was very crowded.

As his guests settled in, Moon asked his sister to help by going after some water. The Moon's sister trudged off in the cold winter night, the wind roaring around her. When she arrived at the water, she found it frozen and had to chip away to fill her buckets.

Finally, Moon's sister returned and looked around the crowded room for a place to sit and warm up but found none. "Where can I sit?" she asked her brother. Moon replied, "Why, there isn't room here for even a mouse! You'll just have to sit on my head!"

Cold and tired, Moon's sister was in no mood for his joke. So she jumped on Moon's head and sits there still, her shadow dimming his brightness. Moon's friends are nearby, dancing across the sky as they talk about what a grand time they had at the party.

Name _____

Moon Diary

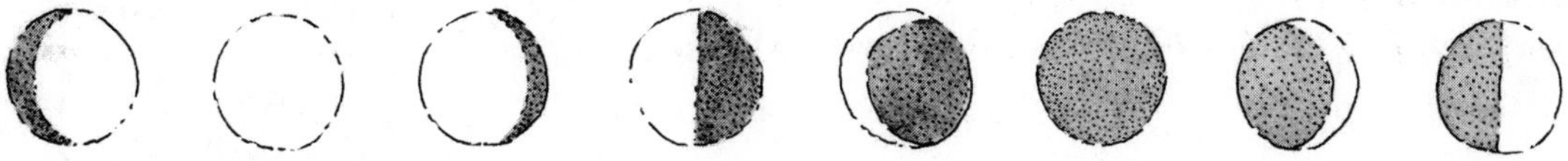

Sunday	Monday	Tuesday	Wednesday	Thursday	Friday	Saturday

_____

_____

_____

Dear _____,

    As part of our class activities on the moon and its phases, your child is keeping a Moon Diary. Here's how you can help reinforce your child's understanding. On _____ (date) , try to observe the moon with your child. Ask your child to draw the way the moon looks in the appropriate space on the diary page and on the moon ticket below. Cut out this ticket and have your child bring it to school the next day. Your child will be adding this picture of the moon to the moon display in our science center.

    Here are some helpful hints for moon viewing:

    ✳ At times, the moon will be visible in the morning or afternoon hours, giving you more options for viewing.

    ✳ If it is cloudy or if you can't see the moon for some other reason, make a note of this on the moon ticket. We'll fill in the information at school.

    Thanks so much for your help with this project, and happy moon watching!

MOON TICKET

Name_____

Draw a picture of the moon
on (date)_____.

Cut out the ticket on the
dotted line and return it to
school on
(date)_____.

Draw a picture of the
moon here.

RESOURCES

FOR CHILDREN

Comets, Stars, the Moon, and Mars by Douglas Florian (Harcourt, 2007). The author's playful poems and illustrations invite young readers to learn oodles about space. Fiction.

If You Decide to Go to the Moon by Faith McNulty (Scholastic, 2005). Lyrical text and lavish illustrations take readers on a wondrous excursion. Fiction.

Moon Man by Tomi Ungerer (Delacorte Press, 1991). The moon, who watches longingly as people on Earth dance, decides to catch a ride on a passing comet to join the fun. Connects with craters (Activity 4) and phases of the moon (Activity 3). Fiction.

The Moon Was at a Fiesta by Matthew Gollub (Tambourine Books, 1994). The moon sees how the sun spends the day, compared to its own quiet life.

Reaching for the Moon by Buzz Aldrin (HarperCollins, 2005) A real-life astronaut, the second man to walk on the moon, shares his adventures in this autobiography. Nonfiction.

So That's How the Moon Changes Shape by Allan Fowler (Children's Press, 1991). Simple, effective photographs help children recognize the patterns of the moon's cycle.

The Stars: A New Way to See Them by H. A. Rey (Houghton Mifflin, 1976) This approachable book is a delight for beginner stargazers. Nonfiction.

Thirteen Moons on Turtle's Back by Joseph Bruchac (Putnam, 1997). Memorable poetry, illustrations, and regard for Native American cultures combine to make this book one you'll pull down from the shelf again and again. Fiction.

What the Moon Is Like by Franklyn Branley (HarperCollins, 1986). A descriptive book about the surface of the moon. Nonfiction.

FOR TEACHERS

ETA Cuisenaire
Renowned for its innovative manipulatives, ETA Cuisenaire now offers teaching tools and materials for science. Contact the company for a catalog: 800-445-5985. Or, visit its Web site: www.etacuisenaire.com/.

Many Moons by James Thurber (Harcourt Brace Jovanovich, 1943). A young princess asks her father to get her the moon. This classic story is too difficult for primary students to read on their own, but it makes a nice read-aloud. Fiction.

The Moon by Seymour Simon (Macmillan, 1984). This book for intermediate readers includes excellent photographs of the moon that will appeal to young children.

Team Moon by Catherine Thimmesh (Houghton Mifflin, 2006). Though the text is best suited for grades 5 and up, the amazing photos captivate readers of all ages. Nonfiction.

TECHNOLOGY CONNECTIONS

Big Space Shuttle directed by William VanDerKloot (Little Mammoth Media, 2003). Designed for ages 5 and up, this DVD documentary provides children with a close-up view of what goes into a single space launch. Run time is 50 minutes.

American Museum of Natural History:
OLogy Our Place in Space
(www.amnh.org/ology/astronomy/stufftodo/index.html)
Packed with links to activities that help children explore space away from the computer—baking, building models, stargazing, and more.

NASA's Educator Features and Articles
(www.nasa.gov/audience/foreducators/index.html)
NASA provides free teaching materials—from educational guides to posters. Be sure to check out this site!

NASA Kids' Club
(www.nasa.gov/audience/forkids/kidsclub/flash/index.html)
Children will enjoy playing the learning games, seeing the photos of the space station crew, and navigating the picture dictionary. You'll enjoy seeing students captivated while learning.

CHAPTER 4

October

Falling Leaves
page 60

Degrees of Weather
page 72

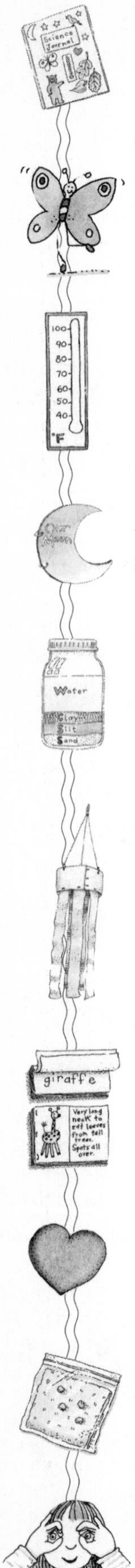

Highlights *of the* Month

Mark these dates, events, and activities on your calendar to help plan and supplement this month's themes.

- Leaves on deciduous trees change color—earlier in more northern areas, wetlands, and mountainous regions.
- Native Americans named the full moon Hunter's Moon because of the light provided for hunting.
- Try to visit a farmers' market. How many kinds of pumpkins and other squashes can children find?
- Identify the trees in your school yard that are changing color. Revisit one tree often. Keep a journal of the changes students see.

Plan Ahead

Prepare for activities in this chapter by gathering leaves and pinecones from the ground. Invite students to bring in leaves they find, too (see Science on Display, page 61). You can keep leaves from drying out by keeping them in a bag with a dampened paper towel.

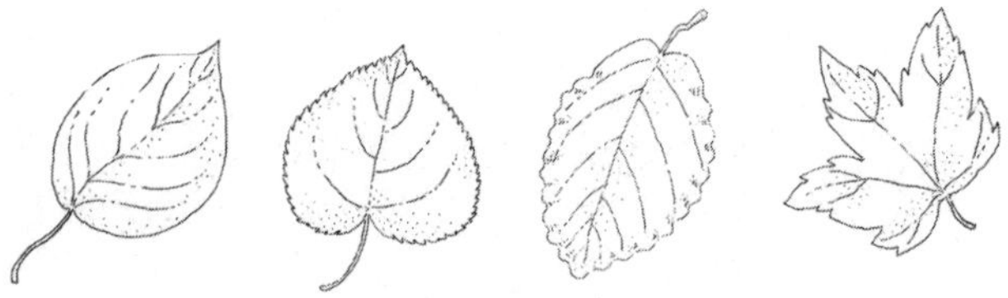

This is a good time to plant tree seedlings in the classroom. You can buy seedlings of many varieties in bulk from the National Tree Trust, (202) 628-8733 or (800) 846-8733, www.nationaltreetrust.org. Or, contact the Arbor Day Foundation, 1-888-448-7337, www.arborday.org.

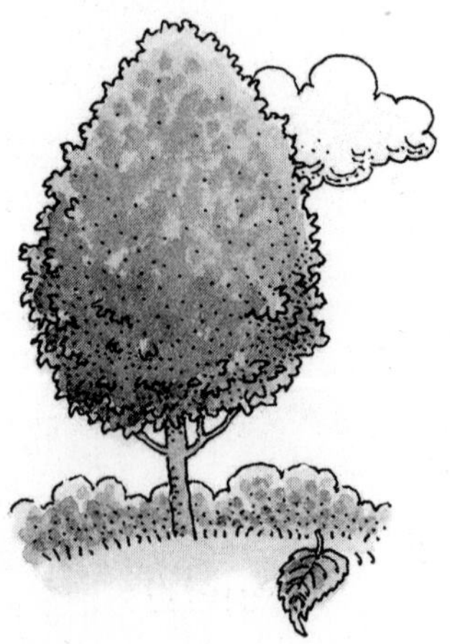

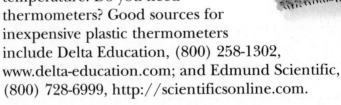

Theme 2 this month focuses on temperature. Do you need thermometers? Good sources for inexpensive plastic thermometers include Delta Education, (800) 258-1302, www.delta-education.com; and Edmund Scientific, (800) 728-6999, http://scientificsonline.com.

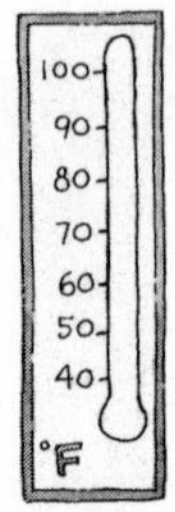

SCIENCE AT HOME

Date _____

This month we are starting two new science themes.

1. Falling Leaves

Children will be investigating the natural cycle of seasons as they collect, observe, and experiment with leaves. You can help your child by looking at falling leaves around your home. (Even in warmer climates, where fall does not bring such noticeable changes in foliage, you can find falling leaves wherever there are deciduous trees.) Ask your child to describe a leaf's edges, colors, size, and shape. How do two or more leaves compare?

2. Degrees of Weather

We will also be investigating the weather this month, focusing on temperature. This is something your child can connect with at home every day. Ask: What's the temperature today? (Hot, warm, cool, cold.) What kinds of clothes will you wear for the weather today? (T-shirt and shorts; pants, sweater, and jacket, etc.)

Wish List

Do you have materials you can donate for our science explorations? For this month's activities, we need:

_____

_____

_____

Reminders _____

_____

_____

Falling Leaves

As quickly as leaves fall in autumn, children love to scoop them up and throw them into the air, crunch them underfoot, pile them up and then run through them, even shape them into "houses." A close look at these leaves provides children with opportunities to learn more about their characteristics and the natural cycle of seasons. A look at a tree's twigs even gives kids a peek at next year's leaves.

Science Concepts and Skills

Concepts: Students will look at the leaves (and trees) around them and recognize that they have observable properties (like size, shape, and color) by which they can be grouped. In addition, students will observe that trees losing leaves is a part of the cycle of the seasons.

Process Skills: observing, classifying, comparing, collecting and recording data, communicating, interpreting

S c i e n c e   D i c t i o n a r y

conifer trees such as evergreens, that have needles and cones

deciduous trees that shed all of their leaves during autumn; the leaves are usually broad, unlike the needlelike leaves found on conifers; oaks, maples, and birches are examples of deciduous trees

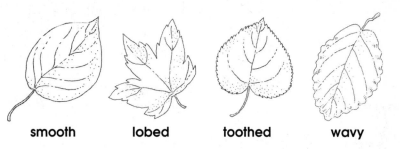

smooth   **lobed**   **toothed**   **wavy**

leaf the part of the plant where it makes its food

photosynthesis the way plants use light to make food

Science on Display

To create a seasonal feeling in your science center, gather leaves in a variety of sizes, shapes, and colors. Laminate the leaves and have students help cut them out. Hang the leaves from the ceiling, group them on a wall, or attach them to a nearby window. Create a tree shape (without leaves) from craft paper. Attach the tree to a wall, where you can leave it up for the entire school year.

While working on this theme, have students write sentences about their leaf discoveries on leaf shapes cut from construction paper and paste them to the tree. You can reuse the tree for other themes, too. Recycle the leaves by having students write on the opposite side.

ACTIVITY 1

Sorting Leaves

As leaves fall, invite students to gather them and take a closer look. What colors and shapes do they see? What part of each leaf was attached to a twig or a branch? Why do students think the leaves fell off? This is a good time to introduce the words in the Science Dictionary (above) and to display them on chart paper for easy reference. Again, as students work, encourage them to write discoveries on paper leaves and paste them to the display tree.

Materials (per group of two or three students)

✳ paper lunch bag

✳ magnifying lens (optional)

Note: Seasonal changes may be most dramatic in the northeastern United States, but leaves fall off of deciduous trees everywhere.

1 Divide the class into groups of two or three for this activity. Give each group a paper lunch bag and ask students to sign their names on the bag. Students will use this bag to store leaves they collect.

2 Spend 10 or 15 minutes gathering fallen leaves from around the school yard. (If your school yard doesn't have any deciduous trees, send home a note asking if children could gather a few leaves from around their houses and bring them to school.) Encourage children to look for leaves that have different shapes, sizes, and colors. Aim to collect at least ten leaves per group.

3 Ask each group to sort its leaves into two piles (for example, pointy/not pointy or big/small) and then invite you over to see if you can determine the sorting rule.

4 Allow time for students to rotate through one another's leaf displays and try to guess the grouping methods.

5 Visit each group again. This time regroup the leaves. Can students determine your strategy?

6 Have students return the leaves to the paper bags for the next activity. (Keep leaves damp so they will not dry out and become brittle. To do this, simply place a damp paper towel in the bag with the leaves and store overnight in a cool place.)

BOOK BREAK
Follow up students' leaf gathering with a book that tells about another reason for a tree losing its leaves. In *Someday a Tree* by Eve Bunting, Alice's old oak tree is losing its leaves. Ask children what is different about this tree. (It's losing its leaves in the spring.) Everyone tries to save the tree, but it is dying. Before you finish reading, stop and ask: What would you do to try to save this tree? Then read on to discover how Alice keeps a part of her tree. (She plants acorns she has gathered from the tree.)

ACTIVITY 2 ∿∿∿∿∿∿∿∿∿∿∿∿∿∿∿∿∿∿∿∿∿∿∿∿∿∿∿∿∿∿∿∿

Leaf Match

Scientists often classify leaf edges as smooth, lobed, wavy, or toothed. Students get a chance to do the same thing in this activity as they categorize their leaves by edge type.

∿∿∿

Materials

❋ Leaf Match reproducible (see page 69)

❋ Leaf Match Science Journal page (see page 70)

❋ leaves from Activity 1

❋ crayons

❋ chart paper

∿∿∿

Note: Before the activity, make a copy of page 69 for each student, plus one extra. Ask a few children to help you color in the leaves on the extra. Laminate and cut out each leaf, then attach them across the bottom of the chart paper. Create two columns for each leaf— one where you will write in words that describe each type of edge and one where students will paste their own leaf cutouts to create picture graphs.

1 Ask each student to select a leaf from the bags of leaves collected for Activity 1.

2 Use the Science Dictionary (see page 61) to introduce the words *smooth, wavy, lobed,* and *toothed,* then display the leaf graph. Ask students to describe the edges of each of the leaves shown. Record students' words in the appropriate columns for each leaf cutout.

3 Have students cut out the four leaf pictures on their reproducible pages and find the edge that most closely matches their own leaves.

4 Invite students to take turns pasting their leaf cutouts in the appropriate bars on the graph. As this is being

done, students can record the same information on their
Science Journal mini-graphs.

5   After all the leaves are graphed, ask students to make a true
    statement based on the graph. (For example: There are more
    toothed leaves on our graph than any other kind of leaf.)
    Write these statements on precut speech balloons and attach
    them to the graph.

ACTIVITY 3 ~~~~~~

Going on a Leaf Hunt

Go on a falling leaf safari to encourage students to apply what
they've learned about leaves.

Materials

✱ construction paper (fall colors) cut into 1-inch squares
    (one per student)

✱ field guide to trees (see Resources, page 71)

1   Go for a leaf walk. Ask students to look for different leaf
    edges on trees they see. Can they spot examples of all four
    leaf edges? (You might want to bring a copy of page 69 for
    reference.) Bring along a simple field guide to show students
    how this kind of book can help them identify trees. Introduce
    the names of some of the trees you see so that children begin
    to associate different species with different shaped leaves.

2   Here are some other activities for your hunt.

    ✱ Find trees that are losing all of their leaves.

    ✱ Find trees that are not losing their leaves.

    ✱ Hold up a leaf and challenge children to find a tree that
        has the same kind of leaf (then let them take turns
        holding up leaves while the rest of you hunt).

    ✱ Cut small squares out of leaf-colored construction paper.
        Give each child a square and challenge him or her to
        find a leaf of the same color.

3 Wrap up your hunt by having children look on the ground for leaves they like. Take the leaves back to the classroom for the next activity.

ACTIVITY 4 〜〜〜〜〜〜〜〜〜〜〜〜〜〜〜

Leaf Collection Quilt

Students turn their leaf collections into a classroom quilt. Prior to starting this activity, ask for a parent volunteer to help sew the finished squares together to create the quilt, or use butcher-paper squares and paste them to a big piece of paper to create a quiltlike effect. (Students can even draw in the stitches.)

Materials (for each small group)

✽ newspaper

✽ leaves from Activity 3

✽ white cotton fabric cut into 10-inch squares (old sheets work great) or substitute with paper squares

✽ 1 paint tray setup for each group, consisting of: a cup of water, several different colors of fabric paint, and a brush for each color. (Clear, 35mm film canisters with snap-on lids make great paint containers.) Choose paints in autumn leaf colors—orange, yellow, pink, red, purple, bronze. It doesn't take much fabric paint to cover the leaves.

✽ smocks

✽ permanent markers (fine point)

1 Have each group cover a work surface with newspaper and put on smocks. Give each group a paint tray.

2 Have students turn their leaves vein-side up, then paint this side of the leaf, being careful to cover the entire surface. Caution students not to put on the paint too heavy or thick.

3 As children finish painting their leaves, have them gently place them paint-side down on the fabric (or paper) squares. Guide students in this step, helping them place the leaves away from the edges of the fabric, since this part will be sewn under. Have students use their fingertips to press down, then remove, the leaves. Being careful not to smudge the paint, help students use permanent markers to sign their squares. Set quilt squares aside to dry. (Check the paint directions for drying times and any special requirements that may be needed to set the paint.)

4 While waiting for the paint to dry, let students assist in the layout of the quilt. How many squares will go across? How many down? Should the squares be arranged in a pattern (by color or leaf type) or randomly? What happens if there are not enough squares to complete a square or rectangle? (You could fill in the quilt with plain squares or squares that have other leaves printed on them, or having a quilt that doesn't finish out in a rectangle, but instead has a stepped edge.) Once students agree on a layout, use a large piece of paper to sketch it out, writing in students' names to show the positions of the squares.

5 When the paint is dry, have students work with the parent volunteer to stitch the squares together.

6 Look at the leaf quilt together. Invite children to identify attributes of their leaves, such as leaf edges, color, size, and so on.

7 Display the completed quilt on a classroom wall or in a reading center, where students can relax with the quilt and leaf through a good book!

Science Celebration

After researching how leaves change color, provide children with patterns representing a variety of leaf shapes and a supply of refrigerator cookie dough. Have students roll out the dough and use the patterns to cut out leaf-shape cookies. Transfer them to cookie sheets. Meanwhile, make a set of leaf paints by mixing 3 egg yolks with 3/4 teaspoon water. Divide the yolk mixture among several different minimuffin tin cups and add a few drops of food colorings in leafy hues (green, yellow, orange, red, and brown) to each. Children can then use new paintbrushes to paint the leaves as desired. Bake leaf cookies according to package directions, eat, and enjoy.

Curriculum Connections

LANGUAGE ARTS
Why Do Leaves Change Color?

To introduce children to the reason autumn leaves turn colors, provide the class with copies of the poems "Autumn Leaves" and "Why Do Leaves Change Colors?" (see page 68). Discuss the meaning of new vocabulary words, such as *chlorophyll, hues, fades, flecks,* etc.

LANGUAGE ARTS
Looks, Smells, Feels

Wrap up this lesson by bringing students together for a sharing session. Begin by asking students to suggest words that describe leaves. List these words on chart paper. On a second piece of chart paper, write the words *looks, smells,* and *feels* across the top. Display the word list and the chart, then invite students to take turns classifying the words, copying the words from the list on leaf-shaped cards, then pasting them under the correct heading. Challenge students to add new words to each column, too.

MOVEMENT
Like a Leaf

For a change of pace, invite students to dramatize falling leaves in different kinds of weather. Introduce the activity by looking at the weather outside. Is it a calm day? Windy? Pouring? If you can, play appropriate music. (Having your music together in one place will make it easy to jump from one musical selection to another. To get started, create a personal jukebox with iTunes. The software is downloadable for free at www.apple.com/itunes/jukebox.)

MATH
Leaves Fall Off

A maple trees loses about 600,000 leaves in the fall! That number might be tough for students to work with, so look at leaves on one branch of a deciduous tree. How many leaves do students think are on a branch? Count the leaves on a low branch. Compare with the estimate. How can students use this number to estimate the total number of leaves on the tree? If possible, revisit the tree throughout fall to see how fast the leaves fall off.

Autumn Leaves

I wonder in September,
and in October, too,
what oaks and elms and maples
and quaking aspens do
to make their leaves
turn red and gold
instead of pink and blue?

—Aileen Fisher

Why Do Leaves Change Colors?

Why do leaves change colors?
The oak tree always lets me know
When autumn has begun.
But why do its dark green leaves
Change colors one by one?

It's chlorophyll that feeds the tree
And makes the leaves look green.
But underneath and out of view
Are hues that can't be seen.

When the summer ends at last,
And days grow short and cold,
The chlorophyll then fades away,
Revealing flecks of gold.

When all the chlorophyll is gone,
Instead of green we see,
Lovely yellow, orange and red,
Bright leaves on the tree!

—Amy Koss

Leaf Match

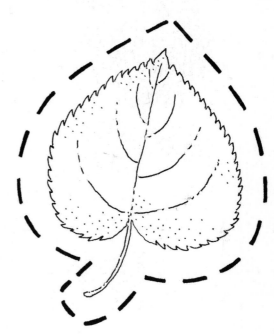

Name _____

Leaf Match

Color in one block for each leaf that is graphed on the big class graph.

What does your leaf graph tell you? _____

_____

RESOURCES

FOR CHILDREN

A Child's Calendar by John Updike (Holiday House, 1999). This collection of poems depicts a child's seasonal activities in a rural setting. Each month is represented by a short poem and two illustrations. Fiction.

It Could Still Be a Tree by Allan Fowler (Children's Press, 1990). Photographs describe the relationship between the seasons and trees. Nonfiction.

Red Leaf, Yellow Leaf by Lois Ehlert (Harcourt Brace Jovanovich, 1991). A colorful book illustrating the growth of a sugar maple tree. Fiction.

Someday a Tree by Eve Bunting (Clarion, 1993). Alice's big old oak tree is loosing its leaves—in the spring. Everyone tries to save the tree, but it is dying. Then Alice thinks of a way to keep part of the tree alive—by planting the acorns she has gathered.

Take a Tree Walk by Jane Kirkland (Stillwater, 2002). Jumpstart learning outside the classroom . . . and take this book with you! Nonfiction.

Why Do Leaves Change Color by Betsy Maestro (HarperCollins, 1994). Readers learn about the changes that take place in trees, causing their leaves to change color and eventually fall. Nonfiction

FOR TEACHERS

Fun With Stencils: Leaves by Paul E. Kennedy (Dover Publications, 1991). A pocket-size booklet containing stencils of six common tree leaves. A fun book to keep in the Science on Display area or in the art center.

Tree Finder by May T. Watts (Nature Study Guild, 1991). A pocket guide to learning about trees and their leaves. Illustrations guide the reader through the process of identification, step by step. Nonfiction.

Trees: A Golden Guide by Herbert Zim (Golden Press, 1952). An easy-to-use field guide to common North American trees. This handy reference was revised and updated in 2001. Nonfiction.

TECHNOLOGY CONNECTIONS

Cool Science for Curious Kids (www.hhmi.org/coolscience/)
Take a visit to Howard Hughes Medical Institute's Cool Science, where children find answers to interesting questions about their world.

Kidsgardening.org (www.kidsgardening.com/teachers.asp)
Find out what is happening in other classrooms around the country via this site's Fruitful Classroom Exchanges. Plus, gain access to garden activities and lessons, information about grants, and free teaching materials.

Smithsonian Kids (www.smithsonianchannel.com)
Smithsonian Kids offers young viewers high-interest programs on a variety of subjects, including natural and social sciences.

Degrees of Weather

During the course of the school year, your students will experience different kinds of weather. What we see outside our windows affects what we wear, what we do, and even how we feel. By including weather study in your curriculum you will be giving students a wonderful opportunity to use simple equipment and understand how tools help us gather data and extend our senses, allowing us to make better observations. During this unit and throughout the year, your students will measure temperature and precipitation. So, come rain or shine, help students discover what weather is all about!

Science Concepts and Skills

Concepts: Students will observe changes in weather and describe their observations in a weather journal. They will begin to notice that, although the weather changes from day to day, over time some things, such as temperature, tend to be constant for the same months from year to year.

Process Skills: observing, predicting, communicating, collecting and recording data

S c i e n c e   D i c t i o n a r y

precipitation any form of water, like snow or rain, that falls to Earth

temperature a measure of how hot or cold something is. We measure temperature with a thermometer

thermometer an instrument for measuring how hot or cold something is; when the liquid inside a thermometer is heated, the liquid expands and moves up the tube; when the liquid cools, it contracts and moves down the tube

weather a description of the conditions outside, including temperature, precipitation, and wind

Science on Display

Find a good spot to place an outdoor thermometer. Look for a place where children can easily read the thermometer from the window. Enlarge a copy of the temperature graph reproducible (see page 80) and tape it near the window. Invite children to decorate the graph by cutting out pictures from magazines that reflect different temperatures and pasting them around the border. (Activity 4, Daily Temperature Graphs, offers ideas for using this graph.)

ACTIVITY 1

Weather Is...

This activity lets students share what they already know about weather and offers a springboard for researching answers to some of the questions they still have. Opportunities like this to ask questions and find answers help children develop important skills they'll use throughout their lives.

Materials

✻ white drawing paper (one piece per student)

✻ crayons, colored pencils, markers

✻ O-rings, stapler, yarn, or other bookbinding materials

Note: *Mark off a 2-inch margin at the top or bottom of the paper. As students prepare to draw their weather pictures, ask them to leave this section blank, so that they can add words later to tell about their pictures.*

1 Ask students to draw a picture that shows weather. Leave your request open-ended so that students' drawings reveal their ideas about weather.

2 As they finish their pictures, have students write "Weather is..." on their pictures and complete the sentence.

3 After giving students time to share their ideas about weather, compile pictures and sentences into a class weather book. Use staples, O-rings, or yarn to bind. (You may want to laminate the pictures before putting them together so they are more durable.) Let students take the weather book home to share with their families. At the end of the school year, take apart the book and put students' pictures in their Science Journals.

4 Review all the things students know about weather, then move on to some of their questions. Ask students what questions they have about weather and compile these on a chart. Discuss ways to find answers to these questions. One strategy you can use to help students pursue areas of interest is to group them by common questions. For example, students who wondered about storms can work together to learn more. This is a good opportunity to team up your students with upper-grade buddies, who can strengthen their own research skills as they help their young buddies find information.

ACTIVITY 2

Weather Reporters

You can help students build on observation, prediction, and other skills by making weather a year-round focus. (You'll find weather-related activities throughout this book.) This activity sets up a class weather-reporting calendar that you can use again and again. Meanwhile, encourage children to keep individual calendars in their science journals.

Materials

✳ butcher paper

1 Create and display a large, blank calendar.

Note: As new weather concepts are introduced throughout the school year, encourage students to incorporate these into their weather observations. Look for evidence of growth over time in students' dated reports.

2 Set up a schedule for weather observations so that for each day of the school week, several students are making and recording weather observations. For example, if you have 25 students, five students will record observations every Monday, five every Tuesday, and so on. This will give students many opportunities to record and share weather observations throughout the school year, and will provide the class with a fairly complete yearlong record of weather.

3 Explain that on their assigned weather days they will be responsible for observing and recording the day's weather. Students can do this with pictures and/or words and should be sure to date all entries.

4 If you do the daily weather as a part of your morning routine, have the assigned observers give the weather report. (Schedule about ten minutes a day for students to observe, record, and report on the weather.)

ACTIVITY 3

Hot or Cold?

Students will discover whether things are heating up or cooling down and, in the process, learn to use one of the most common tools for weather reporting—the thermometer.

Materials

* outdoor thermometer (see Science on Display, page 73)
* plastic thermometers (one thermometer for each group of two or three students)
* plastic drinking cups (two for each small group)
* ice
* warm water
* clock
* Hot or Cold? Science Journal page (see page 79)

1 Ask students if they know how we can tell how hot or cold something is. Guide this discussion to introduce the word *thermometer*. Ask students if they can guess how a thermometer works. Share the definition in the Science Dictionary (see page 73).

2 Explain that you have some thermometers, ice, warm water, and cups. Ask: How do you think we can use these materials to show how a thermometer works?

3 Work with students to design a simple experiment. Write directions for conducting the experiment on a piece of chart paper. Incorporate students' ideas into the simple experiment described here.

   ✻ Set the thermometer on the desk. Read the room temperature. On your worksheet, fill in Test 1 to record this temperature (see page 79).

   ✻ Next, set the thermometer in a cup of ice for two minutes. Watch what happens to the thermometer. After two minutes, read the temperature and record it on your worksheet for Test 2.

   ✻ Now put the thermometer in a cup of warm water for two minutes. Watch what happens to the thermometer. After two minutes, read the temperature and record it on the worksheet for Test 3.

4 Discuss the results of this experiment. Have students complete their worksheets to apply what they've learned.

ACTIVITY 4

Daily Temperature Graphs

By recording temperature over time, students discover patterns and strengthen their predicting abilities.

Materials

   ✻ reproducible (see page 80)

   ✻ red marker or colored pencil

   ✻ thermometer and chart-size thermometer graph (see Science on Display, page 73)

Note: You will be using the Science on Display setup for this activity. Provide each child with a set of four reproducible graphs (copy front and back, if possible), stapled to keep pages together. If possible, introduce the activity at midday, as this is probably the time of day that the temperature peaks. Try to have students record the temperature at the same time each day for the rest of the year. This will allow them to make more meaningful comparisons.

1 Show students the daily temperature graph (see page 80). Explain that everyone is welcome to check out the thermometer and temperature graph each day, but that students will take turns being in charge of recording the temperature on the graph. Together, create a schedule, assigning each child a day to check and record the temperature. Keep the time of day constant. (When each child has had a chance, just start over.)

2 Invite the first person on the schedule to come to the thermometer and read the temperature. Help this child find the correct place on the graph to record the temperature, using the red marker or pencil. Have children fill in the same information on their graphs.

3 Explain that the class will keep a temperature graph for each month of the school year. Ask students to predict how the graphs may change over time. Encourage students to record their predictions in their weather journals and rethink them as they gather additional information. You can also record their predictions on chart paper and post next to the thermometer graph.

4 To go further, you might like to pick a month to have students check the temperature twice a day—once in the morning, then again at the regular afternoon time. What do they notice about the morning temperatures versus the afternoon temperatures?

Curriculum Connections

LANGUAGE ARTS: *Riddle Writing*

What kind of weather can make a person or a puddle? (snow) Invite students to create their own weather riddles. First, share Gail Gibbons's *Weather Words and What They Mean* with students (see Resources, page 81). Follow up by listing weather words from the book on chart paper. Students can add their own words to this list, too, then use the chart as a reference. Students can display riddles in the science area or bind them into a book, slipping answers into pockets they can make on the pages. (Cut envelopes in half and glue one half to each page. Slip answers in the pockets.)

MATH: *Graph Guide*

At the end of each month, use the daily temperature graph to reinforce a variety of math skills. Guide your lesson with questions like the following:

1. On which day was the temperature the highest?

2. What was the highest temperature for the month of _____ ?

3. What was the lowest temperature for that month?

4. What can you say about the temperatures in _____ compared with the temperatures in December?

5. Which of these months: _____, _____, and _____ had the warmest temperatures?

6. Which month had the most days below _____ degrees?

7. Which day in _____ was closest to today's temperature?

Name_____

Hot or Cold?

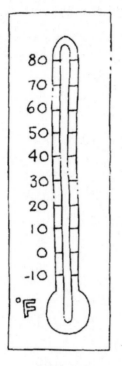

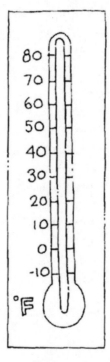

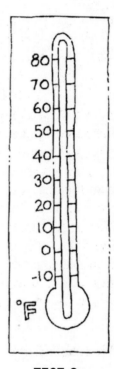

TEST 1
Before the Experiment

TEST 2
Ice

TEST 3
Warm Water

Which thermometer shows the coldest temperature?_____

Which thermometer shows the warmest temperature? _____

Write the thermometers' temperatures in order from coldest to warmest. _____

On the back of this page, draw a picture of what you think a thermometer would look like on a cold, snowy day or on a hot, sunny day.

Name_____

Daily Temperature

Month_____ Week of _____

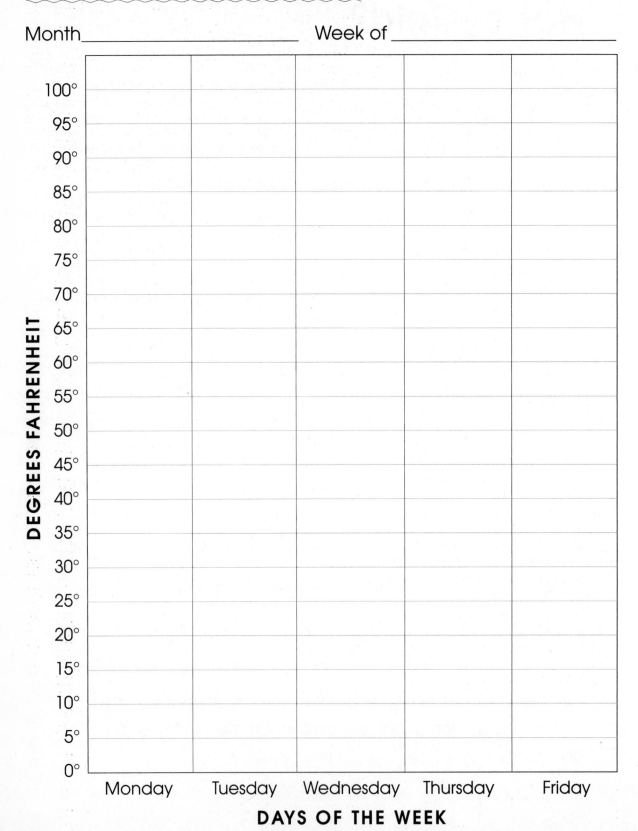

DEGREES FAHRENHEIT

100°
95°
90°
85°
80°
75°
70°
65°
60°
55°
50°
45°
40°
35°
30°
25°
20°
15°
10°
5°
0°

Monday   Tuesday   Wednesday   Thursday   Friday

DAYS OF THE WEEK

RESOURCES

FOR CHILDREN

Cloudy With a Chance of Meatballs by Judi Barrett (Atheneum, 1978). A delightful and preposterous adventure in a town where it rains soup and snows mashed potatoes. Fiction.

How Do You Know It's Fall? by Allan Fowler (Children's Press, 1992). Other books in this series include *How Do You Know It's Spring? How Do You Know It's Winter?* and *How Do You Know It's Summer?* Nonfiction.

Sun Up, Sun Down by Gail Gibbons (Harcourt, 1983). An imaginative look at the many ways in which the cycles of the sun impact life on Earth. Nonfiction.

The Year at Maple Hill Farm by Alice and Martin Provensen (Atheneum, 1978). Events on a farm during each month of the year are colorfully illustrated in this book. Fiction.

Weather Words and What They Mean by Gail Gibbons (Holiday House, 1990). Interesting weather facts add interest to this collection of weather terms. Nonfiction.

FOR TEACHERS

Change It!: Solids, Liquids, Gases and You by Adrienne Mason (Kids Can Press, 2006). Engaging activities help children learn challenging physical science concepts.

"School Weather Station" is a one-stop weather center that invites students to record the daily temperature, rainfall, wind direction—and graph that data over time. Ideal for the youngest meteorologists. For information contact Lakeshore Learning, (800) 421-5354, www.lakeshorelearning.com.

Standards-Based Science Learning Centers by Lynne Kepler (Scholastic, 2006). Hands-on activities with companion reproducible recording pages make it easier to set up science centers, including one on weather.

TECHNOLOGY CONNECTIONS

NOAA Education: Advancing Environmental Literacy (www.education.noaa.gov/index.html) This Web link made available by the National Oceanic and Atmospheric Administration (NOAA) provides links to educational sites and organizations dedicated to science education—links designed for teachers, students (K–5 and 6–12), and everyone else. Be sure to look in on the NOAA photo library: www.photolib.noaa.gov/

NOVA Field Trips: Weather Gone Wild by NOVA (WGBH Boston, 2004). The three virtual field trips in this DVD boxed set include: *Hurricane!, Hunt for the Supertwister,* and *Lightning!* Collection comes complete with teaching suggestions and downloadable educational materials. The set has a total run time of 180 minutes.

82

CHAPTER 5

November

Harvest Time
page 86

Bears in Winter
page 104

Highlights *of the* Month

Mark these dates, events, and activities on your calendar to help plan and supplement this month's themes.

✳ Thanksgiving

✳ The full moon is the Beaver Moon. The wise beaver is preparing for winter.

✳ What kinds of bears (or other animals) are preparing for a long winter's sleep in your state? Research with your students.

✳ Keep an eye out for migrating geese.

✳ Flying squirrels store nuts in tree cavities during the fall. Do they really fly?

✳ String cranberries and popcorn for birds.

Plan Ahead

Students will be making corn-husk wreaths (see page 98). Check with a farm stand or produce department for a supply of corn husks.

Students will be making bird-feeding stations in December. This is a good time to send notes home explaining the project, requesting small donations of birdseed.

Activities in Theme 1 call for pumpkins, cranberries, and Indian corn. You might want to send a note home asking if parents can donate any of these materials.

If you want parent volunteers for any of the activities, such as Making Muffins (page 92), include this request with your note, too.

SCIENCE AT HOME

Date _____

This month we are starting two new science themes.

1. Harvest Time

Pumpkins and cranberries are two festive foods that are common this time of year. Your child will be working with these items to learn about how plants are a source of food. Use mealtimes at home to reinforce this concept. Talk about where different foods you eat come from. Which are plants? Your child can even keep a chart on the refrigerator, drawing in the plant foods served each day at breakfast, lunch, and dinner.

2. Bears in Winter

As we investigate bears this month, your child will be learning about how bears adapt to cold temperatures. Some natural connections will be to look at children's own need for food and shelter, and how these needs are met.

Wish List

Do you have materials you can donate for our science explorations? For this month's activities, we need:

_____

_____

_____

Reminders _____

_____

_____

Harvest Time

Novomber is a time for observing our relationships with nature and with one another. Pumpkins, cranberries, and Indian corn traditionally symbolize this time of year. Some of these foods are shared in celebration with family and friends; some are stored for future meals. This lesson takes a closer look at these foods to help students recognize the many varieties of plant crops and how we use them.

 S c i e n c e   D i c t i o n a r y

fruit the part of the plant that forms around the seeds; fruits are usually wet and fleshy (like peaches and berries) or dry and hard (like walnuts and pea pods); there are some fruits that people often think of as vegetables (like tomatoes)

seed the part of the plant that contains a baby plant (embryo)

Science Concepts and Skills

Concepts: Students will observe objects in their world and recognize properties of these objects. In addition, they will recognize plants as a source of food for humans.

Process Skills: observing, classifying, communicating, predicting, estimating, comparing, measuring, collecting and recording data

Science on Display

Do you still have those autumn leaves from October's activities? Keep them! Cover the top three-fourths of a bulletin board with light blue paper. Finish the bottom fourth with brown paper. Tear the top edge of the brown paper to give it an uneven, earthy appearance. Add some real corn stalks (or cut them from construction paper) to create a cornfield. This is where students will plant their corn kernel–growing bags (see Activity 4: Counting on Corn, page 94). Finally, display a basket of pumpkins and Indian corn. Students will add to this seasonal display in upcoming activities.

ACTIVITY 1

Seasonal Fruit Fun

What could a pumpkin possibly have in common with a cranberry? This set of three activities highlights similarities (and differences) of seasonal fruit.

PART 1: MYSTERY FRUITS

Materials

* ✽ 2 paper grocery bags
* ✽ a small pumpkin
* ✽ several fresh cranberries
* ✽ chart paper and a marker

Note: Before begin-ning this activity, put the small pump-kin in one bag and the cranberries in another. Fold over the tops and staple shut. Write the numeral 1 on the pumpkin bag and the numeral 2 on the cranberry bag.

1 Show students Bag 1 and ask them to guess what's inside. Write their guesses on a chart labeled What's Inside Bag 1?

2 Now ask students what might help them make better guesses without opening the bag. Student suggestions will probably include being able to hold the bag and shake it. Students may also suggest that you give them some hints.

3 Pass around the bag so students can make observations with their eyes, ears, nose, and hands. After everyone has had a chance to hold the bag, have them share their new observations. Could the contents of the bag be something that they already have on the guess list? Is it something that is not on the list? Are there ideas on the list they can safely remove? Discuss new ideas and modify the list.

4 If students have not guessed the contents of the bag yet, begin giving verbal clues. For example: It is a fruit. After each clue let students review and revise the list.

5 Continue until students think they have guessed the mystery object. Then open the bag for all to see!

6 Repeat steps 1 through 5 with Bag 2.

7 Together, compare guess lists for bags 1 and 2. What characteristics did the contents have in common? How were they different?

PART 2: MINI-BOOK

Note: Have chil-dren construct the booklet by cutting on the dotted lines and placing pages 1/8 and 2/7 back to back, 3/6 and 4/5 back to back.

Materials

✳ plastic dishpan

✳ water

✳ balance (scale)

✳ yardstick or meterstick

✳ chart paper

✳ for each small group: a small pumpkin and 1 cranberry

✳ for each student: a copy of the reproducible booklet (see pages 100 and 101); chart paper

Note: *Prepare for this activity in advance by setting up a workstation with a dishpan filled with water and a balance scale. Display a chart on a nearby chalkboard or a wall for each group (see sample, below). Students will record their data for Task 3 here.*

1 Review each of the observation tasks from the reproducible booklet before having students complete pages 1 through 6.

Observation Task 1—Shape, Color, and Texture: Students describe the shape, color, and texture of their group's pumpkin and cranberries on page 1.

Observation Task 2—Weight: Students weigh the pumpkin and one cranberry (separately), and record weights on page 2.

Observation Task 3—Circumference: How big around is a pumpkin? A cranberry? Have each group estimate the circumference of the pumpkin and a cranberry, cutting lengths of string to show how much they think it will take to wrap around the widest part of each fruit. Next, have students use the string to measure the circumference of each fruit. Have each group display the estimates on the left side of a chart and the actual measurements on the right.

Have each group measure estimated and actual lengths of the circumference strings and then complete pages 3 and 4 of the booklet. Were the estimates too short, too long, or just right?

Observation Task 4—Sink or Float: Students predict, then test, whether their pumpkins and cranberries will sink or float. Discuss predictions, then have students complete the appropriate parts of pages 5 and 6. Next, have students test their predictions by placing the fruit in the pan of water, and record results on pages 5 and 6.

Pumpkin Estimate	Pumpkin Measurement	Cranberry Estimate	Cranberry Measurement
1 2 3 4		1 2 3 4	

Note: As with the moon phases, it is a good idea to revisit concepts and give students opportunities to think about what they have learned. To wrap up this part, show students a pumpkin much larger than the ones they tested. Ask them to predict whether this pumpkin will sink or float and to explain their reasoning. Generally, kids believe that larger, heavier objects will sink. Even though they will have discovered that the smaller pumpkins float, some students may be convinced that the larger pumpkin will sink. Explain that whether or not something sinks or floats depends on its density (weight per volume). The pumpkin is not heavy enough (dense enough) to push the water out of the way. As a result, the pumpkin is actually held afloat by the water. Things that are heavier (more dense) than water will sink. In Part 3 you will open up each fruit and look for clues as to why they floated (air pockets).

PART 3: LOOK INSIDE

Materials

* a sharp knife (for teacher use)
* plastic knives
* reproducible booklets (from Part 2)
* for each small group: the pumpkin and cranberries from Part 2, newspaper to protect work areas, handheld magnifying lenses

1 Have students write or draw a picture of how they think the insides of the pumpkin and cranberries will look.

2 Cut open both the pumpkin and the cranberries for each group. Ask students to take a close look at the insides with the hand lenses. Can they find the seeds in each?

　　As students examine the insides of the fruit, ask them about the hollow areas they see. Explain that these are air pockets, which helped the fruit float in Part 2.

3 Have students use the cranberry halves like stamps to make prints in their booklets on page 7. After a close look with a hand lens, ask students to draw life-size pictures of the seeds.

4 Ask students to complete page 8, describing the insides of their pumpkins and drawing life-size pictures of the seeds.

5 As a class, share and reflect on what they have learned about pumpkins and cranberries. Discussion starters include:

* How are pumpkins and cranberries alike?

* How are they different?

* What surprised you the most about the pumpkin? The cranberry?

ACTIVITY 2 ～～～～～～～～～～～～～～～～～～～～～～～～～～

An A-maize-ing Crop

Sweet, flour, flint, dent, pop… all are kinds of corn. By the time Colonists landed in the New World, about 50,000 acres of this corn were being cultivated by Native Americans. Help students get to know this mighty grain with the following activity.

Note: Before beginning the activity, place a small piece of masking tape on the husk of each ear of corn. Write a number on each husk. Assign one student in each small group to be the recorder.

Materials (for each group of 2 or 3 students)

✷ 1 small ear of Indian corn (look for ears with color variation)

✷ large sheet of construction paper (Indian corn colors)

✷ markers

1 Give each small group an ear of corn. Have the recorder in each group look for the number on the husk and write this number in a corner on the construction paper.

2 Now it's time for groups to brainstorm words that describe their ears of corn. Remind them to use all of their senses (except taste in this case). Ask the recorders to write these words on the construction paper.

Note: You'll learn a lot about your students' thought processes by eavesdropping on this part of the activity. You will be amazed at the different approaches they take. Some students may draw lines to form the chart before the brainstorming ever begins, then neatly place words within the chart. Others will write fast and furiously, recording words all over the paper as quickly as their group members can say them.

3 Allow 10 to 15 minutes for brainstorming, then collect the ears of corn and place them where everyone can see them. Let groups take turns sharing their descriptions while others guess which ear of corn is being described.

4 Follow up with a discussion about the activity. Was it easy or difficult to figure out which ear of corn belonged to each group? What words, if any, did each group use? What words were unique to just one group? How is Indian corn different from other kinds of corn? (Have some on hand for a comparison if possible.) How is it the same?

ACTIVITY 3 ~~~~~~

Making Muffins

BOOK BREAK
Read Aliki's *Corn Is Maize* to students (see Resources, page 103), a fascinating story about how Native Americans found and cultivated a wild grass that became a staple in our diets.

From the math of measuring to the science of change, making muffins is naturally multidisciplinary. There are many different strategies for making muffins with students. Here's one approach that works well.

~~~~~~

Materials

  ❋ muffin ingredients (see recipe cards, opposite)
  ❋ muffin pans

~~~~~~

Note: As you prepare for this activity, send home a letter asking families to share favorite muffin recipes. Students can work together to organize, illustrate, compile, and publish the recipes. Make copies for each student to take home. You might also have students take photos of the cooking experience that they can display, include in a class scrapbook, or use to illustrate a class story about the activity (see step 4).

1 Begin by showing students all of the muffin ingredients. Have them name as many as they can and make observations of each ingredient. This will enhance their recognition of just how these ingredients, when mixed together and cooked, change in texture and form.

2 Make task cards by breaking the muffin-making experience into as many steps as you have students (or groups). Tasks can include gathering equipment, measuring a cup of flour, cracking an egg and adding it to the mixture, stirring for one minute, dropping spoonfuls of the batter into baking tins, and so on. This will give every child a chance to help.

3 Guide students in making the muffin batter. When you are finished mixing the batter, have students note which ingredients they can still see and which look different. (For example, the cranberries will still have their shape but will be coated with batter; the flour and other dry ingredients are now mixed together with the liquid.) Record students' observations on a chart.

4 While muffins are baking, have students tell, in their own words, how to make muffins. Write up their cooking story on chart paper.

5 As students enjoy the warm muffins, have them take note, once again, of ways the ingredients have changed. Add their comments to the language experience story from step 4.

Corn Muffins

2 eggs	2 cups cornmeal
2 cups milk	6 T. sugar
$\frac{1}{4}$ cup oil	2 T. baking powder
2 cups flour	2 t. salt

Mix together the eggs, milk, and oil. Set aside. Mix dry ingredients in a separate bowl. Add egg mixture and stir. Pour into greased or paper-lined muffin pans. Bake at 400° F for 20 to 25 minutes. Makes 2 dozen muffins. Variation: Try adding peeled, chopped apple to the mixture before baking.

Pumpkin Muffins

2 eggs	1 cup sugar
$1\frac{1}{2}$ cups milk	$1\frac{1}{4}$ t. pumpkin pie spice
4 T. oil	4 cups biscuit mix
1 cups cooked (or canned) pumpkin	

Mix together the eggs, milk, and oil. Add the pumpkin, sugar, and pumpkin pie spice. Stir, then add the biscuit mix. Mix all ingredients and pour into greased or paper-lined muffin pans. Bake at 350°F for 25 minutes. Makes 2 dozen muffins.

Cranberry Muffins

2 eggs	1 cup sugar
$1\frac{1}{2}$ cups milk	$\frac{1}{4}$ cup orange rind
4 T. oil	4 cups biscuit mix
1 cup chopped cranberries	

Mix together the eggs, milk, and oil. Add the cranberries, sugar, and orange rind. Stir, then add the biscuit mix. Mix all ingredients and pour into greased or paper-lined muffin pans. Bake at 350°F for 25 minutes. Makes 2 dozen muffins.

ACTIVITY 4

Counting on Corn

Students estimate, count, and graph corn kernels for a close-up look at this vegetable's seed.

Materials

* Indian corn (from Activity 1), plus 1 extra ear
* reclosable plastic bag
* Counting on Corn Science Journal page (see page 102)
* colored pencils or crayons

Note: Check to make sure the ears of corn still have numbers on them. Number each bag accordingly.

1 Give each group an ear of Indian corn and the plastic bag that has the same number.

2 Hold up an ear and ask students if they know what we call the part of the corn that we eat. (We eat the seeds, which are often called *kernels*. Kernels are part of the corn seed.)

3 Next have each student estimate how many kernels are on the group's ear of corn and record this number on the reproducible record sheet.

BOOK BREAK
All their work with pumpkins and cranberries is sure to have students thinking about Thanksgiving. Share a story with a twist: In *A Turkey for Thanksgiving* by Eve Bunting, Turkey, for a change, is a guest at a Thanksgiving celebration, hosted by Mr. and Mrs. Moose.

4 Students in each group now work together to remove the kernels from the ear of corn and place them in the plastic bag. (To make it easier for the students to get the kernels off the cob, you might want to pull off the first few. Be sure to place the kernels in the appropriate bags.) Note: Have students save the husks for use in an upcoming art activity (see Curriculum Connections, page 97).

5 When all of the kernels are removed, have students work together to determine the total number of kernels. Ask them to record their methods of calculating. (Some might put the kernels into piles of ten and then count. Others might split up the kernels between themselves, count their piles, and add the sums of the piles together.) Students then record the total number of kernels on the reproducible (ten kernels equals one square) and compare their estimates with the actual amount.

6 Encourage students to apply what they've learned by asking them to estimate the number of kernels on a new ear of corn.

Pass around the ear so all students can get a close-up look. Ask students to record their estimates, then invite them to share their reasoning. For example, a student might compare the size of the new ear with the original ear and adjust the estimate up or down accordingly. Work together to count the kernels, then compare estimates and the actual amount.

ACTIVITY 5

Planting Corn Seeds

Students discover where new corn plants come from.

Materials

✽ corn kernels (from Activity 4)

For each student:

✽ a paper towel

✽ a reclosable plastic sandwich bag

✽ an index card

✽ a thumbtack

1 Hold up a bag of corn kernels. Ask students what would happen if they planted the kernels? (New corn plants should grow from these seeds.) How many new corn plants would they have if each kernel grew? (Suggest that students think back to the last activity. Potentially, this could be hundreds of new plants from one ear!)

2 In preparation for planting, have each student write his or her name and the date on the index card. Then have students return to their small groups with their bag of kernels. Ask each student to take five kernels.

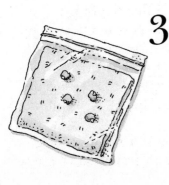

3 Next, demonstrate the steps for planting the kernels inside the plastic bag.

✽ Dip the paper towel in water. Squeeze out the excess.

✽ Fold the damp paper towel to a size that will fit inside the bag.

✽ Place five kernels on top of the towel, then carefully slip the towel inside the bag. Zip shut.

4   After completing these steps, ask students to record
     observations of their kernels on their index cards. Remind
     them to date their entries.

5   Have students use the thumbtacks to attach their planting
     bags and index cards to the science bulletin board (see
     Science on Display, page 87).

6   Students check their kernels daily, recording the date and
     observations on their index cards each time. (Students can
     carefully remove their bags and index cards from the bulletin
     board for this, replacing them when done.)

7   Wrap up this lesson by discussing students' observations. What
     did they see that indicated their kernels had started to grow?
     Did all the seeds start growing on the same day? Did all the
     seeds grow? What will happen if they continue to let the new
     corn plants grow? Is this a good time of year to grow corn
     where you live? Why or why not?

Hint

*To keep the paper towel from drying out, add just enough water to
the bag so that the bottom of the paper towel is touching the water
and acts like a wick.*

HARVEST TASTE TEST

Brainstorm a list of autumn harvest-related foods (apples, corn, nuts, cranberries, pumpkin,
etc.). In a twist on Stone Soup, assign each child one piece (or small amount) of food to
contribute to a class harvest taste-testing celebration. If necessary, modify the foods on
your original list so that the foods collected are easily shared in class (popcorn instead of
fresh corn; cranberry sauce instead of cranberries; and so on). Use the opportunity to have
children comment on the textures, tastes, colors, and smells of each food.

Curriculum Connections

LANGUAGE ARTS
My Great Corn Plants

Use the poem "My Great Corn Plants" (see page 99) to demonstrate how ancient Native American customs and religions consider plants and animals to be special gifts from nature. Ask children to tell how the poet's words helped the plants come to life for the reader. (The poet talks to the plants that are described as having hands.) Explain that when a writer makes a plant, an animal, or an object look or behave like a person, it is called *personification*. Begin a class list of other stories, books, or poems with examples of such personification.

LANGUAGE ARTS
Pop-up Pumpkins

Make pop-up pumpkin books for a variety of writing projects. To begin, make a pumpkin template. Have children trace four pumpkins on construction paper, cut them out, stack them, and fold them in half. Open the pages and place two or three staples along the fold. Make pumpkins stand up by spreading the pages apart.

Story starters follow:

✳ Make an acrostic poem by writing each letter from the word *pumpkin* on a page (not including the title page). Think of a word that begins with the letter *p* that describes pumpkins. Write this on the *p* page. Repeat with each of the other letters.

✳ With younger children, make a *Letter P* picture book by cutting out pictures of things that begin with the letter *p*.

✳ Keep a journal from the point of view of the class pumpkin.

Students can share their books at the reading/language arts center. Place some next to the cornstalk display or in an old bushel basket.

Variation: Make pop-up cranberry books. Use lids from one-pound coffee cans as templates to cut out circle-shaped pages from red paper.

DRAMA
Stalks and Vines

As you read the Native American poem "My Great Corn Plants" on page 99, have children take turns acting out the poem. Some children can be corn plants and squash vines reaching out, while others can walk through the stalks and vines. Have children think up other types of plants they might substitute in the poem and then act out. Comment specifically on the different ways students move and shape their bodies to portray each plant.

MATH
How Many Seeds?

For more estimating practice, have students return to their small groups and number a piece of paper 1 through however many bags of kernels there are. Be sure the bags are zipped shut, then pass them around. Give each group one minute to estimate how many kernels are in each bag. Continue rotating bags until each group has recorded estimates for them all. Then let groups take turns announcing how many kernels are in their original bags.

ART
Make a Corn-Husk Wreath

Make corn-husk wreaths like the one shown at the end of *Corn Is Maize* by Aliki (see Resources, page 103). Students will each need a 10-inch piece of stiff, fine wire (check craft stores) and corn husks (check with a farm stand or produce store).

1. Before beginning the wreaths, show students the husks. Ask if they know what part of the corn plant these are. (The leaves that wrap around the ear of corn.)

2. Prepare the husks by soaking them in water for a few minutes. This will make them easier to fold. While husks are soaking, help students form circles out of the wire by twisting the ends together.

3. Have students tear softened husks into half-inch-wide strips. Then attach to the wire as follows.

   a. Fold a piece of husk in half and hold it behind the wire circle.
   b. Fold the ends over the wire.
   c. Slip the ends through the loop. Pull tight to make a knot.

   d. Repeat steps a, b, and c until the wreath is full.

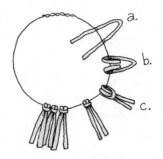

4. Place the wreath between two damp paper towels, then weight down with a heavy book. (This helps the wreaths to dry flat.)

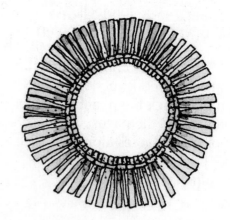

My great corn plants,
Among them I walk.
I speak to them;
They hold out their hands to me.

My great squash vines,
Among them I walk.
I speak to them;
They hold out their hands to me.

—Navajo

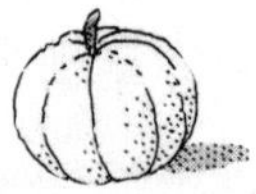

PUMPKIN

Shape________________________

Color_________________________

Texture ______________________

CRANBERRY

Shape________________________

Color_________________________

Texture ______________________

1

Circumference of Our Cranberry

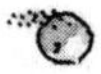

We predicted it would be ________ inch(es) around.

We measured our cranberry and it is ________ inch(es) around.

Our prediction was...

too short

too long

exactly right

4

We predict that our pumpkin will...

SINK

FLOAT

When we put the pumpkin in water, it

SINKS

FLOATS

5

Write five words that describe the inside of your pumpkin.

Draw a pumpkin seed.

8

Cut out on dotted lines, fold on solid lines.

Circumference of Our Pumpkin

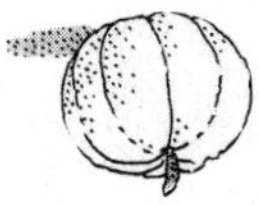

We predicted it would be ________ inches around.

We measured our pumpkin and it is ________ inches around.

Our prediction was
too short
too long
exactly right

3

We predict that our cranberry will...

SINK

FLOAT

When we put the cranberry in water, it

SINKS

FLOATS

6

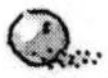

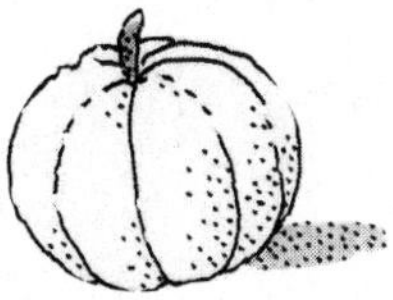

Our pumpkin weighs

____

Our cranberry weighs

____

2

Describe what you think the cranberry will look like inside.

Make a print of your cranberry here. Draw some cranberry seeds.

7

Cut out on dotted lines, fold on solid lines.

Name_____

Counting on Corn

My Estimate   I think our ear of corn has _____ kernels.

My Count   To count the kernels on our ear of corn, we will

_____

_____

We counted _____ kernels
on our ear of corn.

Now color in the number of
kernels that your group counts
on the ear of corn.

On one dozen ears of corn, I
estimate there are _____
kernels.

This is how I estimated:

_____

_____

_____

_____

_____

One square equals ten kernels.

RESOURCES

FOR CHILDREN

Corn Is Maize by Aliki (HarperCollins, 1976). The history of corn and how Native Americans and new settlers of America used it. Nonfiction.

The Harvest Birds/Los Pájaros de la Cosecha by Blanca López de Mariscal (Children's Press, 1995). A farmer gets advice for improving his harvest from helpful birds in this Mexican folktale. Told in English and Spanish. Fiction.

Mousekin's Golden House by Edna Miller (Prentice Hall, 1964). The classic about a mouse who finds shelter in a decaying pumpkin. Fiction.

Pumpkin, Pumpkin by Jeanne Titherington (Greenwillow, 1986). Simple text describes how a child plants pumpkin seeds and watches as they grow. Fiction.

Raccoons and Ripe Corn by Jim Arnosky (Lothrop, 1987). The reader watches as several raccoons raid an autumn cornfield. Fiction.

A Turkey for Thanksgiving by Eve Bunting (Clarion, 1991). In this humorous story, Turkey is a guest for a change at a Thanksgiving celebration, hosted by Mr. and Mrs. Moose. Fiction.

FOR TEACHERS

Apples by Mary Ellen Sterling (Teacher Created Materials, 1990). This theme unit offers a wide range of cross-curricular activities and projects related to a popular harvest food, apples.

Project Seasons by Deborah Parrella (Shelburne Farms; Shelburne, Vermont). This wonderful collection of farming and agriculture activities for elementary students is organized by seasons. To purchase, call (802) 985-8686 or visit www.shelburnefarms.org/basket.asp.

TECHNOLOGY CONNECTIONS

Reading Rainbow: June 29, 1999 by David Wiesner GPN Educational Media (http://shopgpn.com/stores/1/RR_BookLists.cfm) How big can a pumpkin grow? See some that weigh hundreds of pounds! For more information about this episode that explores pumpkin growing and the concepts of fact and fiction, visit GPN Educational Media's Web site.

Harvest Ceremony: Beyond the Thanksgiving Myth National Museum of the American Indian (www.nmai.si.edu/) This information-packed resource (available as a PDF) was created especially for teachers. Use it to build your own background knowledge about the first Thanksgiving—and to help dispel some of the myths that surround the harvest celebration and Native peoples (then and now). The role of corn is a featured topic.

Bears in Winter

This is the time of year when bears prepare for winter. For months now they have been feasting, storing much of what they eat as fat. When the cold settles in and food is scarce, they are

---

Science Concepts and Skills

Concepts: Students will learn that a bear's behavior during this time of year is related to its environment, specifically the cold temperatures and scarcity of food supplies.

Process Skills: observing, communicating

S c i e n c e   D i c t i o n a r y

bear a large mammal; three kinds of bears live in North America: the black bear, the grizzly bear, and the polar bear; all go into a winter sleep; black and grizzly bears enter their period of winter sleep when food is scarce, usually during winter months, but polar bears can enter into winter sleep at any time of the year if food is scarce

den a cave or shelter for an animal; bears go to dens for the winter, where they sleep until spring comes again

dormancy (or winter sleep) the way some animals cope with winter by "sleeping" for part of the winter; a dormant bear's body temperature drops a little below normal (from about 100°F to 88°F) and its heart rate drops to almost 8 beats per minute (from 50 to 80 beats per minute when active); during winter sleep a bear lives entirely off its stored body fat

hibernation a deep sleep that animals go into during winter; true hibernators (such as bats, chipmunks, and many rodents) experience a drop in body temperature that is just above freezing; the breathing rates of animals that hibernate slow down; if disturbed, true hibernators take several hours to rouse, whereas bears remain relatively alert and can get up right away if they need to

migration the movement of some animals from one place to another to find food and shelter

ready to take shelter in caves or under the roots of dead trees, and go into a deep sleep until spring, when food is once again readily available. There is some confusion about whether bears hibernate. Not many animals are considered true hibernators. Unlike true hibernators, which take several hours to rouse from a winter sleep, bears can wake up immediately, for example, if disturbed. A bear's temperature in a winter sleep drops a little, whereas a true hibernator's temperature drops drastically.

Science on Display

Prior to beginning this theme, make bear tracks. Copy the reproducible pattern onto black construction paper, laminate, and cut out. Make as many tracks as you like, forming a trail from the front door, or some other location, to a "den" (an area set aside for this theme). Cover one wall in this area with a piece of craft paper and display the title WHAT WE LEARNED ABOUT BEARS. Students will add to the display in Activity 1: Bear Facts.

ACTIVITY 1 ~~~~~~~~~~~~~~~~~~~~~~~~~~~~~~~~~~~~

Bear Facts

Let your students share what they know and want to know about bears. Then put your young researchers on the right track to finding answers to their questions.

~~~~~~~~~~~~~~~~~~~~~~~~~~~~~~~~~~~~

Materials

✳ 2 pieces of chart paper

✳ mural paper

✳ marker

✳ 2 bear tracks per student, 1 front track and 1 back track each (see reproducible, page 111)

✳ tape

~~~~~~~~~~~~~~~~~~~~~~~~~~~~~~~~~~~~

1 Invite students to speculate about the tracks they see in the classroom (see Science on Display, page 105). Give them clues to the animal's identify, if necessary.

2 Once the bear's identity is revealed, write on one sheet of chart paper "What We Know About Bears." Have students list (or dictate) what they already know about bears.

3 Share a question you have about bears. Write this question on a "front" bear track. Ask students if they have any questions. Pass out front bear tracks and have students write down (or dictate) their questions. Some students may not have questions at this time. This is okay. Just keep the tracks handy so that when they have questions they can write them down.

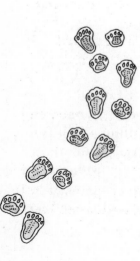

4 Let students share their questions, then tape the tracks to the second piece of chart paper labeled "Questions We Have About Bears." (Add yours, too.)

5 Discuss ways to find answers to the questions. Mention resources like books, field guides, videos, even people, such as a game protector at the nearest fish and wildlife department or a zoologist. Don't forget your class or library computer. (See Resources, page 113.)

6 After tracking down information, students can use back bear tracks to write down the answers to their questions, pull off their front tracks from the question chart, and tape both tracks together on the mural titled WHAT WE LEARNED ABOUT BEARS (see Science on Display, page 105).

ACTIVITY 2

Ready for Winter?

How do humans prepare for winter? How about bears? This activity invites children to learn more about winter survival and to examine their own needs for shelter and food.

BOOK BREAK
Introduce students to the idea of bears getting ready for winter with Jim Arnosky's book *Every Autumn Comes the Bear.* (see Resources, page 113). Guide students in a discussion about bears preparing for winter—what they eat, how they put on weight, how they find dens for the winter, and so on. After your discussion, explain that students will be making a class big book that compares how bears and people get ready for winter. Plan to complete the activity in three days.

Materials

✱ watercolor paints

✱ salt

✱ cups for water

✱ for each student: a large sheet of blue construction paper, 2 pieces of white watercolor paper (half the size of the construction paper), a paintbrush; plain paper

1 On Day 1, have students use watercolors to paint pictures of bears getting ready for winter. Have students sprinkle salt over the paint while it is still wet. As the paint dries, this will create a soft, crystal-like appearance on the pictures.

2 On Day 2, have students paint pictures of something they or others do to get ready for winter. Repeat the salting process.

3 On Day 3, have students use strips of plain paper to write about what is happening in each picture, then attach the strips to their paintings.

4 Help each student fold a large sheet of construction paper in half, glue the bear picture to the left half, and glue the people picture to the right half.

5 Stack all of the folded construction paper pages, punch a hole through all layers at the top and the bottom, and fasten them with O-rings.

6 Read the book together, then schedule students to take the book home overnight to share with their families.

Note: *Make sure students closely observe what happens to the wet paint when the salt is sprinkled. (It seems to disappear.) Talk about what causes the splotchy effect. Introduce the word* dissolve *(to change into a liquid). Ask students why they think the salt dissolved. This is a good opportunity to reinforce the notion that science is all around us. In fact, whatever children choose to do when they are older, they will probably use some science. As they mix different colors of paints, study the symmetry of objects, or use the warmth produced by the friction of their hands to soften and shape clay.*

ACTIVITY 3

A Long Winter's Nap

Students tuck themselves in to understand how the heart rate of a sleeping bear compares with the heart rate of an active bear.

Materials

- chart paper
- marker
- A Long Winter's Nap Science Journal page (see page 112)

Note: *Prepare a chart in advance. Make three columns:* Name, Active, *and* Winter Sleep. *Add the title:* Changing Heart Rates.

1 Show students how to find their heart rate. (With young children it may be easiest to have them put two fingers on the artery in the neck.) Have them count for six seconds, then add a zero to the end of the number to get their heart rate for one minute. (Explain that you are multiplying six seconds by ten.) Practice this a couple of times.

2 Next, take students on a brisk walk—maybe a lap around the school. (The goal is actually to get students' heart rates up.)

3 As soon as you return, have students take their heart rate again. This time, let students come up to the chart and record their names and active heart rates (for one minute).

4 Now it's time for students to tuck themselves in for a winter sleep. Have them lie down (or at least put their heads on

their desks). Turn off the lights (for that cozy den effect) and read a story about bears.

5 After about five minutes, or when you finish reading, have students measure their heart rates again. When they have figured out the heart rate per minute, they can write this next to their names under the Winter Sleep column.

6 Have students compare the numbers on the chart. How do their active heart rates compare with resting? (Even though they will see a drop in their heart rates from active to winter sleep, remind them that the change is even more dramatic with a bear: 50 to 80 while active, 8 during winter sleep.) To get an approximate idea of just how slow 8 heartbeats per minute is, have students tap their hands on their desks once every 8 seconds for one minute.

7 Wrap up this activity by inviting students to imagine that they are bears about to curl up for their long winter naps. What will they dream about? Pass out the reproducibles and ask children to draw pictures or use words to show what they (as bears) are dreaming about.

FORAGING FOR FOOD

Prepare for this activity by putting some bear food (nuts and berries) in plastic snack bags, one for each child. (Label each bag with a child's name.) When the children are out of the room, hide the bags around the classroom. Then, when they return, explain that you want them to pretend they are very hungry bears, fattening up for a long winter's nap. Tell them that if they scrounge around the classroom, they'll find food fit for a bear. (Explain that each child should look for a bag of bear food with his or her name on it.) As students hunt, share a bear story. If students have difficulty finding their food, you can guide them with your story (*...and then the bears tried looking up high for their food*). After they have fattened up, the children-turned-bears can hunt for classroom caves (any available nook or cranny), curl up, and go to sleep until spring.

Curriculum Connections

SCIENCE
Scavenger Hunt

What are other ways animals cope with winter? Have students work with partners on an Animals in Winter scavenger hunt. Give each team a list of five animals. Have students use class and library resources to locate three pieces of information on each animal: Does the animal hibernate, enter dormancy, or remain active in winter? What is the animal's winter habitat? What are the animal's winter sources of food? A starter list follows.

Little Brown Bat (hibernates; in a cave or mine; does not need food for winter)

Black Bear (dormant; finds shelter in caves or in roots under fallen trees; stores food as fat for winter)

Meadow Mouse (active; tunnels under snow; eats seeds, roots, and stems)

Striped Skunk (dormant; winters in fields and woods; eats insects, roots, berries, small animals)

Woodchuck (hibernates; burrows below frost line; doesn't need food)

Snowshoe Hare (active; winters in woods and brush; eats bark, buds, own droppings)

[Source: *Hands-On Nature*, Vermont Institute of Natural Science, 1986]

SOCIAL STUDIES
Bears at Home

In addition to searching for answers to their bear questions, students can take turns working on the Science on Display mural. Lead a discussion about what to include: What kinds of bears live in North America? What kinds of bears live in other parts of the world? (Pandas from China and koalas from Australia are likely to come up. Let students discover for themselves that koalas are not actually bears.) What kind of habitat does each bear live in?

Form committees for each task. You might have a Bear Committee (students who illustrate the bears), a Background Committee (responsible for background features like rocks, trees, streams, and so on), and a Food Committee (responsible for adding bear food: fish, berry bushes, etc.). Set aside some time for committees to gather different media, including paint, fabric, pictures from magazines—whatever is handy and fun.

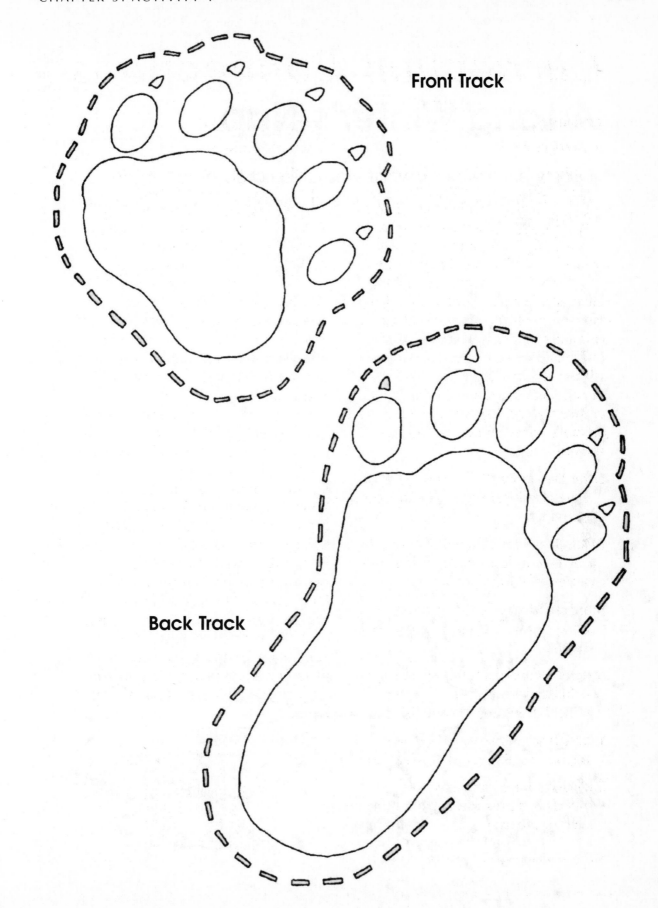

Front Track

Back Track

Name _____

A Long Winter's Nap

If you were this bear, what would you dream about this winter? Draw a picture or write a story about your dream.

RESOURCES

FOR CHILDREN

Bears by Bobbi Kalman and Tammy Everts (Crabtree, 1995). This books describes the eight different families of bears, their anatomical features, and their behavioral traits. Includes color photographs and illustrations. Nonfiction.

Every Autumn Comes the Bear by Jim Arnosky (Putnam, 1993). Beautiful watercolor illustrations and simple text follow a bear through the days before winter sleep. Fiction.

Wake Me in Spring by James Preller (Scholastic, 1994). In this sweet story, Mouse tries to convince his sleepy friend Bear to stay up and enjoy the pleasures of winter, but to no avail. Simple text for young readers. Fiction.

FOR TEACHERS

Bears by Ian Stirling (Sierra Club Books for Children, 1992). Written as a factual book for upper-elementary students, this book provides a lot of good information and would be a great resource for a unit on bears.

Investigating Science Through Bears by Karlene Ray Smith and Anne Hudson Bush (Teacher Ideas Press, 1994). This book includes science and social studies units focusing on black bears, grizzly bears, and polar bears, among others.

CHAPTER 6

December

Ice and Snow
page 118

For the Birds
page 131

Highlights *of the* Month

Mark these dates, events, and activities on your calendar this month to help plan and supplement upcoming activities.

✳ The winter solstice is the first day of winter in the Northern Hemisphere and is the shortest day (number of daylight hours) of the year. Check a calendar or almanac for the date (usually on or around December 21) and write it in.

✳ December's full moon is often called the Cold Moon. Any guesses why?

✳ Recycle holiday gift wrap to make sets of card-matching games for younger children.

✳ On December 17, 1936, the first giant panda arrived in the United States from China. Ask students how big they think a newborn panda is. (About six inches long—the size of a small hamster.)

Planning Ahead

This month's activities look at birds. Contact your local Audubon Society for information about birds that winter locally.

Get a head start on collecting materials for January's activities: Ask families to send in empty shoe boxes.

SCIENCE AT HOME

Date _____

This month we are starting two new science themes.

1. Ice and Snow

Children continue their explorations of weather by looking at the effect of temperature on water. Students will have opportunities to experiment with the changes that occur as something freezes and melts, including water to ice and milk to ice cream!

2. For the Birds

How do birds cope with the cold? Students will be coming to their aid this month by making bird feeders. Bird feeders not only make it easier for birds to find food in winter, but they also offer opportunities for up-close observations. Your child will be keeping a journal as part of a group bird-watching activity in school. Try keeping one at home, too. Record the kinds of birds you or your child spot, when you see them, and what they are doing.

Wish List

Do you have materials you can donate for our science explorations? For this month's activities, we need:

_____

_____

_____

Reminders _____

_____

_____

Ice and Snow

For many, winter means the coolest temperatures of the year. This cooler weather is the result of the Earth's position on the annual path it follows around the sun. In some places, the temperature dips below freezing, while in other parts of the country the temperature may remain in the 70s! No matter where you and your students live, you can investigate the science of change that occurs at this time of year.

Science Concepts and Skills

Concepts: Students will continue to use thermometers as a way to gather data. They will investigate the effect temperature has on water. Students will also continue to notice that although the weather changes daily, over time things such as temperature tend to be constant for the same months every year (winter is cooler).

Process Skills: observing, predicting, classifying, comparing, measuring, collecting and recording data, interpreting

Science Dictionary

freezing when it is cold enough for water to turn to ice

frost frozen water vapor

ice water that has become solid; pure water freezes at 32°F

snow tiny six-sided ice crystals; each crystal is different, but every crystal is hexagonal (six-sided)

winter the time of year when, in the Northern Hemisphere, the Earth's axis is pointing away from the sun; as a result, the sun's rays are hitting this part of the Earth at more of an angle and are scattered over a larger area, so they do not heat as strongly as do the more direct rays of summer

Science on Display

By now, you'll probably want to remove the autumn leaves from the tree. (Well, maybe leave one up to represent those few brown leaves that cling on all through winter.) Students can add snowflakes falling around and on the tree by following the directions here.

SPARKLING SNOWFLAKES

1   Use the lid from a 3-pound coffee can to trace several circles on old manila file folders. Cut them out to make circle templates.

2   Have students trace and cut out a couple of circles on light blue construction paper. They should write their names on one side of their circles.

3   Next, let students brush on "ice crystals" (mix 3 tablespoons salt with ¼ cup water). Let the papers dry overnight.

4   The following day, have students fold and cut their snowflakes as illustrated, next page.

5 Let students tape their snowflakes on and around the Science on Display tree.

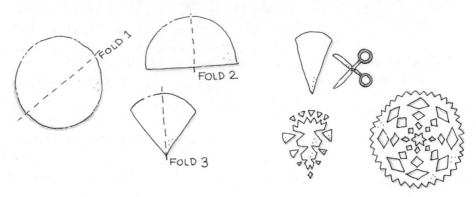

ACTIVITY 1 ━━━━━━━━━━━━━━━━━━━━━━━━━━━━━━━━━━

The Sun and the Seasons

Introduce students to the connection between the sun and the seasons with this activity. Help students understand that in the Northern Hemisphere, winter is when the Earth's axis is pointing away from the sun. The sun's rays are hitting the Earth at more of an angle and are scattered over a larger area, so they do not heat the Earth as much as the more direct rays of summer. You may also want to explain that, meanwhile, the Southern Hemisphere is experiencing its summer.

Materials

* flashlight
* piece of black paper

1 Pass around a sheet of black construction paper for everyone to touch.

2 Now set the black paper on a flat surface. Turn on the flashlight, hold it one to two inches above the paper, and shine it directly on the paper for several minutes. While doing this, ask students to predict what the paper will feel like where the light is shining. (It will be warmer.) Encourage them to give their reasoning. Talk about what the light on the paper reminds them of.

3 Remove the flashlight and quickly let children feel the area where the light was shining.

4 Turn on the flashlight again. This time hold it at a 45-degree angle from the paper. Ask students to compare what the light looks like on the paper this time with how it looked last time. (It will be more scattered and not as bright.) Have students predict how the paper will feel and explain their reasoning.

5 After several minutes, let students feel the paper. Have them compare how the paper feels this time with last time. (It will be cooler than when the light was shining directly above.)

6 Ask: If the light on the paper represents how the sun hits the Earth during summer and winter, which way was winter? Again, ask students to explain their answers. (Some will probably connect the idea that the scattered, less-direct light produced the cooler-feeling paper surface.)

ACTIVITY 2

Freezing and Melting

Students investigate how a change in temperature can change the state of water. After freezing cups of water, students may observe that there is more ice than water. Recognizing that the level of ice is above the water line (marked on the cups) or that the water level is lower than where the top of the ice was, can be an interesting discovery for young students. Water is an interesting substance in that it expands as it freezes. Most other substances contract, or shrink, when they freeze.

As they conduct this experiment, children will see evidence that the water expanded by noting that the level of ice is above the black line. The child's stage of development will determine whether he or she perceives this as being more water or recognizes that the amount of water has remained unchanged.

Materials

* sheet of chart paper and marker (set up chart paper similar to reproducible for this activity)

* tray

* Freezing and Melting Science Journal page (see page 128)

* for each group of two or three students: a thermometer, a clear plastic cup

Note: This is a two-part activity requiring two days to complete. To prepare, use a permanent black marker to make a line a half inch below the top of each cup (on the outside). Number the cups 1 through how ever many groups of students you have. Fill a pitcher with water about an hour before starting, giving the water a chance to come to room temperature. This will ensure that all groups begin the experiment with water that is the same temperature, thus allowing for fair comparisons of results. Finally, divide the class into small groups.

PART 1 (Day 1)

1 Begin this activity by asking the children: What is ice? Let their descriptions, definitions, and experiences with ice guide other discussions during the course of the experiment.

2 Next, ask students what they think will happen if you place a cup of water in the freezer. (If you live someplace where the temperature is cold enough, place the cups of water outside.) Many children will respond that it will turn to ice. How long do they think it will take for the water to become ice? This is a good time to let students set up an operational definition for the experiment. How will they define ice? Will it be when there is some ice starting to form in the water or when the entire cup of water has turned to a solid block of ice? The important thing is that everyone uses the same definition.

3 Hand out reproducibles and have each group predict and record how long it will take a cup of water to turn to ice.

4 Give each group a cup of water filled to the black line and a thermometer. Have students record the number of the cup on their worksheets. Next, they should record the starting time and place the thermometer in the cup. While they wait two minutes to record the temperature, they can write their initial observations of the cup of water on their worksheet. Let them know when it is time to read the thermometers and remind

Note: *What's the science behind ice expanding when it freezes? While most substances contract (shrink) when they cool down, water is unique in that it expands (the water molecules move farther apart). Because of this, students will observe that the ice line on their cups is above the water line.*

them to record the temperature on the worksheet.

5 Place the cups in the freezer for 30 minutes. While students wait, introduce Cool Poetry (see Curriculum Connections, page 126).

6 After 30 minutes, let each group make a quick check of its cup, noting and recording time, temperature, and additional observations. Have students check their cups at regular intervals, noting the point at which they can no longer insert the thermometer in the cup due to the thickness of ice.

7 When the students have reached a definition of ice, let them complete the worksheet.

PART 2 (Day 2)

Materials

* chart, cups of ice, thermometers, and reproducibles from Part 1
* marker

1 Discuss students' experiences from Part 1. What did they learn? (The water froze and turned to ice. Ice forms when the water reaches 32°F, etc.) What would happen if the cup of ice were left out on their desks? Would it take as long for the ice to melt as it did for it to freeze? How can they find out?

2 Discuss ideas for designing an experiment to test how long it takes for the ice to melt. Remember the idea of operational definitions. How would students like to define the end result of this part of the investigation? (What will determine when the ice is melted? Is it when they can insert the thermometer in the water or when there is no ice left in the water?)

3 After recording predictions for how long it will take the ice to melt, have students mark the top of the ice on the outside of the cup. Then, as in Part 1, students should record starting time and observations on their worksheets, then make observations every 30 minutes.

4 Bring students together to compare and discuss the results and what they have learned.

ACTIVITY 3 ～～～～～～～～～～～～～～～～

Making Ice Cream

In this activity, students discover that just as ice changes to water, milk can turn to ice cream.

Note: You may find it helpful to recruit several parents or upper-grade students to lend a hand with this activity. While these helpers assist with measuring and pouring ingredients, remind them to involve the younger students by asking questions along the way, such as "What are we putting in the bag now?" or "How much milk are we pouring in the bag?"

Materials (for each group)

* $\frac{1}{4}$ cup milk
* $\frac{1}{4}$ cup heavy cream
* $\frac{1}{4}$ cup sugar
* $\frac{1}{4}$ t. vanilla
* 2 cups crushed ice or snow
* $\frac{1}{2}$ cup table salt
* 1 quart-size resealable freezer bag
* 1 gallon-size resealable freezer bag
* mittens

1 Place the milk, cream, sugar, and vanilla in the quart-size bag in that order.

2 Zip the quart bag closed, making sure that some of the air is expelled from the bag and that it is zipped completely.

3 Put the quart bag in the gallon bag, along with the ice or snow and the table salt. Zip the gallon bag shut.

4 It's mitten time! Have students put on their mittens (as this next step is pretty cool), then take turns gently kneading the gallon bag. Ask students to predict what will happen to the milk and other ingredients inside. Talk about the changes students see. What does the salt do? (Ice cream freezes at about 27°F, but ice only reaches 32°F. Adding salt lowers the freezing point of water, making it possible to freeze the ice cream.)

5 In about ten minutes, your students will see that the ice has all melted and the mixture in the quart bag has turned from a liquid to a solid and is ready to eat!

Note: Here are some suggested questions to guide a discussion on the technology used in this activity: What tools did students use to make the ice cream? Could they make ice cream without these tools? What might have happened if the smaller bag was not shut completely? What are some other tools used to make ice cream? How do you think ice cream was invented? How do you think ice cream is made in factories? The important thing here is to help children think about what tools are and how we use them.

ACTIVITY 4 ~~~~~~~~~~~~~~~~~~~~~~~~~~~~~~

It's Frosty!

Introduce snow's cool relative, frost. Frost is frozen water vapor. For gardeners and farmers, the proverbial frost on the pumpkin means that the growing season has ended. Even in warmer climates frost can be a problem. When frost threatens orange groves in Florida, farmers build bonfires to prevent cold air from settling around the fruit and causing damage. Sometimes, growers spray their crops with water to create an insulating layer of ice that can actually prevent the plant from freezing! Let students explore this form of water with these activities.

Material

 ✹ a drinking glass

1   Show students the glass before placing it in the freezer.

2   After a half hour, remove the glass from the freezer. Set it on a table where all the children can see.

3   What changes do they see? What is forming on the outside of the glass? Explain that this is frost and that it is similar to snow. (When you take the cold glass out of the freezer, the water vapor immediately surrounding the glass freezes.)

Curriculum Connections

LANGUAGE ARTS
Finger Play

Winter Sweetness
This little house is sugar.
        Its roof with snow is piled,
And from its tiny window
        Peeps a maple-sugar child.

                        —Langston Hughes

Turn the poem "Winter Sweetness" into a finger play:

Line 1: Use fingers to make a pointy triangle roof.

Line 2: Curl fingertips down so that fingers look like fluffy snow piled high.

Line 3: Bring thumbs and fingertips together to create two little round windows.

Line 4: Bring round "windows" to eyes and peep through windows.

Follow up by inviting children to suggest other movements to accompany poem.

LANGUAGE ARTS
Cool Poetry

Here's an activity students can work on while they wait for their water to turn to ice (or for their ice to melt) in Activity 2. Give each student a copy of the Cool Poetry reproducible (see page 129). Explain that they will be writing a form of poetry called concrete poetry. Brainstorm words that describe ice, and have students record these words in the brainstorming box. Next, have them cut out the cube pattern and glue it to an old manila file folder to give it some sturdiness. When the glue is dry, have students select five words they think best describe ice and write one word on each square of the cube. Students can then fold and glue as indicated to make their cubes. For a sparkly touch, brush some of the "ice crystal" salt-and-water mixture over the cube (see Science on Display, page 119). Place cubes in ice trays and display at one of your classroom centers for students to read and enjoy.

MOVEMENT
Melt Down, Freeze Up

Draw a thermometer on the board and mark off degrees in Fahrenheit and Celsius. Show children the point on the thermometer at which water freezes and where it begins to melt. Tell children to pretend they are icicles. Then use a ruler or pointer to indicate a temperature. Try moving the temperature up and down the thermometer at different speeds. Children should freeze or melt according to the temperature and speed of change.

MATH
Let It Snow

Let it snow, let it snow. If you live someplace that gets snow, here are some super snow science activities.

1. Collect a cup of snow. Ask students to predict how much water will be in the cup when the snow melts. Measure the amount of water left after the snow melts. Compare predictions with the actual result. (Did you know it takes about 10 inches of snow to produce 1 inch of water?)

2. Look around the school yard. Is the snow the same depth everywhere? Measure and explain your results.

3. Build a life-size snowperson in the school yard. Measure your snowperson's height and chest daily. Record these measurements on the chalkboard in your classroom. Note the temperature and weather conditions, as well. Wait a week and measure again. Continue until the person is gone. What happened?

ART
Paint Cubes

These easy-to-make, fun-to-use ice cubes will reinforce the idea that as ice warms up it changes back into, in this case, colorful puddles of water. First, mix together powdered tempera paint and water to form a thin paint. Pour the paint into an old ice tray, adding a craft stick to each cube. Repeat with as many different colors as you like. Place the tray in the freezer until paint cubes freeze. Invite children to pop the cubes out of the tray, hold by the stick handle, and paint away. Be sure to reinforce students' understandings of freezing and melting by inviting them to share observations of the paint cubes as they work. How are they changing? How is this like what happened in Activity 2 (see page 121)?

Name _____ Cup Number _____

THEME:
Ice and
Snow

Freezing and Melting

PART 1: Freezing Water

I think the water will turn to ice in _____ minutes.

Time	Temperature	Our Observations

The water turned to ice in _____ minutes.

PART 2: Melting Ice

I think the ice will melt in _____ minutes.

Time	Temperature	Our Observations

The ice turned to water in _____ minutes.

Something I learned from doing this experiment is...

_____

_____

_____

Name_____

Cool Poetry

DIRECTIONS

1. Work with a friend and think of some words that describe ice. How does it feel? What does it look like? Does it make any sound? Write the words you think of in the Brainstorming Box.

2. Follow your teacher's directions to cut out and make the cube.

3. Use words from your Brainstorming Box to make a poem on your cube about ice.

BRAINSTORMING BOX

ICE IS...

Cut on solid lines,
fold on dotted lines.

RESOURCES

FOR CHILDREN

It's Snowing! It's Snowing! by Jack Prelutsky (Greenwillow, 1984). A collection of fun poetry about, what else, snow! Fiction.

Snow (Ready-to-Read. Level 1) by Marion Dane Bauer (Aladdin, 2003). A simple text that simultaneously charms and instructs readers. Nonfiction.

Snow Is Falling by Franklyn Branley (HarperCollins, 1983). An informational book about snow. Nonfiction.

The Snowman by Raymond Briggs (Random House, 1978). A child builds a snowman who then takes the child on an adventure. Fiction.

Snow Sounds: An Onomatopoeic Story by David A. Johnson (Houghton Mifflin, 2006). A book that tickles the imagination awake with onomatopoeic text.

Winter Lullaby by Barbara Seuling (Voyager, 2002). Lovely illustrations complement engaging storytelling. This book is both informative and memorable. Fiction.

FOR TEACHERS

Science Photo Cards: Understanding Weather (Creative Teaching Press). Use this collection of 12 full-color photo cards to help children tackle key weather vocabulary and concepts. For more information, call Creative Teaching Press at (800) 287-8879 or visit www.creativeteaching.com.

Snowballs by Lois Ehlert (Harcourt, Brace, Jovanovich, 1995). This entertaining book will inspire students to make their own snow people and snow animals using snow, of course, and great accessories from around the house. The last couple of pages discuss what snow is and why it snows. Photos of creative snow people add to the fun.

TECHNOLOGY CONNECTIONS

Reading Rainbow: Snowy Day: Stories and Poems edited by Caroline Feller Bauer (HarperCollins, 1986). This DVD provides a great way for children to hear read-alouds of some notable poems (e.g., "Winter Morning" by Ogden Nash). When ready, young viewers can then enjoy LeVar's snowy adventure in Alaska where he travels to learn about sled dogs. For more information, call GPN Educational Media at (800) 228-4630 or visit http://shopgpn.com/stores/1/RR_BookLists.cfm.

Snowflakes (www.its.caltech.edu/~atomic/snowcrystals/) One visit to this site provided by Caltech physics professor Kenneth Libbrecht and you'll be excited about the science behind snow. Make your first stop the photo galleries. Then, look at the FAQ section to supplement your own background knowledge about snow. Libbrecht is the author of several books about snowflakes, including *Ken Libbrecht's Field Guide to Snowflakes* (Voyageur Press, 2006).

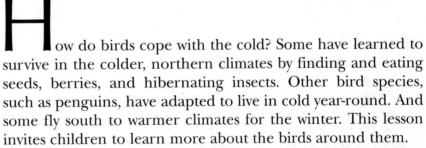

For the Birds

How do birds cope with the cold? Some have learned to survive in the colder, northern climates by finding and eating seeds, berries, and hibernating insects. Other bird species, such as penguins, have adapted to live in cold year-round. And some fly south to warmer climates for the winter. This lesson invites children to learn more about the birds around them.

A local bird-watcher should be able to name birds you can expect to see around the school. Check with your local Audubon Society to see if a member would volunteer to visit and answer children's questions about birds and bird feeding. Have students think of some questions ahead of time. Provide the visitor with a copy of the questions in advance, so that both students and the community resource person will feel prepared.

Science Concepts and Skills

Concepts: Students will observe and begin to recognize the relationship between birds and their environments.

Process Skills: observing, predicting, comparing, classifying, communicating

Science Dictionary

bird a warm-blooded animal that has a backbone, feathers, wings, two legs, and breathes through lungs; there are more than 9,000 species of birds in the world

penguin a mostly black-and-white bird that lives near the oceans in the Southern Hemisphere; there are 18 species of penguins

Science on Display

Gather information about the kinds of birds that live in your area during the winter months. If possible, make pictures of the birds available to students to use as reference.

Remember that display tree? (You may still have leaves and snowflakes on it.) Ask students to select one of the birds to learn more about. To guide students' research, identify a couple of facts you'd like them to find, such as: What does your bird eat? Where does it feed? Have students illustrate their birds, place them on the display where they would likely be found feeding, and attach fact cards. For example, a woodpecker likes to look for insects in the tree. Doves are mostly ground feeders.

ACTIVITY 1

What Is a Bird?

What animal has the warmest and most lightweight coat of all? Has eyes that are almost half the size of its head? Doesn't have teeth? Students discover more about what makes an animal a bird with this activity.

Note: This activity helps children understand that animals are classified into groups based on physical attributes.

Materials

* magazine pictures of animals (mammals, amphibians, insects, birds, etc.—try to make half the pictures of birds)
* chart paper (2 pieces)
* glue stick

1 Gather pictures of animals. You will need one picture per child, plus an extra picture of a bird and an extra of any other kind of animal. Children can help with this preparation. Just guide them in their selections so that you have a good variety.

2 Gather children in a circle. Give an animal picture to each student. Display both pieces of chart paper in the circle.

3 Explain that you would like to place half of the pictures on one side of the chart and half on the other side of the chart. Ask: What are some ways to group these animals?

4 Now glue a picture of a bird on one side and some other animal on the other side. (Your sorting method is birds/animals that are not birds.) Ask: Does anybody have a picture that fits on either side? Have students take turns coming to the chart and telling where they think their pictures belong. If they correctly determine the side it belongs on, let them glue the pictures to the correct side. Continue to do this until all the pictures are glued on the chart, giving children who do not guess the sorting rule the first time another chance.

5 Ask students to explain how they decided where to place their animals. Focus the discussion on attributes of birds (wings, feathers, two legs). List the characteristics students suggest on the bird chart. Together, come up with a title for the chart, such as What Makes a Bird? As students discover more about birds, invite them to add new characteristics to the chart.

ACTIVITY 2

Feed a Friend

Feed them and they will come. Birds burn up a lot of energy in the process of looking for and gathering food, particularly in winter when food is not as readily available and when they need more energy to stay warm. Setting out bird feeders in cold weather helps birds conserve energy and makes it easier for them to survive the winter. Making and setting up bird feeders is also a great way to introduce your students to the birds in their backyards and gives children important experience in caring for animals.

Common Winter Birds

black-capped
chickadee

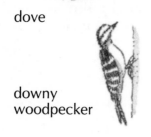

blue jay

cardinal

dove

downy
woodpecker

house finch

nuthatch

Materials

* For each group: a cup of peanut butter, a cup of cornmeal, a margarine container filled with wild birdseed mix

* For each student: a pinecone, a 12-inch piece of yarn, a craft stick, a paper plate

* copies of the Feed a Friend reproducible (see page 142)

1 Tie the yarn to the top of the pinecone as illustrated.

2 Use a craft stick to place peanut butter in the crevices of the pinecone.

3 Roll the pinecone in cornmeal, then in the wild birdseed.

Hanging Bird Feeders: Before hanging up the feeders, discuss reasons for feeding birds during the winter (to provide food for them when food is scarce, to observe birds). Take a walk around the school grounds and look for birds. Decide on the best place to hang the feeders. Remind students that birds need places where they can find shelter (like shrubs and trees). Aim for a spot near your classroom windows, but if not, arrange for students to observe the birds daily. When you have located a good area, hang the feeders. Add a nonmetal dish of water to your bird-feeding station, too, to provide an easy source of water. If you are considering putting food out for ground feeders, be mindful of potential predators like neighborhood cats.

Observing Birds: As you begin watching birds at your feeding station, use a simple field guide like *Peterson First Guide to Birds* to identify them. Once you have determined the kinds of birds using the feeders, try to find pictures of these birds to share with students. Let them compare and contrast the characteristics of these birds. What kind of beak does each have? How do

different beaks help birds? (Digging for worms, eating bugs from beneath bark, cracking seeds, collecting nectar, etc.) What color is the head? How big is the bird? Place these pictures near your bird-watching window, along with copies of the Feed a Friend reproducible page for recording observations.

Note: If you would like to offer some variety in the food you set out for birds, try letting children use heavy string and needles to string unshelled peanuts. Drape these on trees where the pinecone feeders hang. Sprinkle cracked corn and sunflower seeds on the ground (or on a windowsill) to attract birds that might not use the pinecones or peanut feeders.

ACTIVITY 3

Beaks and Birds

How does a nuthatch dig out insects from logs? How does a blue jay crack open the hard shell of a nut? With their beaks, of course! But not just any beak will do. Birds' beaks are adapted to the food they eat. Investigate the specialized nature of birds' beaks to reinforce the concept of adaptation.

Note: To prepare for this activity, place nuts with shells (like walnuts) on several trays (one per group). Paint paper cups brown or cover film canisters with brown paper and fill with seeds (to simulate insects in a log).

Materials (for each group)

 * pliers
 * tweezers
 * nuts (with shells)
 * tray
 * paper cup
 * birdseed

1 Divide the class into groups and give each a set of materials (pliers, tweezers, tray of nuts, cup of seeds).

2 Ask students in each group to take turns using the tools as if they were beaks to grab food. In their journals, ask them to record observations. Which beak is best for grabbing the

BOOK BREAK

Inspire students to look more closely at beaks on the birds at their feeder with *Unbeatable Beaks* by Stephen Swinburne (see Resources, page 144). Post a beak-watch chart at the window. List various functions of bird beaks, such as:

✳ cracks nuts and hard seeds

✳ digs for worms in the ground

✳ hammers holes in trees

✳ sucks nectar from flowers

✳ tears flesh

✳ catches insects in the air

Ask students to jot down the date and time that they see birds with beaks performing these tasks.

nuts? The seeds? (Students will find that it is impossible to crack the nuts with the tweezers and awkward to use the pliers to get the seeds out of the cup.)

3 Ask students what kinds of birds might have beaks that work like pliers? (Birds like blue jays and cardinals that crack open nuts.) Like tweezers? (Birds like nuthatches and woodpeckers that dig out insects from logs or tree trunks.)

4 Encourage children to look closely at the birds that come to the feeders. What kinds of beaks do they have? How do they use their beaks? Look for unusual feeding behavior, too. For example, a nuthatch will take a seed from a bird feeder but won't crack it like other birds. It will take the seed back to a tree and crack it against a crevice. Some birds, like chickadees, are hoarders. They stick seeds in crevices and will remember for a few weeks where the seeds are. Blue jays sometimes store nuts under leaves and in tree crevices, and come back for them, as well.

PROJECT FEEDERWATCH

Your students can contribute to an ornithological study on winter bird populations to find out more about birds that stay around in the winter: what their numbers are, what there feeding preferences are, etc. This bird-watching kit includes a data collection form for recording observations and comments, an educational poster, and a quarterly newsletter that offers updates on the research. For more information, contact the Cornell University Laboratory of Ornithology at 159 Sapsucker Woods Rd., Ithaca, NY 14850; (800) 843-BIRD; www.birds.cornell.edu/.

Science Celebration

Traveling Bird Cup Puppet Show

Give each child a small paper cup (available in a variety of solid colors at party stores). Show them how to glue on paper beaks, wings, and tails to turn the cups into birds. Invite them to add other details with a marker. Children can create informative puppet shows about birds for another class. They might also like to form small groups and put on puppet shows for one another; for example, retelling any of the stories about birds they've read as part of this theme.

ACTIVITY 4

Cold Weather Wear

How do penguins stay warm? In the same way other birds adapt to their environments, penguins have developed a fat layer that keeps them from losing body heat in cold temperatures.

Materials

 * 1 cup solid vegetable shortening
 * 2 quart-size zipper-lock plastic bags
 * large bowl filled with icy water

1 Gather students around to make a fat bag. Put the shortening in the bottom of one of the bags. Turn the second bag inside out, then place it inside the first bag. Zip the two bags together, making sure both sides lock. Let students help squish the shortening around until it completely surrounds the interior bag. You now have a fat bag.

2 Explain that even during the summer, the temperature in Antarctica barely rises above freezing. Use a globe or world map to locate Antarctica.

3 Let students take turns testing the fat bag by slipping one hand in the bag and submerging both hands in the ice water.

4 Discuss their observations. Which hand felt warmer? Why? How would a layer of body fat help keep a penguin warm?

ACTIVITY 5 ⌇⌇⌇⌇⌇⌇⌇⌇⌇⌇⌇⌇⌇⌇⌇⌇⌇⌇⌇⌇⌇⌇⌇

Penguins: A Breed Apart

Students compare and contrast penguins with the birds they see at the feeding station.

Materials

* chart paper (set up in Venn diagram fashion, as illustrated)
* Penguins: A Breed Apart Science Journal page (see page 143)
* several books on penguins (see Resources, page 144)

1 Let students work in small groups to think of ways penguins are the same as birds they have seen at their feeding station or around their homes, and three ways they are different. Have them fill out the Science Journal page. Make sure each group has access to at least one book about penguins.

2 Bring the groups together to share ideas. Help students organize their ideas using a Venn diagram.

3 Discuss some of the similarities and differences, such as, unlike most other birds, penguins do not fly. Ask students if they know how penguins get around. Let them demonstrate their ideas.

4 Guide the discussion to help students understand that penguins may lack the ability to fly, but that they have adapted ways of moving that are much better suited for the environment in which they live. Let students try out some of these penguin moves:

* Penguins use their paddlelike wings to make powerful *swimming* strokes in the ocean.

* Penguins that live where there is snow get around by *tobogganing*. To do this, they fall on their bellies and slide, pushing off with their wings and feet.

* The rockhopper penguin, just as its name implies, *hops* from rock to rock.

* And there's always the famous penguin *waddle*!

Curriculum Connections

LANGUAGE ARTS
Am I a Bird? Big Book

This is a fun project for students to take home and do with their families. Send home the reproducible letter explaining the book (see page 141), along with a sheet of colored construction paper. Students work with parents or other family members to color or cut and paste a picture of a bird or other animal (as indicated in the letter) on the paper. When they bring their pictures back to class, compile them into a big book. Let students take turns sharing their pages, asking: Am I a bird? and listening for classmates to respond yes or no! Make sure the finished big books get sent home overnight, too!

MOVEMENT
Test Your Wings

What does it feel like to be a bird? Let students test their wings to find out. Have them flap their arms for one minute—at a rate of about one beat per second. Anyone tired? Explain that their arms probably ache but that a bird's wings wouldn't because they're adapted for that purpose and can endure this movement for long periods of time. Encourage students to notice the ways different birds at the feeder flap their wings and to record observations in their journals. Does one species seem to flap its wings faster than others? Here are a few to look for:

Chickadee: wings beat 270 times every 10 seconds

Crow: wings beat 20 times in 10 seconds

Pigeons: wings beat 30 times in 10 seconds

Students might like to team up to try flapping their arms as fast as these birds. While one flaps, the other can count and time.

MATH
Seasons

What would it be like to live with penguins and have winter all year long? Discuss such cultures with students. Ask: What would you like (or dislike) most about having 12 months of winter?

If students could create their own seasons, what would their world be like? (Encourage them to think about temperature, precipitation, plants, animals, etc.) Next, let students pick the season they would most enjoy having all year long. Give each child a 2-inch square of white paper to draw something related to a favorite season. On a large sheet of chart paper, list the seasons, then have students glue their squares in the appropriate columns.

DRAMA
A Chorus of Birds

Wake up your classroom with a chorus of birds— and help children discover that each species of bird has a unique song and a preferred time to sing. Prepare by making a bird tag for each child: Using the list that follows, record the name of a bird, the bird's "song," and the time of day the bird sings. Make two or more tags for each bird, as needed for the size of your class.

4 A.M.

robin: cheerio cheery me cheery me

ovenbird: teacher-teacher-teacher

white-throated sparrow: poor Sam Peabody-Peabody-Peabody

5 A.M.

eastern meadowlark: sweet spring is here

eastern wood pewee: pee-a-wee

redwinged blackbird: konk-la-ree

6 A.M.

yellowthroat: witchity-witchity-witchity

black-capped chickadee: chick-a-dee-dee-dee

red-eyed vireo: going up-coming down

yellow warbler: sweet sweet sweet I'm so sweet

chestnut-sided warbler: pleased-pleased-pleased to meet you

7 A.M.

goldfinch: potato chip-potato chip

phoebe: fiby-fiby

white-breasted nuthatch: yank-yank

Start this activity by asking children when they usually hear birds sing. Explain that, in this activity, they will become the birds on their tags, singing at their favorite times (and continuing until the entire classroom is singing). Give children time to team up with other like-species and to practice their songs. Then use a clock with movable hands to wake up your birds.Start at midnight, pausing on each hour. At 4 A.M. the first few groups of birds will start their songs. Continue until the 7A.M. birds join in. Have children sing until about noon, at which time birds usually quiet down. For a variation, learn about the birds in your area. Repeat the activity singing those birds' songs.

A Chorus of Birds is adapted with permission of the publisher: from *Hands-on Nature*, Vermont Institute of Natural Science, RR 2, Box 532, Woodstock, Vermont 05091, © 1986.

Dear _____ ,

Your child is learning about birds in class. Here's an activity you can do at home.

Each student is making one page of a class book. Some of the pages will picture birds and some will show animals that are not birds.

_____ has been assigned a page that pictures

_____ a bird

_____ any other animal that is not a bird.

This can be a family project. Together you can decide on what kind of bird or animal will be on this page. You can cut the picture from a magazine; use crayons, pencils, or markers to draw it; choose a photograph from your collection—use your imaginations! As you work on this project with your child, talk about why this animal is a bird or why it is not a bird. Place the picture on the construction paper included with this letter and ask your child to sign his or her name.

Please have your child bring the picture to school by _____ .

We will put the book together in class and send it home overnight with each child. At the end of the year, each student's picture will be returned.

Have a wonderful time working together!

Feed a Friend

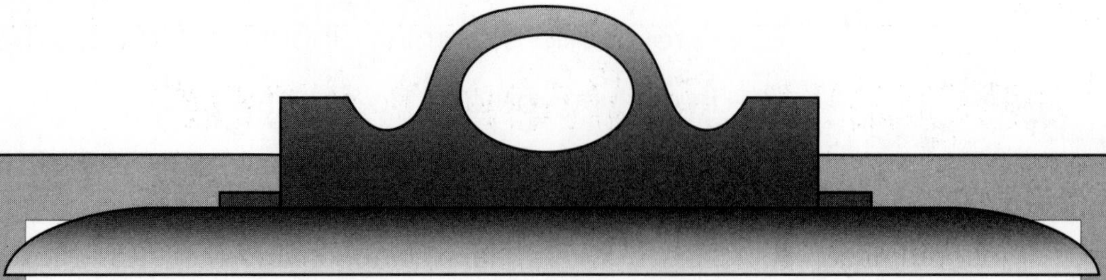

Type of Bird_____

Date Seen_____

At Which Feeder_____

Name of Student Making the Observation

_____

Comments:

_____

_____

_____

_____

Note: Make numerous copies of this page. Place them on a counter or desk near the window and have students fill it out each time they observe feeder birds.

Name _____

Penguins: A Breed Apart

Write three ways penguins and birds are
alike in the space where the circles overlap.

Penguins   **Other Birds**

Write three ways
penguins are different
from other birds.

Write three ways other
birds are different from
penguins.

RESOURCES

FOR CHILDREN

An Egg Is Quiet by Dianna Hutts Aston (Chronicle Books, 2006). A superb introduction to miraculous eggs, oviparous animals, and life cycles. You'll want to pore over the watercolor illustrations again and again. Nonfiction.

Antarctica by Helen Cowher (Farrar, Straus, and Giroux, 1990). This story focuses on the interaction among the animals who live in Antarctica (Adelies and Emperors, Weddell and leopard seals, and skuas). Fiction.

How Do Birds Find Their Way? (Let's-Read-and-Find-Out Science 2) by Roma Gans (HarperTrophy, 1996). An inviting introduction to bird identification, navigation, and habitats. Includes maps and charts. Nonfiction.

A Nest Full of Eggs by Priscilla Belz Jenkins (HarperCollins, 1995). A boy watches a robin build its nest, hatch its eggs, and raise its young. Includes descriptions of the different types of nests built by various birds. Fiction.

Night of the Pufflings by Bruce McMillan (Houghton Mifflin, 1995). Beautiful color photos show children in Iceland guiding pufflings to the sea as they make their first flight. Nonfiction.

Unbeatable Beaks by Stephen Swinburne (Holt, 1999). Vivid collages set off the interesting, informational text about bird beaks and how they function. Nonfiction.

FOR TEACHERS

"Chick-U-Bator" is a clear-domed mini-incubator that can be used to hatch quail, pheasant, chicken, or duck eggs in the classroom, available through ETA Science Catalog. To order a catalog, call (800) 445-5985. Or, visit the Web site: www.etascience.com/.

Mr. Popper's Penguins by Richard and Florence Atwater (Dell, 1986). This is a classic read-aloud about a man who receives a penguin from his friend, the Antarctic explorer Admiral Drake, and the surprises he encounters raising the penguin and its chicks. Fiction.

TECHNOLOGY CONNECTIONS

BRIDGE

Sea Grant Ocean Sciences Education Center (www.vims.edu/bridge/)

This site has done the Web research you don't have time to do. Just select the grade level (K–6) and find a link to activities and lesson plans on the ocean science topics you teach— weather, sea life, bird migration, coral reefs, and more.

CHAPTER 7

January

The Night Sky
page 148

Push and Pull
page 160

Highlights *of the* Month

Mark these dates, events, and activities on your calendar to help plan and supplement upcoming activities in this month's themes.

✳ New Year's Day

✳ The Quadrantid's Meteor Shower is an event that occurs annually during the first week of January. The meteors are best seen by early risers at around 5 A.M. Look to the northern sky.

✳ Winter nights are great for stargazing. Look for Ursa Major, the Great Bear, home of the Big Dipper. Show students the representation of the constellation below and ask: What do you think this group of stars looks like? Explain that different cultures looked at the stars and saw different things. In the group of stars pictured here, some saw a big bear.

✳ January's full moon is known as the Wolf Moon.

✳ On January 3, 1888, a patent was given for the first artificial drinking straw. When you drink through a straw, are you pushing or pulling liquid? See pages 160 to 174 for more Push and Pull activities.

Plan Ahead

Start collecting magnets for this month's activities. Edmund Scientific offers assorted magnets. For information, call (800) 728-6999 or visit the Web site http://scientificsonline.com.

SCIENCE AT HOME

Date _____

This month we are starting two new science themes.

1. The Night Sky

Stars fill children and adults alike with a sense of wonder. In this month's activities, your child will take a close look at stars. Watch for a related family activity page that your child will be bringing home. To extend the learning, share a story about the stars at your child's bedtime. Try making up a story about a constellation (like the Great Bear) or find one in a book. Invite your child to tell a star story, too.

2. Push and Pull

We'll also be exploring what makes things move—including your child! Together, identify things that move in your daily lives. Watch for a family activity sheet about this, too.

Wish List

Do you have materials you can donate for our science explorations? For this month's activities, we need:

_____

_____

_____

Reminders _____

_____

_____

The Night Sky

For the young child, stargazing means looking up into the night sky and being filled with a sense of wonder about those faraway lights. January is a great month to learn about the stars. It gets dark early, and the nights are often clear, allowing students to watch the stars come out before bedtime. Inviting students to become stargazers is a way to connect them to the past and to the future. People in earlier times used the patterns and location of the stars to navigate their way through their world. Today we continue to took to the stars for answers about our universe.

Science Concepts and Skills

Concepts: Students will describe the stars as bright objects that can be seen in the night. They will also begin to recognize that people have given names to some of the patterns formed by the stars, forming imaginary pictures called constellations.

Process Skills: observing, communicating, inferring, predicting

S c i e n c e   D i c t i o n a r y

constellation a pattern of stars that forms an imaginary picture; there are 88 recognized constellations, but only a few of these can be seen year-round; constellations that can be viewed all year are called *circumpolar constellations* because they are found in the area of the night sky located around the poles of the Earth; Ursa Major (contains the Big Dipper) and Ursa Minor (contains the Little Dipper) are circumpolar constellations in the Northern Hemisphere

shooting stars these are not stars at all; they are meteors, or glowing chunks of rock moving through space at great speed; a "shooting star" may be spotted on any night, but there are times of the year when there are meteor showers and many meteors per hour can be seen; one of the most productive meteor showers of the year happens during the first days of January (see Highlights of the Month, page 146)

star a ball of gas that can be seen in the night sky as a small point of light; stars come in different sizes and colors; the star nearest to our planet is the sun; stars differ from the planets and our moon in that they give off their own light (planets and the moon shine because they reflect light from the sun)

Science on Display

Transform your science area into a space station! Cover a bulletin board with dark blue craft paper, then use a white crayon to outline a few favorite constellations. Let children take turns applying star stickers to correctly indicate the stars' placement in the constellations. (Provide pictures for them to use as reference.) Label each constellation. Add a construction-paper frame and use glitter paint to make knobs and dials that suggest you are peering through a space-station window.

Add a Starry Stories tape to the space station. There are several good resources listed at the end of this chapter for star legends. Record the stories on audiotape. (Upper-grade students might volunteer to tape the stories for you.) Next, make a simple picture of each constellation, laminate them, and staple them together to make a booklet for students to use while listening to the tape. Display the storybook and tape in the center with simple directions for starting the tape.

ACTIVITY 1 ~~~~~~

Shimmering Stars

Note: Students will be making star-shaped mobiles. To reinforce the pieces, you might want to copy the patterns on plain paper and then have students glue that paper to heavier stock like construction paper or used manila folders, then cut out the stars.

What do your students see when they look up at the stars? This activity encourages students to take a close look and to use specific language to describe what they see.

~~~~~~

Materials

* Shimmering Stars Parent Letter and Science Journal page (see page 157)

* star patterns (see page 158)

* string

* tape

* glitter

* glue

* chart paper cut into a large star shape

~~~~~~

1   A couple of nights before you begin your unit on stars, send home the parent letter/activity sheet.

2   When all students have had a chance to complete the stargazing activity at home, ask them to share their observations. How many stars do they think are in the sky? (Billions!) How would they describe a star to someone who had never seen one? Make a list of the words and phrases they use to describe stars.

3   This is a good time to introduce the definition of a star. The Science Dictionary provides one definition (see page 149). Students might like to add their own ideas, too.

4   Give each student a copy of the star patterns page (see page 158). Have them write the word *stars* on the largest star and one word that describes stars on each of the smaller stars. Students can refer to their journals and the take-home activity for ideas.

5   When they are finished, have students cut out the stars, then lightly brush glue over the surfaces and sprinkle with glitter.

6 Help students use thread and tape to join the three small stars to the larger star. Punch a hole in the top of the large star and push a length of thread through the hole. Dangle students' shimmering stars around the room.

ACTIVITY 2

Stargazing

Students discover why we only see the stars after dark.

Note: Before the activity, use the star patterns on page 158 to make seven stars on white or yellow paper, then laminate for durability.

Materials

* 7 flashlights (You may want to include a note in this month's Science at Home newsletter asking to borrow some.)
* 7 paper stars (use star patterns, page 158)

1 Tape the laminated paper stars to the floor to form the pattern of the Big Dipper, as illustrated on page 152.

2 Ask seven volunteers to stand on each of the stars. Give each of these students a flashlight.

3 With the classroom lights still on, have these students point the flashlights at the ceiling and turn them on. Ask the other students (stargazers) to describe what they see. Can they see the light from the flashlights on the ceiling? (Probably not.)

4 Now ask stargazers to make a prediction: How will the light from the flashlights look if you turn out the classroom lights? Give them time to share their predictions before going on.

5 Now turn out the classroom lights. Ask students to describe how the light from the flashlights looks now. (The light will be visible, appearing as small circles of light.)

6 Lead a discussion comparing the visibility of the lights from the flashlights after the room was darkened with the visibility of the stars after it begins to get dark at night. Help students to understand that the stars are always out there, but we don't see them during the day because of the brightness of the

BOOK BREAK
Wrap up Activity 2 by reading *The Big Dipper* by Franklyn Branley (see Resources, page 159). Before you begin reading, pick seven new students to hold the flashlights. Read the book with the lights out and the Big Dipper shining overhead.

sun's light (classroom lights in this experiment).

7 Select seven different students to hold the flashlights and stand on the stars.

8 Have your stargazers observe the lights on the ceiling again. How many lights (stars) do they count on the ceiling? Explain that, long ago, people used the stars to help them get from one place to another. They imagined that groups of stars formed pictures and they gave these pictures names. These imaginary star pictures are called constellations. What imaginary picture can they see on the classroom ceiling?

9 Ask students if they have ever seen the constellation called the Big Dipper. Explain that the pattern of stars on the ceiling looks like the Big Dipper. Ask students how they think this constellation got its name. Help them to see the handle and the bowl of the dipper.

ACTIVITY 3 〜〜〜〜〜〜〜〜〜〜〜〜〜〜〜〜〜〜〜〜〜〜〜

Seasons and Stars

winter

spring

Materials

* ✻ pencils
* ✻ black tempera paint and brushes
* ✻ white crayons
* ✻ heavy white paper cut into 8-inch squares
* ✻ large sheets of construction paper
* ✻ glue stick
* ✻ writing paper cut into 8-inch squares

Note: Before the activity, make at least five stencils of the Big Dipper. To do this, copy the Big Dipper pattern (see illustration, left) onto old manila file folders or blank 5-by-8-inch index cards. Laminate, then use a hole-punch to indicate position of stars. This idea would also extend nicely to the constellations that you choose for the Starry Story booklets (see Science on Display, page 149). Students can use the stencils to create constellations while listening to the stories.

summer

fall

1 Show students the pictures of the Big Dipper in its summer and winter positions. Ask students why they think the position would change. Do the stars move? (No, but the Earth moves, causing the constellations to appear as though they are moving from east to west in the night sky.)

2 Place the large drawing of the Big Dipper on the floor. Explain that this is how the Big Dipper looks in the sky during the winter months.

3 Now have students form a circle around the picture. Explain that they each represent the Earth as it makes its yearly trip around the sun. Have students walk around the dipper, paying special attention to the handle of the dipper. As students move around the circle, does the handle point away from them? Toward them? To either the left or right sides? Help students understand that the reason the Big Dipper looks like it is in a different position is because we on Earth have changed position.

4 Now have students sit in a circle around the picture. Ask for students' help in labeling the rest of the seasons, showing the position of the Big Dipper during those seasons.

5 To finish this lesson, share the Micmac Indian legend of Great Bear and how it moves through the sky (see page 154). Ask students how they think the Indians got the idea for this story. (The story describes the apparent movement of the constellation through the year.)

Curriculum Connections

LANGUAGE ARTS
Night Comes

Ask children to recall what they know about moods, including any moods they've ever felt. Explain that in stories and poems, a poet or a writer uses words to create different moods for us to feel. Read the poem "Night Comes" together. Invite children to suggest words that describe how they felt (afraid, brave, etc.). Review the poem carefully to discover which words helped to create these moods.

SOCIAL STUDIES
A Story to Share

Explain that there are 88 named constellations, but that different groups of people sometimes gave constellations different names and made up their own stories about these stars. The Big Dipper, which is actually within a larger constellation called Ursa Major, the Great Bear, has many stories associated with it. According to Chinese legend, the dipper was an instrument that would measure food equally and fairly during times of famine. The early people of Great Britain saw the Big Dipper as King Arthur's chariot. Here is a retelling of a Native American legend about the Big Dipper told by the the Micmacs of Nova Scotia. Display a picture of this constellation as you share the story with students.

BEAR HUNT
from the Micmac Indians of Nova Scotia

Long, long ago, there was a great bear who, when the weather turned cold, went to sleep for a very long time. When the great bear finally woke up in the early spring, he was very hungry. The bear left his den in search of food but was spotted by hunters, who were very hungry, too. The hunters chased the bear, but the bear was quick and difficult to catch.

All through the spring and summer, the bear continued to move while the hunters chased him. As summer turned into fall, some of the hunters grew tired of the chase. They stopped hunting the bear. By late autumn the three remaining hunters finally caught the bear and killed him. The bear's blood stained the tree leaves causing them to turn bright red. The dead bear could be seen in the sky, lying on its back, all winter long. But in the spring, the spirit of the great bear entered another bear. This bear woke up hungry, too, and went out looking for food. And once again, hungry hunters spotted the bear and the hunt began again.

Two other books that tell tales of the Big Dipper are *Her Seven Brothers* by Paul Goble (a Cheyenne legend) and *Follow the Drinking Gourd* by Jeanette Winter, the story of slaves who used the constellations to find their way to freedom. (See Resources, page 159.)

ART
Stories that Sparkle

Ask students to think about the stories they've heard about the Big Dipper. Have them think back to when they used the flashlights to form the Big Dipper on the classroom ceiling, too: What pictures came to their minds when they saw the pattern of light on the ceiling? Then have students follow these directions to create shimmering night skies and star stories.

1. Put the Big Dipper pattern on a piece of white paper. Mark the placement of each star with a pencil.

2. Color a star with white crayon wherever there is a pencil dot.

3. Paint over the whole paper with black tempera paint. (The white stars will pop out from the black background thanks to the resistance of the crayon's waxiness to the water-based paint.) Let the painting dry.

4. Write a new story about the Big Dipper. (Ambitious stargazers may want to rename the constellation and make up a completely new story.) Allow students to work individually or collaboratively on their stories, using their journals to jot down ideas and write rough drafts. Mount the story and the painting on a large sheet of construction paper. Display around the science or reading area.

5. Record Starry Stories, Volume Two, featuring students' new star stories (see Science on Display, page 149).

MOVEMENT *Star Catchers*

This game originated in Equatorial Guinea and Zaire. Start by dividing the class into two groups: stars (one third of the students) and catchers (two thirds)—you may want to adjust these proportions. Mark off two boundaries, about 20 feet apart. Have the stars stand together at on end and the catchers stand in the middle, between the two ends. The catchers start the game by chanting "Star light, star bright, how many stars are out tonight?" Stars respond with "More than you can catch!" Stars then run as fast as they can to the opposite end, trying to avoid being tagged by a catcher. Stars who are caught become catchers and the game continues until all stars are caught.

MATH *Counting on Stars*

Make constellation graphs, showing the number of stars in each. Some questions to guide a discussion follow:

✶ How many stars are in each constellation?

✶ Which one has the most? The fewest?

✶ How many more stars in _____ than _____ ?

✶ Are there more stars in ___ or ___ ?

✶ How many fewer stars in ___ than ___ ?

✶ How many stars altogether?
Follow up with an opinion graph: What is your favorite constellation?

Star Catchers adapted from *The Multicultural Game Book* by Louise Orlando (Scholastic Professional Books, 1993) by permission of the author.

Night Comes...

Night comes
leaking
out of the sky.

Stars come
peeking.

Moon comes
sneaking,
silvery-sly.

Who is
shaking,
shivery-
quaking?

Who is afraid
of the night?

Not I.

—Beatrice Schenk de Regniers

Dear _____,

   We are becoming a class of stargazers. You can reinforce science concepts at home by stargazing with your child.

   Spend a few minutes looking at the stars together. Ask your child to describe how the stars look. Have your child record three of these words on the form below and return this paper to class by _____. Your child will be using these words for class activities.

   Thank you, and happy stargazing!

Shimmering Stars

Date_____

Stargazers' Names_____

_____

1. Write a word in each star to describe the stars you saw tonight.

2. Finish the sentence:

When I looked at the stars _____

_____

Star Patterns

RESOURCES

FOR CHILDREN

The Big Dipper by Franklyn Branley (HarperCollins, 1991). An introduction to the pattern of stars known as the Big Dipper. Nonfiction.

"Coyote Helps Decorate the Night" retold by Harold Courlander, in *From Sea to Shining Sea: A Treasury of American Folklore and Folk Songs* (Scholastic, 1993). This Hopi tale from the Southwest details how Coyote helped scatter stars in the night sky. Fiction.

Follow the Drinking Gourd by Jeanette Winter (Knopf, 1988). This story tells how slaves used the drinking gourd constellation (the Big Dipper) to make their way north to freedom. Fiction.

Her Seven Brothers by Paul Goble (Bradbury, 1984). A Cheyenne legend about how the Big Dipper came to be. Fiction.

Stargazers by Gail Gibbons (Holiday House, 1992). This easy-to-read book explains constellations and telescopes. Nonfiction.

Switch on the Night by Ray Bradbury (Knopf, 1983). "Once there was a little boy who didn't like the Night." So he surrounds himself with lanterns and flashlights, and lights up the house at night with every lamp in the house. Then he meets Night and learns about switching on the crickets, the frogs, and a skyful of stars. Nonfiction.

FOR TEACHERS

Find the Constellations by H.A. Rey (Houghton Mifflin, 1988). This book will come in handy for pictures of constellations. Also contains a few constellation myths.

Stars: A Golden Guide by Herbert Zim (Golden Press, 1985). A simple field guide to stars.

David Levy's Guide to the Night Sky (Cambridge University Press, 2001). A rather extensive guide to night sky phenomena, this book will help you locate constellations and learn the features of the moon, and much more.

TECHNOLOGY CONNECTIONS

Lunar Cycle 1: Calendar
Science NetLinks (part of Thinkfinity)
(www.sciencenetlinks.org/tool_index.cfm)
    Access dozens and dozens of lesson plans and teaching tools that support standards-based science instruction. The activity Lunar Cycle 1, found in the Tools section of this site, challenges children to use photos of the moon at different phases to complete the pattern of one lunar cycle.

Astronomy: Our Place in Space
American Museum of Natural History
(www.amnh.org/ology/astronomy/)
    Colorful graphics and interesting information covers a variety of interests: Mars, gravity, our sun, and more.

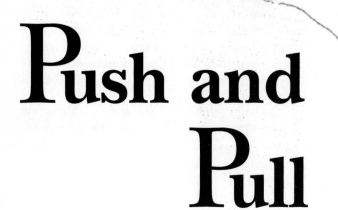

Push and Pull

What makes things move? Moving is something that young children know a lot about. They spend much of their time making things move—pushing toy trucks through sand and pulling sleds through the snow, blowing bubbles across the yard and throwing balls through hoops.

The concept introduced in this theme—that the forces of push and pull result in motion—is developed in different kinds of activities. Your students will be looking for examples in their daily surroundings, moving their own bodies to imitate the forces of push and pull, listening to stories, and building models. Research about how we learn has indicated that presenting an idea in a variety of ways and making connections between these presentations will enhance learning. After you finish an activity, help students make these important connections by reminding them of how the same concept was presented in earlier activities.

 S c i e n c e   D i c t i o n a r y

push and **pull** forces that cause motion

magnet an object made from iron and ore that can push or pull objects made of iron or steel

Science Concepts and Skills

Concepts: Students will recognize that they can make things move by pushing or pulling them, and that they can change the speed and direction of that movement. They will also discover that magnets can be used to make things move without actually touching them.

Process Skills: observing, classifying, comparing, communicating, predicting, measuring, collecting and recording data, interpreting

Science on Display

Remember the moon border you started in September? If you've kept this activity going, the border has most likely moved beyond the science display and is taking over another part of your classroom. Well, here's another fun border idea that will personalize the topic of movement for your students. Create a background for your border out of black craft paper, cut about 6 inches high and however long you need to wrap around a wall or two. Dip the tires of a toy truck in some bright yellow paint and make tracks along the top and bottom edges of the border. Students can now complete the border as part of Activity 1.

ACTIVITY 1

Look at Us Move

Students discover there are many ways to move from here to there.

Note: To complete this activity you will need a copy (or photocopy) of students' school pictures (small, wallet-size).

Materials

* old magazines (students will be cutting out pictures from these)
* students' school pictures
* glue sticks
* chart paper

1 Help students brainstorm ways they get from one place to another. List their ideas on chart paper, and post.

2 Give students copies of their school pictures. They will need to cut out the head portion of their pictures, then set the photos aside.

3 Pass out blank 3-by-5-inch cards. Ask students to look through the magazines and cut out pictures that show people moving. Have students stick to pictures that are about the same size as their cards. It's okay if there's some overhang but the intent is to have all students' cutouts close to the same size. (Hint: Sports magazines are a good source of movement pictures.)

4 Have each student cut out a picture, then cut out the head of the person (or one of the people) in the picture.

5 Next, have students glue their magazine pictures to the cards, then add their own face pictures, gluing them where the original heads had been. If students are using photocopies of school pictures, they might like to add color with multicultural-colored crayons.

6 Let students share their pictures—explaining the movement in their pictures—then glue them to the border.

(You can also try this activity without the children's participation, choosing instead to surprise them one morning with pictures of themselves on the move! Expect a lot of talk about their various "moving" situations!)

ACTIVITY 2 ~~~~~~~~~~~~~~~~~~~~~~~~~~~~~~~~~~

Push and Pull Play

Students act out ways we use the forces of push and pull.

1 Have students stand up and find some space where they can move without touching anyone else. (This is a good outdoor activity if weather permits.)

2 Explain that you are going to name some movements for them to act out that use the forces of push and pull. Here are some to get you started, but feel free to add more.

* pulling a box from a tall shelf

* pushing a friend on the swings

* pulling a banana off of a bunch

* pushing a huge box

* pulling your little sister in a wagon

* pushing a broom

ACTIVITY 3

Let's Go Sledding

If you live in a snowy area, sledding will probably be something your students do a lot. But if you live in a milder climate, sledding may not be a familiar activity. Either way, this activity invites children to make some predictions and observations, and challenges them to put the forces of push and pull to work.

Materials

* 1 shoe box with lid for each group of two or three students (the larger the shoe box, the better)

* small, empty boxes (tiny gift boxes or the kind wooden matches are packed in)

* a box filled with string, paper clips, rubber bands, pieces of Velcro, pipe cleaners, thin wire, buttons, tape

* Let's Go Sledding Science Journal page (see page 170)

Note: Paint the outsides of the boxes white, turning them into snowy slopes for sledding!

1 Show students the lid from one of the shoe boxes and one of the small boxes. Place the small box on the lid and ask how you could make the small box move across the lid, from one end to the other. Listen to their ideas and try them out. (These will probably include giving the small box a push or blowing on the small box. Encourage students to recognize that the push helped move the box.)

2 Now ask students if any of them have ever gone sledding. If they have, let them describe the sleds and the kinds of places they went sledding. If none of them have ever gone sledding, try to have some pictures on hand to share.

3 Demonstrate the idea of sledding by setting up a shoe-box hill, as illustrated. Set one of the small boxes on the edge and let it slide.

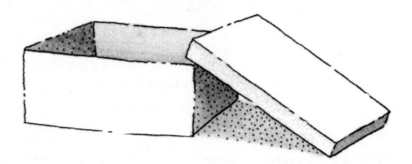

4 Now ask students if they can think of a way to get the sled back up to the top of the hill. (Most obvious response will be to pick up the box and set it back on top of the lid.) If they were sledding for real, how would they get the sled back up? (Pull the sleds uphill.)

5 Now, present this challenge: How can we get the sled (small box) to the top of the hill (lid) without picking it up with our hands? (Possible solutions include taping string to the box and pulling it up, and attaching a paper clip to the box and using a magnet to move the box.)

BOOK BREAK
Share *Dr. DeSoto* by William Steig, the story of a celebrated dentist (who happens to be a mouse) whose system of pulleys enables him to do dental work on larger patients. Allow time afterward for the inspired discussion that is sure to follow (see Resources, page 175).

6 Let students share ideas for several minutes, then break them into small groups to come up with a solution. Show them the various materials they can use (see Materials). They may suggest other materials, too.

7 Give students time to experiment with materials and create ways to move the sled back to the top of the hill. As with many activities, some groups will need and want to spend much more time on this than others. Groups that finish early can work on the Science Journal page describing and/or illustrating their designs.

8 Give each group a chance to show off its design, describing the kinds of movements that are happening to get the sled to the top. If possible, set up hills and sleds in the science display area so that students can try out one another's designs.

9 If students are really enjoying this activity, don't stop! Let them try adding loads to their sleds. Does it make a difference how the sleds move down the hill? How does the effort needed to get the full sled to the top of the hill compare with the empty sled?

10 Use sledding as a springboard to a discussion about how technology effects our daily lives:

   ❋ Why do you think someone invented a sled? (To reduce work.)

   ❋ What are some uses for a sled?

   ❋ What is something that you could do with a sled to help you at home?

Brainstorm other inventions that help us move things.

ACTIVITY 4 〜〜〜〜〜〜〜〜〜〜〜〜〜〜〜〜〜〜〜〜〜〜〜〜

Magnetic Attractions

Students investigate objects that are attracted to magnets.

〜〜〜〜〜〜〜〜〜〜〜〜〜〜〜〜〜〜〜〜〜〜〜〜

Materials

   ❋ small bar magnets

   ❋ Magnetic Attractions Science Journal page (see page 173)

   ❋ assorted objects such as paper clips, coins, straws, washers, crayons, pieces of aluminum foil

〜〜〜〜〜〜〜〜〜〜〜〜〜〜〜〜〜〜〜〜〜〜〜〜

Note: This is one of those activities that is a lot more manageable if the materials are easily accessible. If possible, use small trays that can hold enough magnets and test materials for each person in a small group of two or three students.

1 Give each student a copy of the Science Journal page. Have students write Yes or No to indicate their predictions about whether or not each item on the list will stick to a magnet.

2 Once students have recorded their predictions, invite them to test the objects and record their results. After testing the six objects on the list, students can find four more objects to test. They should write the name of each object in the space provided, record their predictions, then test each object.

3 When all groups are finished, gather students together. List the first six objects on chart paper and ask students to answer Yes or No to this question: Does (the object) stick to a magnet? If discrepancies occur, take time to retest.

4 After you have recorded the results for the first six objects, have students help you list additional objects they tested. Record Yes or No for these items, as well.

5 Using information collected from this experiment, what can students say about the kinds of objects that will stick to a magnet? (Do all metal objects stick to a magnet? Shiny objects?) Many children will predict that anything made of metal will stick to the magnet, but this is not the case. Objects made of iron, nickel, or cobalt (or alloys of these metals) are attracted to magnets. Objects made of aluminum and lead are not. Discuss students' ideas and compile and display a list of the characteristics of things that stick to magnets.

ACTIVITY 5 ~~~~~~

Move It With Magnets

Students explore how a magnet can make something move without touching it.

Materials

 * magnets (at least three different sizes, shapes)
 * paper clips
 * Move It With Magnets reproducible (see page 174)
 * large sheet of light-colored construction paper (trace each magnet across the top of this paper)

1 Give each small group a magnet and some paper clips. Challenge them to use the magnet to make the paper clip move. Give them a couple of minutes to try this, then have them share their observations.

2 Now show them some of the other magnets . Will they all pull a paper clip? (Students will want to test this out, too.)

3 Ask: Do you think all magnets pull with the same strength or are some magnets stronger than others?

4 Have students brainstorm ideas for testing the strength of each magnet's pull. Then give each small group three different magnets to test. Direct students' attention to the large sheet of paper on which you have traced the magnets. Ask them to predict which magnet will have the most pulling power. Have students sign their names (or make a check mark) under the tracings to indicate their predictions.

5 Demonstrate how to use the reproducible to test pulling power: Place the magnet on top of the magnet outline, and the paper clip on top of the picture of the paper clip. Move the magnet, one block at a time, toward the paper clip. Continue to do this until the paper clip is pulled toward the magnet. (The paper clip does not necessarily have to move all the way to the magnet.) Make a mark where the front of the magnet lies on the paper. Have students work in their groups to test the magnets themselves, repeating the procedure for the other two magnets and completing the question at the bottom of the reproducible to tell which magnet had the most pulling power.

6 After all groups have tested their magnets, come together to discuss the results as a class. Look back at the predictions. How do these compare with the results? Why would it be important for some magnets to be stronger than others?

Curriculum Connections

SOCIAL STUDIES
People Who Move

Take a walk around school to look for people who are moving things. Before setting out, have students share their ideas of what they might see. Bring a clipboard to record who students see, what they are moving, and a description of the movement. Have students collect each person's autograph on this record sheet, as well. (Hint: The day before your walk, brief people you might see at work. Explain what students will be looking for. This way they will be ready to show off a part of their work.)

As an extension, have students work with a parent to find people around their home or neighborhood who are moving things. A sample letter and record sheet is provided (see page 169). When students return findings to class, compile a class book about moving.

MOVEMENT
Tug-O-Game

Measure out a long length of smooth rope or clothesline. Mark off the center point on the rope with a knotted piece of cloth. Place two parallel lines of masking tape (approximately 3 feet apart) on the ground to mark off a neutral zone.

Have an equal number of children hold onto each end of the rope so that the cloth is in the center of the neutral zone. At a signal, the teams begin pulling, trying to get the cloth into their territory. Switch teams several times so that every child has a chance to win.

ART
Sliding Sleds

Use reproducible on pages 171 and 172 with students to create sledding scenes. Here's how:

* Glue page A to a file folder and let dry.

* On page B, cut the long and short dotted lines, then set aside.

* When page A is dry, cut out each piece, being careful not to cut off the tab at the end. Fold the tab along the dotted line, toward the strip.

* Next, insert the tab from the long strip through the long cut line on page B, and slip the other end of the long strip through the short cut line. Pull the strip through to the other side. Glue the sled to the tab.

* Pull and push the long strip to make the sled move.

Dear _____,

    In class, your child is learning about the forces of push and pull, and how they help things move. You can reinforce your child's understanding by taking some time together to watch for people who are moving things. This might be around home, in the neighborhood, at the grocery store, wherever you and your child happen to be.

    Please help your child record what you see together on the chart below and return this paper to class by _____.

    Thank you for your help.

Name _____

Look at Us Move!

WHO	WHAT IS BEING MOVED	DESCRIPTION OF MOVEMENT

Let's Go Sledding

Group Members _____

_____

Solve This Problem: The sled is at the bottom of the hill.
How can you get it back to the top without picking it up
with your hands?

Draw a picture here to show how you can solve the problem.

Use words here to explain your solution.

_____

_____

_____

_____

_____

Directions

1. Glue this page to a file folder. Let dry.

2. Cut out pieces 1 and 2 along the dark lines.

3. Fold the tab in along the dotted line.

4. Cut on the dotted lines on page B.

5. Slip the tab through the long cut on page B. Glue your sled to the tab.

6. Slip the strip through the short cut on page B. Pull the strip through to the other side.

7. Cut out small pictures of people from magazines. Or make your own. Paste them to the sled. Now push and pull to make your sled move.

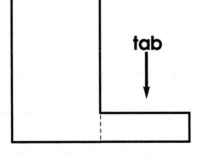

tab

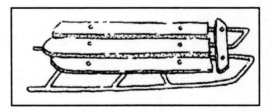

①   ②

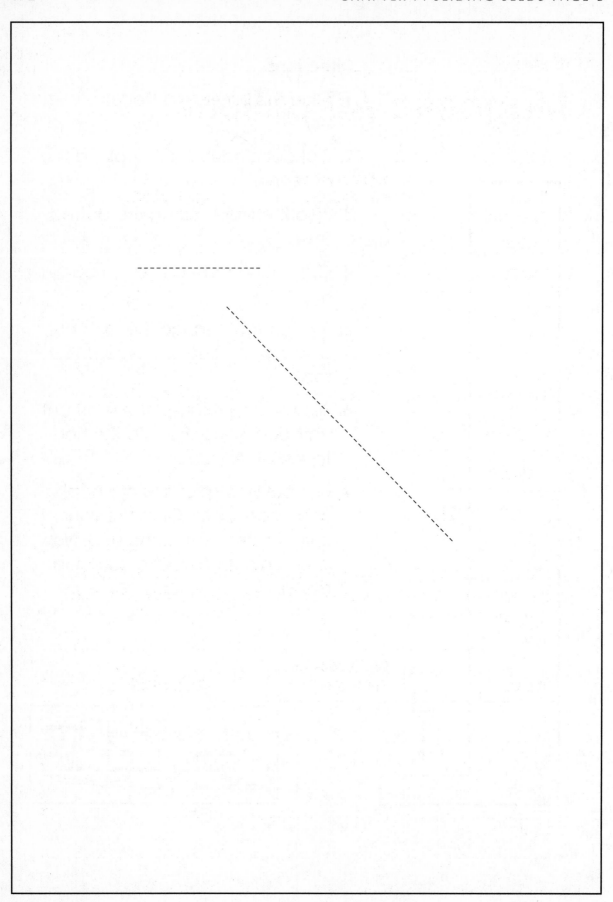

Name_____

Magnetic Attractions

Object	Will it stick to the magnet?	Did it stick?
1. paper clip		
2. coin		
3. straw		

Object	Will it stick to the magnet?	Did it stick?
4. washer		
5. crayon		
6. aluminum foil		

Think of four more objects to test. Write the names of the objects here. Write your prediction first. Then test with the magnet.

Object	Will it stick to the magnet?	Did it stick?
7.		
8.		
9.		
10.		

Name _____

Move It With Magnets

Trace magnet here.	Trace magnet here.	Trace magnet here.

Which magnet has the most pulling power?

_____

RESOURCES

FOR CHILDREN

Amazing Magnetism (Magic School Bus Chapter Book) by Rebecca Carmi (Scholastic, 2002). Ms. Frizzle challenges Mr. O'Neatly's class to a science contest. Learning and fun ensues while The Friz teaches her students about magnetism. Fiction.

Dr. DeSoto by William Steig (Farrar Straus Giroux, 1990). A celebrated dentist, who happens to be a mouse, uses a system of pulleys to enable him to do dental work on larger patients. Fiction.

Forces Make Things Move (Let's-Read-and-Find-Out Science 2) by Kimberly Brubaker Bradley (HarperTrophy, 2005). An enjoyable and straightforward introduction to some challenging science concepts. Nonfiction.

Mike Mulligan and His Steam Shovel by Virginia Lee Burton (Houghton Mifflin, 1939). Mike and his steam shovel, Mary Anne, help Popperville build a new town hall. Includes diagrams of levers and other parts that help Mary Anne get the job done. Fiction.

What Makes a Magnet? (Let's-Read-and-Find-Out Science 2) by Franklyn M. Branley (HarperTrophy, 1996). Accessible explanations and cheerful illustrations help to convey the properties of magnets. Includes directions for hands-on activities.

FOR TEACHERS

Magnets & Electricity (Teacher Created Materials) A compilation of hands-on science activities designed to make lesson planning easier. For more information, contact Teacher Created Materials at (800) 858-7339. Or visit the Web site: www.teachercreatedmaterials.com.

Simple Machines Made Simple by Ralph E. St. Andre (Teacher Ideas Press, 1995). Students build levers, pulleys, and other gadgets while they learn about simple mechanics. The book includes activities for slightly older children that can be adapted for primary students.

TECHNOLOGY CONNECTIONS

Hard Hat Harry's 6-Pack (Good Times Video, 2005) This collection of videos features cars, machines, and trucks. Hard Hat Harry DVDs are intended for the youngest learners. (Each video has a run time of about an hour.)

If You Give a Mouse a Cookie (Reading Rainbow) explores what happens when one action sets a series of actions in motion. There's also a neat segment on how bowling balls are made. For more information, call GPN Educational Media at (800) 228-4630 or visit http://shopgpn.com/stores/1/RR_BookLists.cfm.

The New Way Things Work 3.2 (Dorling Kindersley, 2006) Based on David Macaulay's book, this multimedia extravaganza shows how 150 machines work through lavish illustrations, animations, and live-action videos. Children familiar with the book will recognize their guide, the Great Woolly Mammoth.

Inventor's Workshop
PBS Kids
(http://pbskids.org/cyberchase/games.html) Third graders will enjoy creating their own fabulous inventions online at Cyberchase's Inventor's Workshop. You'll enjoy lessons and activities that connect to the NCTM standards.

CHAPTER 8

February

In the Shadows
page 180

Healthy Hearts
page 194

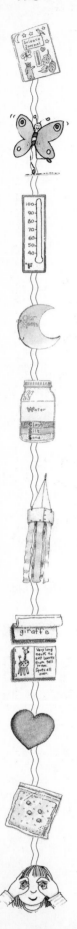

Highlights *of the* Month

Mark these dates, events, and activities on your calendar to help plan and supplement upcoming activities in this month's themes.

* February 2 is Groundhog Day.

* February 14 is Valentine's Day.

* National Heart Month

* The February full moon is the Snow Moon or Hunger Moon.

* Challenge children to locate Punxsutawney on a map. (Hint: It's in Pennsylvania.) What is this city known for?

* Two other names for groundhogs are woodchucks and whistlepigs. Where would you find a groundhog?

Plan Ahead

The first theme this month focuses on shadows, and since Groundhog Day falls on February 2, be prepared to have students listen to the news that morning. What do they think the groundhog's weather prediction will be? (See note on page 183.)

You'll need a stethoscope for the Healthy Hearts activity. Inexpensive stethoscopes are available from Delta Education, (800) 258-1302; www.delta-education.com.

SCIENCE AT HOME

Date _____

This month we are starting two new science themes.

1. In the Shadows

Your young scientist will be learning more about the nature of shadows this month (and watching to see if the groundhog's prediction comes true!). You can reinforce learning at home by noticing together which objects make shadows and which don't.

2. Healthy Hearts

Helping children learn about healthy habits when they are young makes it easier for them to continue to have healthy habits as they grow. This month, we'll be focusing on the heart. Watch for a family activity page that invites you and your child to compare heart rates.

Wish List

Do you have materials you can donate for our science explorations? For this month's activities, we need:

_____

_____

_____

Reminders _____

_____

_____

In the Shadows

According to weather lore, if the groundhog emerges from its burrow on the morning of February 2 and sees its shadow, we can expect six more weeks of winter weather. If he doesn't see it, there will be an early spring. Use the groundhog's forecast as an invitation to your young scientists to learn more about the true nature of shadows.

 # Science Dictionary

opaque something you can't see through, like a notebook

shadow a dark shape that is made when an object blocks out the light

translucent something you can see through, but not clearly, like wax paper

transparent something you can see through clearly, like window glass

Science Concepts and Skills

Concepts: Students will observe that light travels in a straight line unless it strikes an object. They will recognize that some objects that are hit by light block it completely, creating a shadow of the object. They will also recognize that not all objects create shadows when light hits them.

Process Skills: observing, inferring, predicting, comparing, communicating, classifying, interpreting

Science on Display

Note: So that students can better see the shadows they make, turn out the lights over the area if possible. If this is not possible, try stacking boxes (like the kind that reams of copy paper come in) to build a workstation. The boxes will help cut down on some of the extraneous classroom light.

When getting ready to begin a study of shadows, select some small objects that make interesting shadows, such as an eraser, a crayon, a paper clip, a key, and a small toy. Trace the shadows on a piece of poster board, coloring them in with black marker. Place these objects, along with other objects, in a shoe box labeled Only the Shadows Know. Across the top of the chart write: Can you guess what made these shadows? Explain to students that the shadows were made by objects in the box. Invite them to first guess which object made which shadow, then use the flashlight to solve the mystery. (You might want to have students take turns at this display, working in small groups of two or three at a time.) Freshen the activity now and then by adding new shadow pictures to the chart and objects to the box.

ACTIVITY 1

What Is a Shadow?

Students make shadows to learn more about light and what happens as light hits objects.

Materials

* flashlight
* chart paper
* marker

1   Hang chart paper on a wall or chalkboard. Darken the room and shine the flashlight directly onto the paper.

2   Ask students to describe what the light looks light. (It will appear as a circle of light.) Have them describe the path of the light from the flashlight to the paper. (They should see a straight beam of light.)

3   Now invite a student to hold one hand in the light beam about halfway between the flashlight and the chart paper. (Kids will love this!) What happens to the light on the chart paper? (The light beam is interrupted by the hand, and a dark area, a shadow of the hand, appears on the paper.) Ask a second student to trace around this hand shadow. Then let the first student sign his or her name by the shadow picture. Both students can return to their seats.

4   Ask students to try to guess what would happen to the shadow if a hand is placed closer to the flashlight. Listen to their guesses, then try it out. Have another student place a hand in the beam of light, this time within a couple inches of the flashlight. Ask students to describe what they observe. How does this second hand shadow compare to the first hand shadow? (This shadow will be bigger. The closer an object is to the light source, the darker and larger the shadow that is produced.)

5   As with the first hand shadow, ask another child to trace around the second hand shadow, then let the student whose hand it is sign by the tracing.

6   Time for more guessing. Ask students to predict what will happen if the hand is moved farther away from the light source. Listen to predictions, then invite a new student to place his or her hand fairly close to the chart paper. Students should describe how this shadow compares with the first two. Repeat steps of tracing and signing hand shadows.

7   Finish up by asking students to describe how a shadow is made and how shadows can change in appearance. To guide the discussion, ask students to identify the light source (flashlight) and explain what makes the shadow. (The light cannot pass through the hand. Where this light is blocked out, a dark area in the shape of a hand is made.)

8   Invite students who did not get a chance to help each other make, trace, and sign their shadows.

ACTIVITY 2

Groundhog Day

What do classroom groundhogs have to say about their shadows?

BOOK BREAK
Around the beginning of February, read *Groundhog Day!* by Gail Gibbons. (See Resources, page 193.) After reading, ask children to share their ideas about the reliability of a groundhog's predictions.

Materials

* groundhog pattern (see page 190)
* used manila file folder
* craft sticks or pencils
* air-drying clay
* heavy white paper
* brown paper lunch bags
* crayons
* tape

Note: Do this activity before Groundhog Day. Prior to the activity, make stencils of groundhogs by copying the pattern on file folders. Introduce the activity on February 1 (or as close to this date as possible), asking students what they know about Groundhog Day.
If they don't already know, tell them the story. Ask them to make a page in their Science Journals for recording the groundhog's prediction and their own predictions, and tracking the weather for the next six weeks.

1 Let students trace the groundhog pattern onto white paper, then cut out and color their groundhogs.

2 Next, have students tape the groundhog to a craft stick or pencil, then insert the stick into a ball of clay.

3 Give each student a brown paper lunch bag. This will be the groundhog's burrow. Students can name their groundhogs and write the names on the bag.

4 Have students place groundhogs in the bags, fold over the tops, then set the bags on a windowsill.

5 The following morning, have students lift their groundhogs out of the burrows, set them on the windowsill, and observe whether or not the groundhogs see their shadows. Remind students to record observations in their weather journals.

6   Gather students together to discuss their observations. Did all of the groundhogs see their shadows? Why or why not? (They should all have the same result.) How do their groundhogs' predictions compare with the predictions of the groundhogs in the news? Why would the results be the same or different?

7   Your groundhogs may want to return to their burrows if they see their shadows and sleep for the next six weeks. Or if they didn't see their shadows, you can roll down the paper bags and let the groundhogs enjoy the early spring.

ACTIVITY 3

Mystery Shadows

Materials

* overhead projector
* file folder
* collection of shadow-producing mystery objects (keys, paper clip, banana, baseball card, beads, coins, watch)
* paper bag
* Mystery Shadows Science Journal page (see page 191)

Note: Before this activity, tape the file folder on the light stem of the overhead projector, creating a screen so that students cannot see the objects that you place on the overhead.

1   Explain that you are going to be putting different objects on the overhead projector. Ask students to use the shadows as clues to guess what the objects are.

2   After you have made shadows with all the objects in the bag, ask students which objects were the hardest to identify and why. Then ask which objects were easiest to identify and why. What do all the objects have in common? (They all block light and make shadows.)

3   Divide the class into small groups. Give each group a flashlight and each student a copy of the reproducible Science Journal page. Turn out the lights (or otherwise darken the room) while students complete the reproducible.

4   Display and discuss students' drawings. Which shadows were easy to identify? Which were difficult? How did they change

the size of their shadows? As students may recall from Activity 1, when an object is farther away from the light source, the shadow will be smaller. So one student might have held the object farther from the light source while the other traced the shadow.

ACTIVITY 4

What Makes a Shadow?

Students compare and classify shadow-making objects with nonshadow-making objects.

Materials (for each group)

* flashlights (or can be done on a sunny windowsill)

* set of objects to test: opaque objects (piece of aluminum foil, small piece of cardboard), translucent objects (piece of wax paper, piece of paper towel), transparent objects (clear plastic lid, clear plastic sandwich bag)

* What Makes a Shadow? Science Journal page (see page 192)

Note: Before the activity, place objects for each group in the plastic sandwich bags. The objects on the Science Journal page record sheet correspond to those listed above. You'll find a couple of blank spaces on the chart in case you want to add other objects to the bag.

1 Let students work in small groups for this activity. Give each small group a plastic bag that contains the objects and give each student a reproducible.

2 Tell students that the first thing they need to do is observe the items in the bag and predict whether or not each object will make a shadow. They should record their predictions on the reproducible.

3 After students have made their predictions, give each group a flashlight and turn out the lights. (Or direct each group to find a sunny location where they can test for shadows.)

4 The students should test each object and record on the reproducible which objects made shadows and which did not.

5 After they have tested the materials in the bag, including the bag itself, they should go on to the next two challenges on the reproducible (find one more object that makes a shadow, find one more object that does not make a shadow).

BOOK BREAK

Challenge students to identify more mystery shadows with *Guess Whose Shadow?* by Stephen Swinburne. (See Resources, page 193). The photographs in this book will keep children guessing about what objects made the shadows. Then turn students' own shadow pictures into a class shadow book and challenge another class to identify the objects.

6 When all groups are finished, let students help you list the items that made shadows and those that did not (including their "Challenge" finds). Some questions to guide a discussion of these results follow.

✳ What do all the objects that make shadows have in common? (These objects are solid. They block out light.)

✳ Does light pass through all of these objects in the same way? (No. Some, like the wax paper, are *translucent* and only let some light through. Other materials, like the clear plastic lid, are *transparent*. They let all of the light pass through. Children may describe these differences as light not being as bright—translucent objects—or light being bright—transparent objects.)

✳ What do all the objects that don't make shadows have in common? (We can see light through these objects.)

Curriculum Connections

LANGUAGE ARTS
Look at My Shadow

After reading the poem "Look" (see page 189), challenge children to see if it's possible to have their own shadows measure 10 feet tall (using the sun or a different light source). Experiment with other objects, too, to make shadows of varying lengths. Then have children rewrite the poem substituting the name of the objects for the word *my* and the new length in feet for the word *ten*. Have children illustrate their sentences and bind the pages into a class book of shadow measurements.

10 feet

MOVEMENT
Shadow Friends

Pair up students and let them take turns being their partner's shadows—imitating everything their partners do. This will take a little practice. Encourage students to make their movements slowly, at least at first, so that their shadows can keep up.

MATH
Measuring Me

Here's an activity to take outside on a sunny day. On a chart, record each student's name and height. Make two columns for recording length of students' shadows. Select two times during the day (one early in the morning or later in the afternoon, the second between noon and 1 P.M.) to go outside and measure shadows. Let the kids work in pairs to measure their partners' shadows. Have students record the length of their shadows in the appropriate column. (Write in the time of day at the top of each column.) Use the chart to help students answer questions like: When were the shadows the longest? Shortest? Is everyone's shadow the same length? Was the teacher's shadow the same as the students' shadows? What was the light source outside?

DRAMA
Hand Movies

Long before moving pictures appeared in the movies and on television, people were enjoying making moving pictures with hand shadows. To have students try their hand at this ancient art, you'll need a strong light source, such as a high-intensity study lamp, or the light from a film projector. Darken the classroom, if necessary, then shine the light beam on the wall or onto a white sheet that's been draped over a door. Invite children to take turns placing their hands in the light to demonstrate any hand shadows they already know. Then, share new hand shadows for them to try. Finally, encourage children to create new shadow shapes of their own. A good source for hand shadow ideas is *The Little Book of Hand Shadows* by Phila H. Webb (Running Press, 1990).

Look

Firelight and shadows
dancing on the wall.
Look at my shadow
TEN FEET TALL!

—Charlotte Zolotow

Groundhog Pattern

Name _____

Mystery Shadows

Directions: Find something in your classroom to make a mystery shadow. Draw the shadow here. Ask your teacher and classmates to guess what made the shadow.

Find a way to change the size of your mystery shadow. On the back of this paper, draw a picture of the new shadow. Explain how you changed the shadow's size.

Name _____

What Makes a Shadow?

Object		Prediction (Will this object make a shadow?)	Result
	aluminum foil		
	cardboard		
	wax paper		
	paper towel		
	clear plastic lid		
	clear plastic sandwich bag		

Find one more object that makes a shadow. Write its name here. Is it opaque, translucent, or transparent?

_____

How can you tell? _____

_____

_____

RESOURCES

FOR CHILDREN

Groundhog Day! By Gail Gibbons (Holiday House, 2007). What do groundhogs have to do with the onset of springtime? Gail Gibbons sheds light on the subject. Nonfiction.

Guess Whose Shadow? by Stephen Swinburne (Boyds Mills Press, 2002). A playful introduction to the hows and whys behind shadows. Nonfiction.

Nothing Sticks Like a Shadow by Ann Tompert (Houghton Mifflin, 1988). Shadows go wherever you go, don't they? Woodchuck and Rabbit explore the question. Fiction.

Shadows (Rookie Readers) by Deanna Calvert (Scholastic, 2004). A fun-to-read book with simple text and playful illustrations. Fiction.

Substitute Groundhog by Pat Miller (Albert Whitman & Company, 2006). Groundhog has the flu and needs to find a substitute. Can any of his animal friends take his place? Fiction.

FOR TEACHERS

Shadow Magic
Uncle Milton
> Just hang the glow-in-the-dark screen on the wall, set an object directly in front of it, and flash the strobe light. This simple-to-use shadow-casting set is perfect for hands-on learning. To learn more about this product call (888) 742-2484 or visit: www.unclemilton.com/. (For extra fun, download free shadow templates from the Web site. Templates include: butterfly, fish, ghost, pumpkin, robot, and rocket.)

TECHNOLOGY CONNECTIONS

Punxsutawney Groundhog Club
(www.groundhog.org/teachers/)
> Head straight to Punxsutawney, PA, for the scoop on everybody's favorite groundhog—or, visit this Web site! The Teachers' Corner provides links to activities and lesson plans that support learning about the history and traditions that surround Groundhog Day.

Chinese Shadow Puppets
Boston Children's Museum
(www.bostonchildrensmuseum.org/educators/curriculum.html)
> Extend classroom learning about shadows even further by studying and making Chinese shadow puppets. Then, peruse this Web site provided by the Boston Children's Museum. It's a treasure trove of lesson plans, learning activities, and curriculum units that relate to the study of the art, science, and culture.

Healthy Hearts

Valentine's Day is a time when we share messages from the heart. What better time to introduce your students to messages important for the heart? It is clear that helping young children understand the importance of practicing healthy habits, such as good nutrition, lots of exercise, and proper rest when they are young, will make it easier to continue those healthy habits as adults. So this year, give your students a very special valentine.

Science Concepts and Skills

Concepts: Students will begin to develop an understanding of the relationship between having a healthy body and eating the right foods, getting exercise, and relaxing.

Process Skills: observing, predicting, collecting and recording data, communicating, measuring, comparing, classifying, interpreting

Science Dictionary

heart a muscular organ that pumps the blood through the body; the average adult heart rate (number of beats per minute) is 70; this means that the heart is contracting or pumping blood about 70 times each minute; for children ages 6 to 8 the average beats per minute is 65 to 130 (resting)

nutrition the kinds of foods we need to stay healthy, including proteins, carbohydrates, fats, vitamins, minerals, and some fiber; examples of these nutrients are found at right

pulse the way arteries throb when the heart contracts

Science on Display

Cover your bulletin board with bright red craft paper. Then let students help make a border of hearts that resemble the candy conversation hearts found this time of year. Here's how.

Give each student one of the candy hearts. Make a list of the messages. Now let students brainstorm other messages to add to the list. Next, have each student trace and cut out a heart from pastel-colored paper, then choose a message to write on the heart. (Make heart stencils by copying the pattern on this page.) Have students display their hearts on the bulletin board to create a border. (Depending on the size of the bulletin board, you may need students to make more than one paper heart each.) After you are finished, students can eat their candy hearts. (Remind them, of course, that it's not good for them to eat too much sugar!)

Students can use the remainder of the board to display theme-related messages about the heart on heart-shaped paper. These might include heart facts, health tips, poems, riddles, and so on. Allow time for students to browse through their classmates' messages—and learn from each other.

ACTIVITY 1 〜〜〜〜〜〜〜〜〜〜〜〜〜〜〜〜〜〜〜〜〜〜〜

Heart Work

Introduce your students to this awesome organ by letting them experience how hard their hearts work.

〜〜〜〜〜〜〜〜〜〜〜〜〜〜〜〜〜〜〜〜〜〜〜〜〜〜〜〜〜

Materials

* Heart Work Science Journal page (see page 202)

* stethoscopes (see Plan Ahead, page 178)

* alcohol swabs

〜〜〜〜〜〜〜〜〜〜〜〜〜〜〜〜〜〜〜〜〜〜〜〜〜〜〜〜〜

1 Ask students to guess how large their hearts are. After listening to their ideas, have them each make a fist. Explain that their hearts are about the size of their closed fists.

2 Keeping their fists closed, students should place one fist where they think their hearts are in their bodies. Show them with your own fist that the heart is located to the left of center inside their chests.

3 Explain that their hearts are important muscles because they keep blood pumping through their bodies. In order to do this, their hearts must be strong. To demonstrate, tell students that you are going to say *lub dub*. When you say *lub* they should open their fists; when you say dub they should close their fists. Try to time your *lub dubs* so you are doing one per second.

4 Let students practice the rhythm a couple of times, then explain that they will do this for the next minute. Start timing and keep them in rhythm by chanting *lub dub, lub dub....*

5 At the end of one minute, ask students how their hands feel. (Their expressions and groans during the above task will let you know! Their hands will feel tired.) Do they think they could do this for five minutes? An hour? Now they know why the heart must be strong: so that it can keep pumping night and day, without ever stopping.

6 Finish up by introducing students to the stethoscopes. Demonstrate how to use the instrument, then let them take turns listening. (Wipe the ear pieces with alcohol swabs after each child's turn.) Ask them to describe the sounds they hear, then have students complete Part 1 of their journal pages.

ACTIVITY 2

Listen to My Heartbeat

Students investigate their heart rates after rest and exercise.

Materials

* chart paper
* glue stick
* blue and red crayons
* Science Journal page from Activity 1

Note: Before the activity, use the chart paper to set up a graph like the one illustrated here.

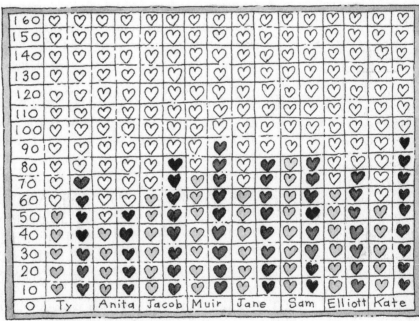

blue : resting
red : after exercise

1 Start this activity after children have been sitting for a while. Give each child a copy of the reproducible worksheet. Ask them to predict how many times they think their hearts beat in one minute and write this number in the place provided on the worksheet.

2 Explain that one way to find out the number of times your heart beats is to locate your pulse. Demonstrate this for the children by placing your index and middle fingers on the pulse point in your neck. Help students to do the same. Remind them that when they locate their pulse point, they only need to lightly place their fingers on this spot.

3 Tell them to try counting the number of beats in six seconds. Keep time for them while they count silently. Do this a couple of times or until they have the hang of it.

4 Now tell them this time they will be counting to find their heart rates for one minute. Again, time for six seconds. At the end of this six seconds have students add a zero to their count and record this number on their journal pages. (You are multiplying their count in six seconds by ten to determine heartbeats per minute.) Next to their names on the class graph, they can then color in one heart for every ten seconds with blue crayon. For example, if the heart rate is 90, color in nine hearts.

5 The next step is to have students predict what effect exercise will have on their heart rates. Listen to their ideas and have them jot down predictions on their journal pages. Then select an activity for students to do for one minute, such as jumping jacks, a brisk walk with you up and down a staircase, etc.

6 After one minute of exercise, count beats, add zero, and record on the worksheet. As before, have students complete this part of the worksheet, then color in one heart for every ten, this time with red crayon.

7 Work together to create a key for the graph. Draw or glue a blue heart next to the graph and ask: What do the blue hearts represent? (Heart rate before exercise, or resting.) Draw or glue a red heart next to the graph and ask: What do the red hearts represent? (Heart rate after exercise.)

8 Guide a discussion of the results with the following questions:

* Are the heart rates the same before and after exercise?

* Why do they think the heart rates are higher after exercise?

* Does everyone have the same heart rate?

* What is the class range in resting heartbeats? In active heartbeats?

9 Have students complete Part 2 of their Science Journal pages.

COMMUNITY HELPERS

Heart Workers

Tell students that they will be learning about their hearts. What are some questions they have about their hearts? Provide heart-shaped cutouts for students to record these questions. Brainstorm people who might be able to answer their questions (the school nurse, a pediatrician, an aerobics instructor, someone trained in CPR). Make a list of their ideas, including specific names if they have any (for example, a parent who is a doctor, the school nurse). Invite someone from their list to visit. Have students write their questions on extra paper hearts. Give these to the visiting expert in advance.

ACTIVITY 3

Match the Beat

Students compare the number of times their hearts beat per minute with the heart rates of other animals to understand the relationship between size and rate.

Note: Before the activity, cut apart the animal cards and glue them to index cards or construction paper. On the remaining four cards, write these numbers: 20, 70, 200, 500.

Materials

* ✻ reproducible animal picture cards (see page 204)
* ✻ 8 index cards or squares of construction paper
* ✻ watch or clock
* ✻ tape

1 Show students each of the animal cards. Ask students to help you place the cards in order from the smallest animal to the largest animal. Tape these cards in a row on the chalkboard.

2 Now show the four number cards. Let students read the numbers on the cards. Explain that these numbers represent the average heartbeats per minute of the four animals shown on the picture cards. Ask students to predict which heart rate goes with each animal and explain their reasoning. (They should be able to match 70 with the person card based on their prior experiences with finding their own heart rates in Activity 2!)

3 After discussing their ideas, reveal the answers (elephant—20; child—70; rabbit—200; mouse—500) and tape the number cards under the matching animals. Let them try to clap their hands, as they did in Activity 1, to each heart rhythm.

4 Redirect students' attention to the two sets of cards. Ask if they notice any patterns. Guide them in making the connection that the larger the animal, the slower the heart rate.

5 Tell students that they will observe this connection again when they collect heart rates at home. (Typically, the adult heart rates they collect will be slower than their own heart rates, for the same reason.)

Science Celebration

HEALTHY HEART SNACKS

Use a heart-shaped cookie cutter to cut heart shapes from bread. Have children spread the bread with healthy treats (natural jellies and jams, natural peanut butter, nonfat cottage or cream cheese). Provide other healthful toppings such as low-fat grated cheese, fresh vegetable shavings, fresh, canned, and dried fruit bits, and sesame seeds. If possible, print index cards with basic nutrition information for each food, so children can see which vitamins and minerals they are each enjoying.

Curriculum Connections

MATH
Hearts at Home

As an extension to Activity 2, students can compare their heart rates to an adult's. The reproducible take-home sheet (page 203) includes a letter of explanation to parents and a record sheet. Students can work with an adult at home to determine resting and after-exercise heart rates. When students return their papers to class, discuss and compare the results. Some activities to help students analyze their data follow.

❋ Let students share their results. Whose heart rate is faster, the child's or the adult's?

❋ Graph results. Overall, do children or adults have faster heart rates? (Typically, young children have faster heart rates than adults.)

❋ What could explain the difference between children and adults? (In general, the smaller the organism, the faster the heart rate.)

MOVEMENT
Healthy Heart Exercise Course

Once you have established with your students that exercise is important for maintaining a healthy heart, let them work together in small groups to create an exercise course that promotes aerobic exercise. Decide on a location for your course—the classroom, gym, or maybe even outside! Explain that students will work in groups to plan a form of exercise for different stations. Examples of activities could include jumping jacks, jogging in place, jumping rope, etc.

Give each group a numbered sign (1 through however many groups/stations there are). After students decide on the exercises (and clear them with you), have them put directions on their signs (using words and/or pictures). Display signs to create a course, then invite students to take turns going through. You might even consider inviting other members of the school community—the principal, gym teacher, school nurse—to help model the importance of exercise for everyone.

Name_____

Heart Work

Part 1

Six words that describe my heart are:

_____

_____

_____

_____

_____

_____

Part 2

1. I think my heart beats _____ times per minute.

2. My heart rate when I am resting is _____ beats per minute.

3. I think my heart rate after I exercise will be _____ beats per minute.

4. My heart rate after I exercise is _____ beats per minute.

On the back of this paper draw a picture of you doing a favorite exercise.

Dear _____,

    We are learning about the human heart in class: how it works and how to keep it healthy. You can help your child understand more about hearts by doing this activity together. Please have your child return the completed activity to class by _____.
Thank you.

Name _____ Date _____

Hearts at Home

Ask your child to show you how to take a heart rate (by placing your index and middle fingers on the pulse point in your neck). Take each other's resting heart rate, counting beats in six seconds. Add a zero to the numbers to get beats per minute. Write your heartbeats here:

Name_____ Resting Heart Rate_____

Name_____ Resting Heart Rate_____

Now, if you can, do some light exercise together, such as taking a walk, doing some jumping jacks, or jumping rope for a minute. Afterward, take each other's heart rates, counting beats in six seconds, and adding a zero to the numbers to get beats per minute. Write your heart rates here:

Name_____ Active Heart Rate_____

Name_____ Active Heart Rate_____

Compare your heart rates. Whose heart rate is faster?

_____

Talk about why this might be. Write a possible explanation on the back of this page.

RESOURCES

FOR CHILDREN

A Drop of Blood by Paul Showers (HarperCollins, 1989). What makes up a drop of blood and what it does for us are two of the questions answered in this easy-to-read book with kid-friendly illustrations. Nonfiction. (Also check out *Hear Your Heart* by the same author.)

The Magic School Bus Inside the Human Body by Joanna Cole (Scholastic, 1989). Ms Frizzle is off on another adventure, leading her students on an exploration of how our bodies work. Nonfiction.

See Inside Your Body by Katie Daynes (Usborne, 2006). A lift-the-flap book that helps children learn about the body's inner workings. Nonfiction.

The Skin You Live In by Michael Tyler (Chicago Children's Museum, 2005). A simple and affecting message about skin . . . and diversity. Fiction.

Uncover the Human Body by Luann Colombo (Silver Dolphin Press, 2003). This book's three-dimensional format and instructive text make it one that kids will read and reread. Nonfiction

FOR TEACHERS

Adorable Wearables Human Body by Donald Silver (Scholastic, 2005). Use the wearable models to help young children learn about muscles, bones, digestion, the five senses, and more.

Blood and Guts: A Working Guide to Your Own Insides by Linda Allison (Little Brown, 1976). A factual and humorous look at the workings of the human body. Intended for an older audience but with lots of information and activities that can be adapted for primary children. Includes a separate chapter on the heart.

Easy Make & Learn Projects: Human Body by Donald M. Silver (Scholastic, 2000). The models, manipulatives, and mini-books in this resource provide engaging ways to help kids learn about the body's systems. Includes patterns and step-by-step directions.

First Human Body Encyclopedia (Dorling Kindersley, 2005). A wealth of diagrams, photographs, and illustrations that help to explain the workings of the human body and its various systems.

My Body by Patricia Carratello (Teacher Created Materials, 1980). Describes body parts—including the heart—and how they work. Includes reproducible patterns for children to make a life-size replica of the human body.

TECHNOLOGY CONNECTIONS

Nervous System Guide
National Science Teachers Association
(www.nsta.org/publications/interactive/nerves/)
Boost lessons on the nervous system with the interactive features at this site provided by the National Science Teachers Association. An amazing opportunity to show students simulations of the functioning of nerve cells, reflexes, brain waves, and more. While this site is most suited for older students, it's well worth the trip for exciting the interests of younger scientists.

Learn and Live
American Heart Association
(www.americanheart.org/presenter.jhtml?
identifier=3028650)
A visit to this site provides access to grade-specific learning activities and reproducibles. You can also access an associated site that's been developed by the American Heart Association and National Football League to help children live active lives:
www.WhatMovesU.com.

CHAPTER 9

March

Windy Weather

Flying Things

Highlights *of the* Month

Mark these dates, events, and activities on your calendar to help plan and supplement upcoming activities in this month's themes.

✳ The arrival of spring—vernal equinox—occurs either on March 20 or 21 (check your calendar for the exact date each year). On this day the number of daylight hours equals the number of hours of darkness.

✳ March's full moon is often called the Worm Moon, most likely because of the emergence of worms from the mud after the ground has thawed. Ask students to think of another good name for the March moon.

✳ Look for signs of spring!

Plan Ahead

Ask students to begin collecting pictures of flying things. They'll use these for activities in Theme 2 this month.

Place orders for seeds now, if you plan on doing the seed activities in Chapter 10 (see pages 254 to 268). Some seed catalogs you and your students might want to request follow.

W. Atlee Burpee & Co., 300 Park Avenue, Warminster, PA 18974, (800) 333-5808; www.burpee.com.

Seed Savers Exchange, 3094 North Winn Road, Decorah, IA 52101, (563) 382-5990; www.seedsavers.org.

Seeds of Change, PO Box 152, Spicer, MN, 56288, (888) 762-7333; www.seedsofchange.com.

Native Seeds/SEARCH, 526 North Fourth Avenue, Tucson, AZ 85705, (866) 622-5561; www.nativeseeds.org.

SCIENCE AT HOME

Date _____

This month we are starting two new science themes.

1. Windy Weather

Our class is continuing to explore the weather in our world, this month taking a closer look at wind. You can help your child understand the concept of the wind's strength and direction at home just by noticing the wind when you're outside together. How strong is it? In what direction does it seem to be blowing?

2. Flying Things

From airplanes to birds and butterflies, children are captivated by flying things. This month, we'll be investigating some of the principles of flight. Encourage your child's interest and understanding by talking about some ways flying things you see are alike and different.

Wish List

Do you have materials you can donate for our science explorations? For this month's activities, we need:

_____

_____

_____

Reminders _____

_____

_____

Windy Weather

When March comes in like a lion, it goes out like a lamb. When March comes in like a lamb, it goes out like a lion. This piece of weather lore makes reference to the changeable and sometimes blustery weather of March. Your students will enjoy characterizing the personality of the wind, and, by doing so, will discover the impact wind has on their daily lives.

Science Concepts and Skills

Concepts: As a result of these activities, students will observe changes in the wind and learn that the wind can vary in strength and direction. They will learn that there are instruments to measure the strength and direction of the wind. In addition, students will recognize the wind as a force strong enough to push objects.

Process Skills: observing, predicting, measuring, collecting and recording data, interpreting, inferring, communicating

S c i e n c e   D i c t i o n a r y

Beaufort scale a measure of how strong the wind is blowing. Wind speed is often estimated using this scale

calm: smoke rises (0 mph)

light air: smoke drifts (1–3 mph)

slight breeze: vanes move (4–7 mph)

gentle breeze: leaves and twigs move (8–12 mph)

moderate breeze: branches move, flags flap (13–18 mph)

fresh breeze: small trees sway, white caps on water (19–24 mph)

strong breeze: large branches move; flags beat (25–31 mph)

moderate gale: flags extend (32–38 mph)

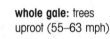
fresh gale: twigs break (39–46 mph)

strong gale: signs, antennas blow down (47–54 mph)

whole gale: trees uproot (55–63 mph)

hurricane: widespread destruction (64+ mph)

storm a very strong wind that usually includes rain, snow, or hail, and sometimes thunder and lightning

wind moving air; as air is warmed by the sun it rises, and colder, denser air moves in to replace it; the direction and strength of the wind is influenced by geographical features like mountains, deserts, and bodies of water; the direction of the wind, determined by where the wind is blowing from, often affects our weather

wind vane instrument used to show wind direction

Science on Display

Use this month's display area to post a large calendar that features the winds of March. Cover the board with blue craft paper. Make a border out of cotton balls that are stretched out to appear cloudlike. At the top of the paper, write: "Is March a lion or a lamb?" Read the question with students and ask if anyone knows what it means. Describe how people have described the calm and gentle winds as being like a lamb, and the strong winds roaring like a lion.

As with the moon calendars (see Chapter 3, page 45), have students sign up to observe the wind each day in March (weekends, too) and draw either a lion or a lamb on the calendar to characterize the wind. Use the reproducible calendar (see March: Lion or Lamb?, page 219) to have students keep their own windy weather journals. (Have students fill in the dates on their calendars first.) At the end of the month, review the class and individual calendars. How would students answer the question at the display now?

ACTIVITY 1 〰〰〰〰〰〰〰〰〰〰〰〰〰〰〰〰〰〰〰〰〰〰〰〰

Huff and Puff

Note: You will need at least one cotton ball per student, plus a bag of cotton balls if you wish to use them on the graph. (You can substitute small circles of white paper.) Before the activity, tape the craft paper sheets to the floor, leaving plenty of room between each so that students do not get in one another's way.

Students do some huffing and puffing to learn about the power of the wind.

〰〰〰〰〰〰〰〰〰〰〰〰〰〰〰〰〰〰〰〰〰〰〰〰

Materials

* cotton balls
* 2 sheets of colored craft paper (two different colors) for graphing
* craft paper (one 3-foot-long sheet for each small group)
* masking tape
* glue stick

〰〰〰〰〰〰〰〰〰〰〰〰〰〰〰〰〰〰〰〰〰〰〰〰

BOOK BREAK
Take time out for a familiar and fun story about wind power, the story of "The Three Little Pigs." Students can join the wolf with their own huffing and puffing. Afterward, invite students to take turns dramatizing this story. Simple props could include straw, cardboard bricks, and sticks.

1 Begin by asking students to describe wind. What is it? Can they see it? If they can't see it, how do they know it is there? (They can see objects that are being moved or pushed by the wind; they can feel it in their hair or on their skin.) Have them look out a classroom window and identify signs of wind (or the absence of it).

2 Next, give each student a cotton ball. Explain that they are going to be moving the cotton ball from one side of their group's paper to the other side. The challenge is that they cannot touch the cotton ball with any part of their bodies. What ideas do they have for moving their cotton balls? If no one suggests blowing on it, you can explain that because you are learning about the wind, you would like them to move the cotton balls by blowing on them.

3 Ask students to blow as hard as they can (like lions), trying to get the cotton ball to the other side with as few puffs as possible. Let one student demonstrate while the others keep count of the number of puffs. Show students where they will record this information on their papers. Now have one student demonstrate how to blow the cotton ball gently across the paper (like a lamb). Again, show them where to record this number.

4 Divide the class into groups of three or four and assign each group to a piece of chart paper on the floor. Explain that they will take turns: while one student is puffing, one or two will be counters, and one will be the recorder. Conduct several trials so each child has a chance to blow on the cotton balls. Have students record how many strong puffs and how many gentle puffs it took to move the cotton ball across the chart paper.

5 After all groups are finished, bring students together to compile and graph the data. Make two graphs: Number of Strong Puffs and Number of Gentle Puffs. Have students glue cotton balls or paper circles by their names to represent the number of puffs it took them to move the cotton ball.

6 Start a discussion about the results by asking: What did this activity teach you about the wind? (That wind can be calm or strong. That wind can move objects by pushing them. The stronger the wind, the quicker it moves objects.)

ACTIVITY 2 ～～～～～～～～～～～～～～～～～～～～～

Wind Power

Extend students' observations by testing objects outside.

Materials

* an assortment of objects (foam balls, golf balls, wooden blocks, sheets of newspaper, empty plastic milk bottles, and so on)

Note: Plan on doing this activity at least twice, choosing a day when the wind is gentle, and a second day when the wind is stronger.

1 Take students and objects outside. Let students work together in groups to select several objects and test how easily they are moved by wind power. You might discuss ways to conduct these mini-experiments or let groups make their own plans.

2 After each group has had a chance to test and observe several objects, bring students together in a sharing circle. Explain that they are going to make two groups of objects: those that were moved by the wind and those that were not moved by the wind. One at a time, have groups sort their objects. Record the names of objects in each group, then ask: What do the objects that were moved by the wind have in common? What do those that were not moved by the wind have in common?

3 Finally, ask students to describe the strength of the wind on this day. Record their words on the chart from step 3.

4 Repeat the activity on a day when the wind's strength is different.

5 Compare the charts. Are there objects that did not move on a calm day but were pushed by the wind on a breezy day? Ask students to explain the differences in the two charts: What kinds of objects are moved most easily by the wind? What kinds of objects are more difficult for the wind to move? Is there any kind of wind that could move these objects? This is a good time to introduce the Beaufort scale (see Science Dictionary, page 211).

ACTIVITY 3

Make a Wind Sock

Students make a weather instrument that will help them measure the strength of the wind.

BOOK BREAK
Share *Storms* by Seymour Simon. Ask students to think about how the storms are the same. How are they different? Discuss students' own storm experiences. What have they observed? How did they feel? What did they do to stay safe?

Materials (for each student)

    ✷ a 16-by-5½-inch piece of tagboard (an old manila file folder cut in half lengthwise works nicely)

    ✷ a large paper clip

    ✷ 3 pieces of kite string, each 12 inches long

    ✷ 6 pieces of crepe paper, each 18 inches long (strips of fabric the same length will work, too)

    ✷ colored markers, construction paper, watercolor paints (your choice)

    ✷ hole-punch

    ✷ stapler

1 Explain that students are going to construct an instrument that helps show the strength of the wind.

2 Give each student a piece of tagboard to decorate using markers, watercolor paints, or construction paper. Weatherproof students' decorated board by laminating.

3 Help students roll their laminated tagboard into cylinders, and staple the edges together.

4. Have students staple the six long strips of crepe paper around the cylinder as illustrated.

5 Use the hole-punch to make three holes evenly spaced around the top edge of each child's cylinder.

6 Have students thread and knot one piece of the string through each of the holes, then tie and knot all three pieces of string around one end of the paper clip.

7 Take students outside to try out their wind socks. They should hold the wind socks away from their bodies. How can they tell if the wind is blowing? (The wind sock will move.) Have students describe the strength of the wind by observing their wind socks. How does this wind rank on the Beaufort scale?

8 Hang the wind socks around the room for a week or so, then let the students take them home so that they can use them to observe and describe the wind at home, too.

ACTIVITY 4 ～～～～～～～～～～～～～～～～～～～～～～～

Make a Wind Vane

Students make another instrument to help them learn more about the wind.

～～～～～～～～～～～～～～～～～～～～～～～～～～～

Note: Before the activity, make a hole in the center of the bottom of each cup.

Materials (for each student)

    ✱ reproducible wind vane pattern (see page 222)

    ✱ straw

    ✱ pencil

    ✱ straight pin

    ✱ small ball of clay

    ✱ tape

* small plastic cup (recycle yogurt cups or use the kind sold for bathrooms)
* tagboard (4-inch square plus extra to reinforce arrow)

Note: Encourage students to include descriptions of the wind in their Science Journals. (They can add extra pages for this.) They might illustrate how the wind blew their wind socks and record words that describe the wind or draw pictures of their wind vanes, indicating the direction of the wind on a particular day. Remind students to include the date and time on all entries.

1 Ask students how they can tell which direction the wind is coming from.

2 Ask them if they have ever seen a barn or house with an arrow on its roof. Introduce the term *wind vane* (see Science Dictionary, page 211) and explain that people use this kind of instrument to find out the direction of the wind. Take time to discuss various uses for this information. Who would want or need to know about the wind and why?

3 Have each student cut out the arrow on the reproducible and paste it to a piece of tagboard.

4 While their arrows are drying, students can mark the cups with compass directions: north, east, south, and west.

5 After their arrows are dry, students cut them out again.

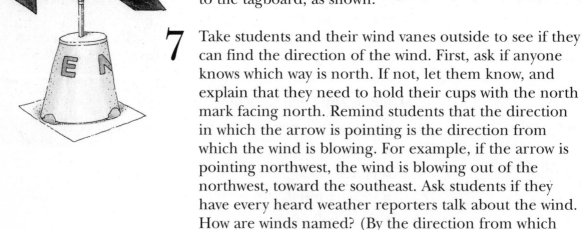

6 Assist students with the next step: Use two small pieces of tape to attach the straw to the center of one side of the arrow, as shown. Insert the straight pin through the middle of the straw, then stick it into the pencil's eraser top. Push the other end of the pencil through the hole in the top of the cup. Place the cup upside down on the tagboard square. Use pieces of the clay to secure the cup to the tagboard, as shown.

7 Take students and their wind vanes outside to see if they can find the direction of the wind. First, ask if anyone knows which way is north. If not, let them know, and explain that they need to hold their cups with the north mark facing north. Remind students that the direction in which the arrow is pointing is the direction from which the wind is blowing. For example, if the arrow is pointing northwest, the wind is blowing out of the northwest, toward the southeast. Ask students if they have every heard weather reporters talk about the wind. How are winds named? (By the direction from which they are blowing.)

ACTIVITY 5

Which Way Is the Wind Blowing?

Materials

* wind vanes (see Activity 4)

* reproducible (see page 223)

Note: Plan on doing this activity over four consecutive days, allowing about 15 minutes a day.

1 Share this saying with students:

> A wind from the west,
> Brings weather at its best;
> A wind from the east,
> Brings rain to man and beast.

Explain that typically winds from the west bring good weather, while winds from the east bring bad weather. Remind students that people used wind vanes to find out which direction the wind was coming from so they would know if good or bad weather was on the way. Ask: What are some ways we learn whether good or bad weather is coming our way?

2 Have students cut apart the reproducible page to form a booklet. On Day 1, students use their wind vanes to find the wind direction, then record this information on page 1, along with the date. The following day, students illustrate and/or describe the weather that followed their wind observations. They then make a Day 2 wind observation and record it on page 2 of the booklet, the next day recording the weather. Repeat for Day 3.

3 At the end of the week, look over the books together. Do students notice a pattern?

Curriculum Connections

SOCIAL STUDIES
What's the Meaning?

Ask students about wind vanes they may have seen. (It would be helpful to collect pictures of wind vanes prior to this lesson.) Many have an animal or some other figure that sits above the arrow. Ask students why they think people have wind vanes with different figures. Explain that sometimes a figure was a meaningful symbol. For example, a blacksmith might have a wind vane with a horse on it. Here are some other figures found on the tops of wind vanes: a lobster, a moose, a fish, a sailboat, and an ice cream cone! Using the wind vanes they made as models, have students illustrate (and construct if they want) wind vanes with figures that have meaning to them.

LANGUAGE ARTS
Words for Wind

"The Spring Wind" (see page 221) is full of sensory images. After children listen to the poem, comb through the lines together to discover the words the poet uses to help us see, feel, hear, and touch the different winds. Brainstorm and chart other words for winds in each season. Let students use the chart as a reference to write their own windy word poems.

ART *Wind Works*

Students can use their own wind to create works of art using tempera paints and straws. Spread newspaper over the work area. Give each student a sheet of heavy white paper. Use eyedroppers to place paint on students' papers. Now give each student a straw. Tell them that instead of brushes, they are going to blow through the straws to move the paint around the paper. Encourage them to blow both gently and hard through the straw. Does it make a difference how the paint moves on the paper?

Name_____

March: Lion or Lamb?

Guess which type of wind we will have most often in March: _____ calm and gentle (lamb) _____ strong (lion)

Each day, feel the wind. If it is gentle, paste a lamb in the box. If it is strong, paste a lion in the box.

Sunday	Monday	Tuesday	Wednesday	Thursday	Friday	Saturday

In March there were _____ lion days (strong winds) and _____ lamb days (calm winds). The wind in March was more like a _____ than a _____.

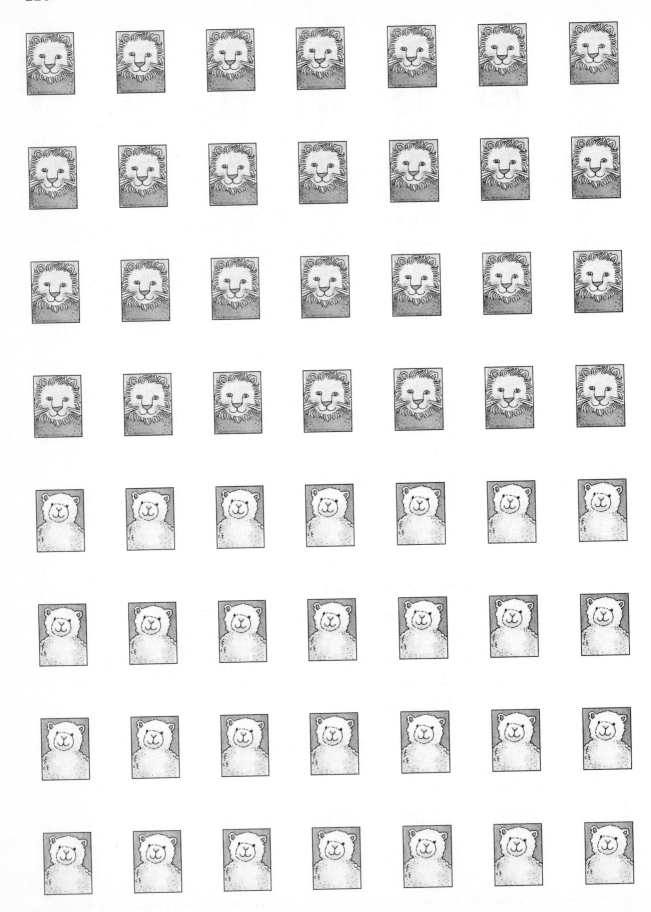

The Spring Wind

The summer wind
is soft and sweet
the winter wind is strong
the autumn wind is mischievous
and sweeps the leaves along.

The wind I love best
comes gently after rain
smelling of spring and growing things
brushing the world with feathery wings
while everything glistens, and everything sings
in the spring wind
after the rain.

—Charlotte Zolotow

Name _____

Make a Wind Vane

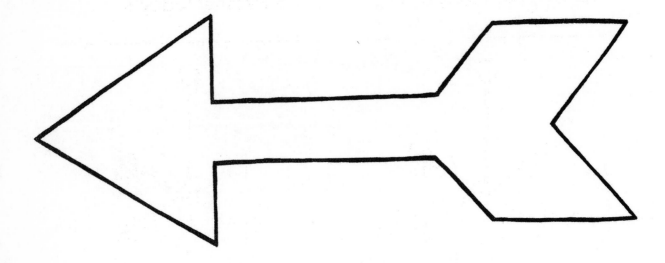

Draw a wind vane in the space below.

Which Way Is the Wind Blowing?

Date_____

The weather today is

_____

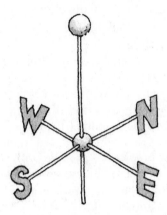

Draw an arrow on this wind vane to show the wind direction today.

1

Date_____

The weather today is

_____

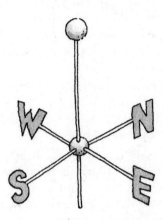

Draw an arrow on this wind vane to show the wind direction today.

2

Date_____

The weather today is

_____

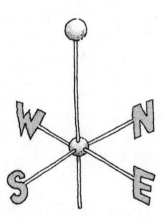

Draw an arrow on this wind vane to show the wind direction today.

3

Date_____

The weather today is

_____

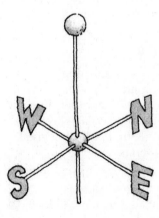

Draw an arrow on this wind vane to show the wind direction today.

4

RESOURCES

FOR CHILDREN

Feel the Wind by Arthur Dorros (Crowell, 1989). Bright illustrations and simple text explore causes, effects, and use of wind. Fiction.

I Wonder Why the Wind Blows and Other Questions About Our Planet by Anita Ganeri (Kingfisher, 1994). Part of the "Science Facts" series, this book answers children's most common questions about weather and other natural phenomena. Nonfiction.

Mirandy and Brother Wind by Patricia McKissack (Knopf, 1988). Mirandy tries to capture the wind to help her move with grace and win the Cake Walk competition. Fiction.

The Random House Book of Poetry for Children edited by Jack Prelutsky (Random House, 1983). This comprehensive poetry anthology includes a variety of beautiful poems about the wind's power, music, and mystery. Fiction.

Storms by Seymour Simon (Scholastic, 1989). Vivid color photographs bring storms to life. Nonfiction.

The Sun, the Wind and the Rain by Lisa Westberg Peters (Holt, 1988). A young girl explores the erosional effects of the wind (and the sun and rain) at the beach. Fiction.

Weather and Climate by Barbara Taylor (Kingfisher Books, 1992). This is challenging reading for primary-grade students, but provides a lot of good information that could be selectively read aloud. Nonfiction.

FOR TEACHERS

Anemometers (for measuring wind speed) and handheld wind vanes (for determining wind direction), as well as other simple weather instruments, are available from Didax. To order call (800) 458-0024 or visit www.didax.com.

Weather: A Thematic Unit by Diane Williams (Teacher Created Materials, 2004). This literature-based theme unit includes plenty of suggestions for books, stories, and poetry, as well as supporting activities related to weather and wind.

TECHNOLOGY CONNECTIONS

Weather Wiz Kids
(www.weatherwizkids.com/index.htm)
Meteorologist Crystal Wicker developed this Web site to give children and educators easy access to interesting information about weather. Includes many photos and kid-friendly charts and graphs.

Franklin's Forecast
The Franklin Institute Science Museum
(www.fi.edu/weather/)
Check out the Resources for Science Learning page—with links to sites that invite young learners to access a variety of weather technologies (tools they need to make weather predictions just like professional meteorologists). Plus, access to links that cover topics such as weather folklore, severe weather, and climate.

Flying Things

Young children are naturally captivated by objects moving through the sky: airplanes and helicopters, birds and butterflies, dandelion seeds and hot-air balloons. Flying things invite children to move as they do—arms outstretched like a plane or flapping like a bird—and to wonder what it would be like to move through the sky just as flying things do. As your students explore the winds of March with the activities here, they will observe how objects glide, float, and twirl through the air.

Science Concepts and Skills

Concepts: Students will begin to recognize that flying things can move through the air as a result of being pushed. They will also be able to provide examples of how people have borrowed the idea of flying from objects in nature, and will be able to distinguish between naturally flying objects and flying objects made by people.

Process Skills: inferring, observing, comparing, classifying, predicting, measuring, making models

Science Dictionary

drag the air resistance that happens as an aircraft moves forward; opposite of thrust

gravity a downward pulling force

lift a force that helps keep flying things aloft, or in the air

thrust the force that pushes an aircraft forward

Science on Display

Send students into space without leaving the classroom with this display. Use a large cardboard appliance box to create the figure of an astronaut. Cut the ends and one of the sides from the box, leaving three pieces which will stand like a screen. Ask a student to lie down on one of the cardboard panels, positioning legs so they look like they are floating. Trace around the student.

Draw a helmet around the outline of the head. Cut out a space for the face large enough for students to fit their faces in.

Let students add the finishing touches to this stand. I like to assign committees to work on these kind of projects—one to paint the background of the box black, another to cut out stars from foil or white paper and glue them to the black background, and a third to paint the space suit and helmet.

Prop up the astronaut stand in the science area. Over the next week, take a snapshot of each of your students posing as an astronaut. See Space Stories, page 231, for a related activity.

ACTIVITY 1

Things that Fly

Students compare flying things to develop a basic understanding of the principles of flight.

Materials

* pictures of flying things (collected by students; have extras on hand)
* Things that Fly Science Journal page (see page 232)

1 Have each student bring a picture of a flying thing to sharing circle. Let them identify their flying objects.

2 After everyone has had a chance to show their picture, ask students to think of ways to sort these pictures into two groups. Try out their ideas. (Suggestions for groups could include: things with wings/things without wings; living things/things that are not alive; things that will carry people/things that will not carry people; and so on) For each group, have children state how the flying things are the same.

3 Ask students to look at the variety of flying things they have collected. Ask: "Which of these things do you think was flying before the others?" Listen to their ideas, then work together to create a time line of flight with students' pictures (tape pictures to adding-machine tape or to other strips of paper). Mention that Wilbur and Orville Wright made history in 1903 when they flew for 12 seconds in a gas-powered plane. Ask students where they think people got the idea to fly. (In the 1400s, Leonardo da Vinci studied flight. He created hundreds of designs for flying machines, including a helicopter!)

4 Have students sort the pictures again into two different groups (such as flying objects from nature/flying things made by people). Can they find a flying object with wings in both groups? Can they find an example of a flying object that glides? Encourage children to recognize how flying objects made by people imitate flying objects found in nature. Let students complete the Science Journal page.

ACTIVITY 2

Wonderful Whirlybirds

Students discover what wings can do.

Materials (for each student)
* reproducible whirlybird pattern (see page 233)
* paper clip
* 2 sheets of copy paper
* chart paper

BOOK BREAK

Read *How People Learned to Fly* by Fran Hodgkins (see Resources, page 234). Have a chart on hand that lists the alphabet letters. After you have read the book, challenge students to think of as many flying things as they can. Write these flying things next to the corresponding alphabet letters. You probably won't be able to finish this at one sitting, so leave the chart in the science area and encourage students to add names of flying objects on their own, too. (Or revisit the chart together another day.)

1 Hold the piece of copy paper flat and above your head. Tell students you are going to let go of the paper. What do they think will happen? (It will drop to the ground.)

2 Let go of the paper. When it has fallen to the floor, ask students to describe what they observed.

3 Now crumple a second sheet of copy paper into a ball. Hold the flat paper in one hand and the crumpled ball in your other hand. Again, ask students to predict what will happen when you drop both.

4 Drop both pieces of paper. Ask students to compare how the two pieces of paper fell. Ask: Why does one piece float down to the ground and the other piece drop straight down? (The flat piece of paper offers more resistance to the air. The air pushes up against the paper as it falls. This helps to keep the paper aloft for a longer period of time.)

5 Let students cut out their whirlybirds. Have them add the paper clip to the bottom strip of the whirlybird (as illustrated), but hold off having them fold the wing strips. Instead, ask students to hold their whirlybirds so both strips are upright. They should hold the whirlybird as far above their heads as they can, then wait for the countdown (3, 2, 1, drop). Have them describe the way the whirlybird moves and record their observations in their journals.

6 Now ask students if they have any ideas for how to make their whirlybirds stay in the air for a longer period of time. (Many will recognize the potential wings and quickly suggest folding the strips to make wings.)

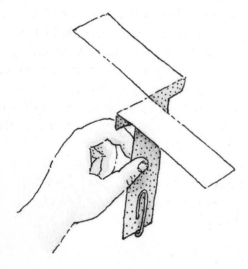

7 Tell them to go ahead and fold the strips to create wings. Count down and launch! (Again they should drop the whirlybirds from high above their heads.) How does the flight of the whirlybird this time compare with its first flight? (This time the whirlybird will spin through the air. Like the piece of paper in step 1, the wings provide air resistance, allowing the whirlybird to stay aloft longer.)

8 Students will want to play with their whirlybirds for a while. Encourage their explorations by giving them one or more of the following challenges: Does the direction of the whirlybird's spin change if you reverse the wings? What happens if you remove the paper clip? Color your whirlybird. What does it look like now when it spins?

ACTIVITY 3

Rocket Balloons

Note: This is a fun activity, and one that will get your students thinking about variables—those things that could make a difference in the observed results. For example, some students will probably question whether the amount of air in the balloon affects how far it will travel. (It does!) Whenever your students raise such questions, encourage them to pursue answers.

In Activity 2, students discovered how the principles of drag, lift, and gravity work. In this activity, students will learn about thrust, or the way flying objects can be pushed. This is a good opportunity to revisit concepts developed in the lesson on push and pull (see Chapter 7, page 160).

Materials

* string (about 25 feet)
* tape
* 2 chairs

For each student:

* balloons (all the same kind—same size, shape, etc.), 1 paper lunch bag, a straw, a spring-type clothespin

1 Give each student a paper bag to decorate like a spaceship. In the meantime, set up a rocket balloon launch area. Cut a piece of string to 25 feet in length. Wrap one end of the string with tape (this will make it easier to slip the string through the straws). Set the two chairs about 20 inches apart. Use tape to attach the string to the back of one of the chairs. Eventually you will want to have the chairs far enough apart (about 20 feet) so that when you tape the other end of the string to the second chair back, the string is taut.

2 When students have finished their bags, have them tape one straw each to one of the skinny sides of their bags (as illustrated on the next page).

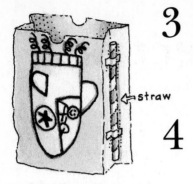

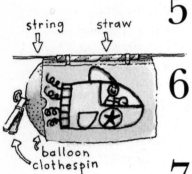

3 Next, give each student a balloon and a clothespin. Assist students in blowing up their balloons (good time for an upper-grade helper), then pinching them shut with the clothespins. Have students slip the balloons into the paper bags, so that the end that has the clothespin is facing out.

4 Invite one student to bring the bag and balloon to the launch area. Slip the end of the string that is not taped to the chair through the straw on the bag, then tape down that end to the back of the other chair.

5 Move the bag and balloon to the center of the string. Ask students to predict what will happen when the clothespin is removed. Which way will the rocket balloon travel?

6 Let the student remove the clothespin while classmates observe. Ask students to describe what happened to the bag and the balloon. (As the air rushes out of the balloon, the bag is pushed forward, in the opposite direction.)

7 Give all students a chance to launch their rockets. (The purpose of putting the first bag in the middle was to challenge students' to predict which way the bag would travel. Now that they know, students can launch the bags from one end, with the open end of the bag where the balloon sticks out facing the nearest chair.)

8 After launching all of the rocket balloons, discuss how the bags moved across the string. This is a good time to tie in related vocabulary, including thrust and drag (see Science Dictionary, page 226).

9 Repeat the activity (the kids won't mind), and this time let students measure how far their rocket balloons travel.

FLYING TOY MUSEUM

Invite each child to bring to school one toy that really flies (or a model of a flying vehicle, such as a toy airplane or a flying action figure). Ask each child to explain the features of his or her toy to the class and/or demonstrate the toy's flying ability. Afterward, dangle the toys from strings attached to ceiling wire to create a hanging museum of flying toys.

Curriculum Connections

ART
A Roomful of Flying Things

After Activity 1, have students glue their pictures of flying things to tagboard (or pieces of old manila file folders). After the glue dries, have students cut out the pictures and color the back sides (the tagboard side) to look like the front. Help students make a small hole through the top of their flying-thing pictures (you may just want to poke a hole yourself using a pin). Give each student a paper clip that has been opened to an S shape to slip through the hole in the picture. Stretch a length of lightweight string around the classroom and hang the flying things from it.

LANGUAGE ARTS
Space Stories

Remember those astronaut photographs of students? Have students glue their photos to colored construction paper and write stories about imaginary flights. Students can add finishing touches to their pictures and stories with star stickers and glitter paint. These photo stories make a fun hallway display or a class book to share with families.

MATH
Pilot a Plane

Invite students to pilot paper airplanes they make, then keep flight logs of test runs. First, demonstrate how to fold a simple paper airplane (see Resources, page 234). Have students fold their own planes, then pair up to test them out. How far can their planes fly? Create and make copies of a simple flight log with space for the following information: Pilot's Name, Copilot's Name, Distance I Think My Plane Will Fly, and Distance Traveled (with space for Test 1, Test 2, etc.). After the test, bring students together to share their results.

Follow up by asking students why they think flight was invented as a means of transportation. Compare and contrast it with other forms of transportation (car, bus, train, horseback, bicycle, etc.). Ask students to predict how many classmates have flown. (This could include planes, helicopters, even hot-air balloons.) Create a graph with columns for different forms of transportation, including flying things. Have students take turns adding their names to the graph in the appropriate columns, then discuss the results. (Are there more flyers than nonflyers? How many more students have traveled by _____ than by _____?)

Name_____

Things that Fly

Name two things
you have seen fly.

_____

_____

One way these flying things
are the same is:

_____

_____

_____

One way these flying things
are different is:

_____

_____

_____

Draw a flying thing
from nature here.

Draw a flying thing made
by people here.

Whirlybird Pattern

Directions:

1. Cut out the rectangle.

2. Cut on the dotted lines.

3. Your teacher will explain how to fold your whirlybird.

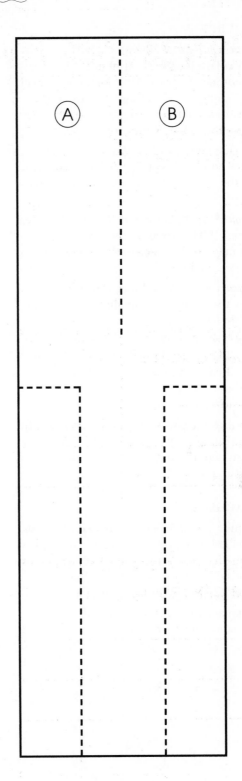

RESOURCES

FOR CHILDREN

The Big Balloon Race by Eleanor Coerr
(HarperTrophy, 1992). Ariel stows away on
her mother's hydrogen balloon and discovers
that piloting this aircraft takes a lot of work. A
historical account of balloonist Carlotta
Myers's 1882 race. Nonfiction.

Flying by Donald Crews (Greenwillow, 1986). This
picture book follows the flight of an airplane
from the time it takes off until it lands again.
Fiction.

The Glorious Flight by Alice and Martin Provensen
(Viking, 1983). Based on the true story of a
flight made in 1909 across the English
Channel. Fiction.

Hot-Air Henry by Mary Calhoun (Morrow, 1981).
Henry the cat takes a solo flight in a hot-air
balloon. Fiction.

*How People Learned to Fly (Let's-Read-and-Find-Out
Science 2)* by Fran Hodgkins (HarperCollins,
2007). Readers will learn about history . . .
and about man's determination to be carried
by the wind.

The Paper Airplane Book by Seymour Simon (Puffin,
1988). Designs for paper airplanes plus the
science behind what makes them glide, do
tricks, and more. Nonfiction.

FOR TEACHERS

Flight by Judy Vaden (Teacher Created Materials,
1981). This comprehensive theme unit for
intermediate students includes activities that
can be adapted for younger children.

Kids' Paper Airplane Book by Ken Blackburn
(Workman, 1996). Directions and materials
for making 16 paper airplanes.

TECHNOLOGY CONNECTIONS

Build and Fly Activities
New England Air Museum
(www.neam.org/education/build.asp)
A helpful site for learning more of the
science, history, or technology related to
flying. You can search the collections for the
type of craft you'd like to learn more about.
Or, you can access the Build and Fly Activities
page that provides easy access to hands-on
activities sure to delight the imaginations of
novice aviators.

The Greatest Paper Airplanes (KittyHawk Software,
2005; [602] 678-0923). With a focus on the art
of paper folding, this program features fold-
by-fold plans for 50 flying machines. Includes
animated lessons on the history of flight and
the principles of aerodynamics, plus throwing
tips.

Young Eagles
Experimental Aircraft Association
(www.youngeagles.org/games/)
The Young Eagles program is designed to help
children learn about flight and have real-life
opportunities to fly in aircraft. To learn more
about programs in your area, call (877) 806-
8902 or visit the Web site listed above. At the
Web site, young aviation enthusiasts can learn
all about airplanes and play several fun games,
including Pitch, Yaw & Roll, which teaches
players how to fly a plane.

CHAPTER 10

April

Rain Comes and Goes
page 238

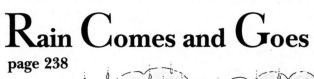

Seeds and Soil
page 254

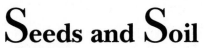

Highlights *of the* Month

Mark these dates, events, and activities on your calendar to help plan and supplement upcoming activities this month.

✳ Arbor Day was first celebrated in 1872 in Nebraska—more than one million trees were planted that year. Start a school tradition: Plant a tree every year.

✳ Earth Day is celebrated around April 22. It was first observed in 1970 to promote clean air and water, and to emphasize taking responsibility for the environment.

✳ Looking for a class activity that will help you to celebrate Earth Day? Read *Earth Book for Kids: Activities to Help Heal the Environment* by Linda Schwartz (The Learning Works, 1990).

✳ Take a survey: What do students in your class (grade, school) think is the biggest environmental problem? Plan an activity to help.

✳ April's full moon is the Pink Moon, for the first flowers of spring.

✳ Read a puddle poem like "Country Rain" by Aileen Fisher (from *Out in the Dark and Daylight*). Go puddle hopping. Make footprint patterns.

Plan Ahead

Begin collecting large jars with lids and soup cans for Activity 2 in this month's first theme (Rain Comes and Goes). You'll need a jar with two lids and a soup can for each group of students.

Ask students to save and bring in paper-towel and gift-wrap tubes for the rain stick–making activity on page 247.

SCIENCE AT HOME

Date _____

This month we are starting two new themes.

1. Rain Comes and Goes

As part of a unit on rain and the water cycle, each child will be charting rainy days this month. You can help your child complete the calendar by noting weekend weather together.

2. Seeds and Soil

As part of an investigation on what plants need to grow, your child will be planting seeds and recording observations in a journal. For a simple growing activity at home, try planting a pizza garden in a pot. Oregano and sweet basil are two herbs that are easy to grow.

Wish List

Do you have materials you can donate for our science explorations? For this month's activities, we need:

_____

_____

_____

Reminders _____

_____

_____

Rain Comes and Goes

Ap(A)pril showers bring May flowers. April's showers also bring plenty of opportunities for your young scientists to explore water. Children love to play in water, but they don't always appreciate what rain can do. This introduction to the water cycle will have children looking forward to rainy days so they can catch raindrops and march through puddles, then watch those same puddles disappear and reappear as clouds in the sky.

Science Concepts and Skills

Concepts: Students will observe that rain is drops of water and can be one of many changes in weather that may occur from day to day. They will describe and measure rain and include these observations in their weather journals. They will also begin to recognize that rain, as the liquid state of water, can change states as it evaporates. This is a part of the water cycle.

Process Skills: observing, inferring, predicting, comparing, collecting and recording data, measuring, communicating, making a model, interpreting

S c i e n c e   D i c t i o n a r y

clouds billions of tiny water drops or ice crystals; as water vapor rises into the atmosphere, it cools; as it cools, it condenses and turns into water drops or ice crystals; the droplets or ice crystals combine with particles of dust or dirt to form a cloud; the shape, size, and color of a cloud can help us forecast the weather

water molecules warm up they move, and evaporate, faster

precipitation the solid (snow, hail, frost) and liquid (rain) states of water that fall from the sky

rain gauge the instrument used to measure rainfall

condensation the process by which vapor cools and turns into drops of water

evaporation the process by which water (a liquid) turns into water vapor (a gas); heat speeds up evaporation, because as

water cycle the movement of water from clouds to the Earth, and back to the clouds again; the rain falling today is made up of the same water that fell to Earth as rain millions of years ago

Science on Display

Note: Students will use the reproducible calendar and raindrop cutouts to keep their own records (see pages 250 and 251). Have them record predictions, then attach raindrops to show rainy days. Note the weather on weekends to help children complete their calendars. Remind children to keep calendars in their journals.

Turn part of the science area into a raincoat factory. In a box, place a variety of materials for students to test their water-repelling power. You might include wax paper, copy paper, construction paper, cotton fabric, vinyl scraps, sandpaper, aluminum foil, and more. Keep a small can of water and several eyedroppers near the box. Invite students to explore the water-repelling properties of each material by placing drops of water on the material. What do the drops do on each kind of material? Students can work together to make groups of materials that repel and materials that don't repel (absorb).

At some point, students can design their own raincoats. Let them each cut out a raincoat (see reproducible, page 249), then decorate it using assorted materials (from markers and crayons to pieces of wax paper, vinyl, etc.). Remind students to write their names on the back of their raincoats, then laminate and hang them on a clothesline across the science area. Have students attach a description of their raincoats. Students will enjoy using a plant mister to spritz their raincoats with water for effect.

Along with the raincoats, set up a class calendar to chart rainy days in April. Have students cut out large raindrops and place them in a box near the calendar. Students can take turns gluing the raindrops onto the calendar on rainy days.

ACTIVITY 1

What Is Rain? (Part 1)

Begin this unit by collecting students' ideas about rain.

Materials

* 5 sheets of light blue craft paper (each cut into one big drop shape)

Note: If possible, try to begin this activity with a rainy-day walk. Check weather forecasts to see when rain is expected. (A light sprinkle is fine.) Make sure children are dressed to take a walk in wet weather. Before the activity, label each of the paper drops with one of the five senses.

1 Take students outside for five or ten minutes while it is sprinkling. Bring along a clipboard to record their observations. While you are outside, ask the following questions to help students focus on the five senses:

TASTE: Catch some raindrops on your tongue. How does the rain taste?

SOUND: Listen to the rain. What do you hear as the drops hit the ground? What does it sound like when you walk through wet grass or a puddle?

SIGHT: How do things look when they get wet? What does rain look like as it comes down through the air? Look for a drop on a leaf or a piece of grass. Try to catch one on your sleeve. What does the drop look like?

SMELL: Take a deep breath through your nose. What words describe the smell of rain?

TOUCH: Catch some raindrops on your face and in your hands. How does the rain feel on your skin? How does the wet ground feel?

2 Back in the classroom, brainstorm words that describe rain, using each of the five senses. Record students' responses on the paper drops. For example, on the drop labeled "sound" you might write *splash, drip, splat,* etc. (Use the notes as reminders.) Do this for each of the senses. Dangle drops around the science display area or tack to a bulletin board.

What Is Rain? (Part 2)

Follow your walk with this demonstration of how rain forms.

Note: Set up materials for this activity in advance. Set one jar with two lids in the middle of each work table. Place a few ice cubes in a can and set that on the table, too. Divide the class into small groups and assign each to a table.

Materials (for each small group of students)

* large glass jar with two lids (only one needs to fit)
* metal can (empty soup cans work well)
* ice cubes
* hot water

1 Explain to students that you will be pouring some hot water into each of the jars. One of the students in each group will loosely place the lid on the jar—without grabbing the jar. A second student will immediately place the second lid upside down on top of the first lid. As soon as this has been done, a third student will set the can with the ice cubes on the top lid.

2 When students know which task they will be doing, go around and add about 1 inch of hot water to each group's jar.

3 After the cans with ice are in place, students should begin observing what is happening in the jar. Encourage them to record brief observations, though they may not want to take their eyes off the jars. Guide them through a discussion, pointing out that some of the hot water will **vaporize** or evaporate, but as it rises and meets the cooler air, produced by the ice on the lid, the water vapor will **condense** and form droplets near the top of the jar. The inside of the glass around the top of the jar will get a little steamed up, like a **cloud**. Droplets on the first lid will start to merge together as they cool even more, and eventually, **rain** back to the bottom.

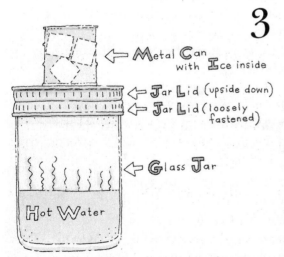

← Metal Can
   with Ice inside
← Jar Lid (upside down)
← Jar Lid (loosely fastened)
← Glass Jar
Hot Water

4   Help students make connections between this experiment and how rain falls from clouds when warmer air cools and forms drops, which eventually fall like the drops in the jar.

ACTIVITY 2 〜〜〜〜〜〜〜〜〜〜〜〜〜〜〜〜〜

Build a Rain Gauge

Students learn how to collect, measure, and reuse rainwater.

Materials

Note: Label the large can Rainwater.

      ✳ a large, empty, clean coffee can and lid

      ✳ empty soup cans (one per group)

      ✳ rulers

      ✳ masking tape

      ✳ Build a Rain Gauge Science Journal page (see page 252)

      ✳ rocks

1   Explain that people who study the weather measure how much rain we get. The instrument they use to measure rain is called a rain gauge. Show students an empty soup can and ask them to suggest ways to use the can to measure rainfall.

2   Divide the class into groups and give each a set of materials. Have group members write their names on a piece of masking tape and put the tape on the bottom of the can. Set the cans outside, away from buildings and trees, where they can fill up with rain. Suggest that they support the cans with rocks so they won't tip over in the wind.

3   After each rainfall, bring the cans inside. Let students use rulers to measure the amount of rain and record their results on their Science Journal page.

4   When they are done measuring the rain each time, have students pour the rainwater into the large coffee can. Use this rainwater to make a Rain Mobile (see page 246). As students continue to collect rainwater, they can use it for Activity 3 (see page 243) and to water classroom plants.

ACTIVITY 3 ～～～～～～～～～～～～～～～～～～～

Contemplating Clouds

Students observe that not all clouds look the same. You might want to use the illustrations in the Science Dictionary to introduce words for different clouds during this activity (see page 239).

Materials

＊ paper and pencil

1 Invite students to observe clouds under various kinds of weather conditions.

　＊ On a sunny day students can sit outside in the school yard, watching and drawing clouds. Have them label these pictures Sunny Day Clouds.

　＊ On a day when the weather is rainy or threatening rain, have students observe from a window. Again, they should draw one or two clouds on a piece of paper and label these pictures Rainy Day Clouds.

2 Also ask students to describe the clouds by color, size, and shape. Make sure they notice the differences between the sunny day clouds and the rainy day clouds.

3 To reinforce the idea that billions of tiny drops come together to make a cloud, give each student a piece of torn paper. Ask students to make as many dots with their pencils as they can on the paper. These dots should be tiny and close together. Explain that the dots they are making are like the droplets of water in a cloud.

4 After you feel students have had enough time to make these dots (about five minutes), ask them to stand up, holding their papers in their hands. Remind them of how the water droplets in the rain experiment cooled and moved closer together (Activity 1, Part 2). Tell students that they are going to act like these droplets, moving closer together. Invite one table or row of students to move together so that their papers can touch. Have them move together toward the blue display paper in the science area (see Science on Display, page 239), and then glue their pieces of paper onto the blue paper, so all the dotted papers are touching.

BOOK BREAK

"One Monday morning the king, the queen, and the little prince came to visit me. But I wasn't home," begins the young boy in the enchanting book *One Monday Morning* by Uri Shulevitz (see Resources, page 253). The story opens with the boy daydreaming at the window, as rain comes down. While the king, the queen, the prince, and a few other royal characters attempt to visit, the rain eventually clears up, and the sun comes out.

5 Repeat with the remaining groups of students, always so that the cloud papers on the board are touching one another.

6 When the dot cloud is complete, let the children go up for a close look. How many droplets (dots) do they see in the cloud? Too many to count! Share with them that each cloud has billions of droplets, which is a lot more than the dots in their cloud! But just like their cloud, the droplets in the air move close together to make the cloud.

ACTIVITY 4 〰〰〰〰〰〰〰〰〰〰〰〰〰〰〰〰〰〰

Where Do Puddles Go?

Students try to find out where puddles go, reinforcing their understanding of the water cycle as introduced in Activity 2.

BOOK BREAK
Read *The Cloud Book* by Tomie dePaola. This book describes different kinds of clouds and the weather associated with them. You'll find folk sayings about clouds and weather, too, which students will have fun discussing. Follow up by asking students if they know of any ways to predict the weather. Does someone have a dog that crawls under a bed when a storm is approaching? Has anyone ever heard that cows lie down if it's going to rain?

Materials (for each pair of students)
  ❋ a clean foam meat tray
  ❋ water
  ❋ an eyedropper (or small paper cup)
  ❋ pencils

1 Let each pair of students create a puddle on a foam tray. To do this, each student should empty one eyedropper full of water onto the tray.

2 One student then traces around the puddle with a pencil.

3 Students carefully place their trays on a windowsill and record their predictions about what will happen to the puddles.

4 Have students check the trays every half hour to hour. (The warmer the location is, the more frequently they need to check.) Each time students check their trays, they should trace around the puddles in pencil.

5 Students will quickly discover that as the puddles dry , they shrink. Ask students where they think the puddles are going. (As the water molecules in the puddle warm up, they move faster and further apart, turning into water vapor. Review with students that these are the same results as in the rain experiment in Activity 1.)

6 Your students can expand their understanding by setting some puddles in sunny, warm locations and others in cool places that are out of direct sunlight. Which puddles dry up (evaporate) more quickly? They will discover that those puddles in the warmer, sunnier locations dry up more quickly.

Note: This would also be a fun activity to take outdoors after a rain. Let students trace around puddles on the playground with chalk. Are all of the puddles the same size? Why do puddles form in different sizes? Have students predict which puddles will dry up first. Revisit the puddles several times to check their predictions. If the puddles are on sidewalks or a paved play area, students can draw chalk circles around the puddles every half hour or so and watch as they get smaller.

Curriculum Connections

MOVEMENT
Creating List Poems

The poem "Sound of Water" is particularly strong because all the watery-sounding words are also action-packed verbs (see page 248). Have students create their own action-word list poems to describe topics of their choice. For example, students might make a list of verbs that tell what hands and fingers can do (slap, clap, wave, tickle, point, etc.) or a list of verbs that describe what dinosaurs did (stomp, chew, tear, roar, etc.). Use this activity to help students add powerful words to their writing.

Invite children to pantomime the action suggested by the words. As you read the poem again, have children act out the verbs. Afterward, talk about the different ways students interpreted the same action words.

LANGUAGE ARTS
Make a Rain Mobile

Plan to make these mobiles in three parts—Part 1 following Activity 1, and Parts 2 and 3 following Activity 2.

Part 1: Let each student trace and cut out three raindrops (provide a simple pattern) out of light blue construction paper. Ask students to write two words that describe rain on each drop, one word on each side, for a total of six words. Laminate these drops to give them a wet and shiny appearance (or paint with white glue diluted with water). Punch a hole in the top of each drop.

Part 2: Give each student two large sheets of white construction paper. Ask them to describe the color of clouds on rainy days (mostly gray). To achieve a rainy-day look, have students paint water over both sheets of paper. Next, they dip their brushes into the water, then in black watercolor paint, and brush across the paper. This allows the paint to blend across the surface of the paper. Set papers aside to dry.

Part 3: When the papers are dry, have students tape pages, painted sides together, then draw a cloud shape. (Clouds should fill the paper.) While the sheets are still taped together, have students cut out their cloud shapes. They can now untape their clouds.

Show students how to tie string through the holes. (Make strings different lengths.) Tape each string to the unpainted side of a cloud cutout. When all three are taped, glue the cloud sheets together, painted sides out. Punch holes in the tops of the clouds and sprinkle the room with showers.

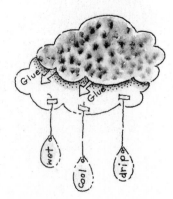

MATH
A Puddle Problem

Challenge your students to solve this problem: Find a way to measure a puddle. Let children work in small groups to devise and test solutions. Allow children time to share their ideas. If no one has suggested it, show students how to measure a puddle by taking a piece of string and laying it around the puddle. When the string is completely around the puddle, cut the string. Pull the piece of string out straight and measure it with a yardstick or meterstick. Let students try guessing the size of some puddles, then use this technique to measure them.

If the weather isn't cooperating, make puddles indoors by cutting puddlelike shapes from light blue paper and laminating them. Place in a math or science center and let students measure the puddles using the string method, then lay them in a row from smallest to largest.

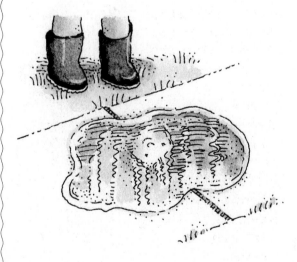

ART
Mini Rain Sticks

This cooperative activity gives students a chance to experience the sounds of other cultures. Rain sticks originated with African and South American cultures. People used natural objects to create these instruments that imitated the sound of rain.

Gather together paper, glue, tape, cardboard tubes (from paper towels and gift wrap) plus beans, rice, pebbles, sand, and other noise-making materials. Follow these directions to make mini-rain sticks with your students.

* Trace two circles that are a half inch larger around than the diameter of the cardboard tube. Make half-inch cuts around each circle.

* Place one circle on one end of the tube, folding down the edges. Tape or glue down the edges to secure this end of the tube.

* Add beans, rice, beads, even small pebbles to the tube (a handful or two total).

* Use the second cardboard circle to cap the other end of the tube and tape or glue in place.

* Decorate the rain stick, then seal it by wrapping it in clear contact paper.

Let students share their rain sticks at the science area, quietly exploring this instrument's relaxing sounds.

Sound of Water

The sound of water is:
Rain,
Lap,
Fold,
Slap,
Gurgle,
Splash,
Churn,
Crash,
Murmur,
Pour,
Ripple,
Roar,
Plunge,
Drip,
Spout,
Skip,
Sprinkle,
Flow,
Ice,
Snow.

—Mary O'Neill

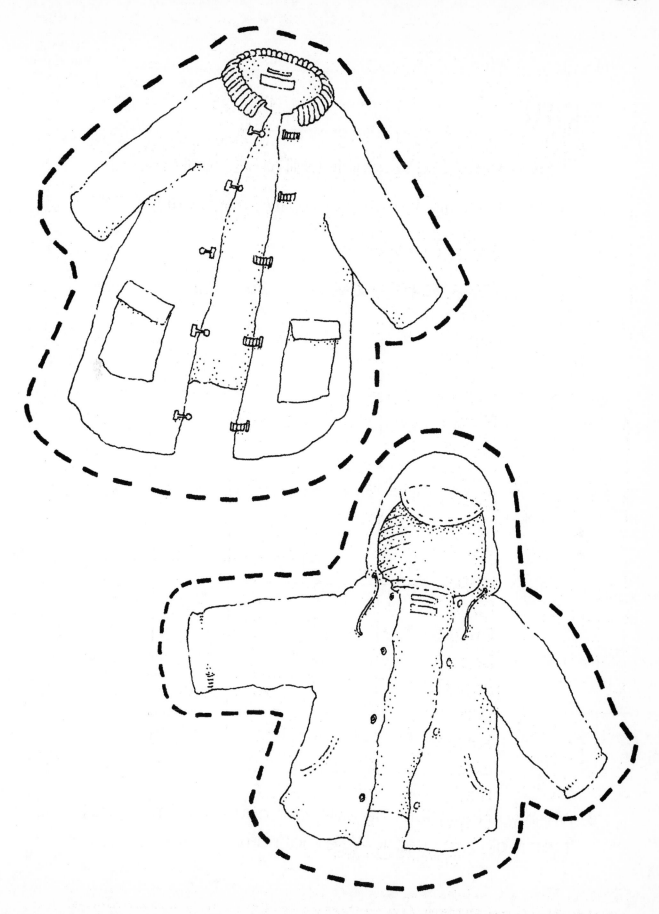

Name _____

April

1. How many days do you think it will rain in April? _____

2. First fill in the dates in April. Each day it rains, cut out
a raindrop and glue it to that day.

Sunday	Monday	Tuesday	Wednesday	Thursday	Friday	Saturday

3. When you complete the calendar, count how many days
it really did rain in April. Write that number here. _____

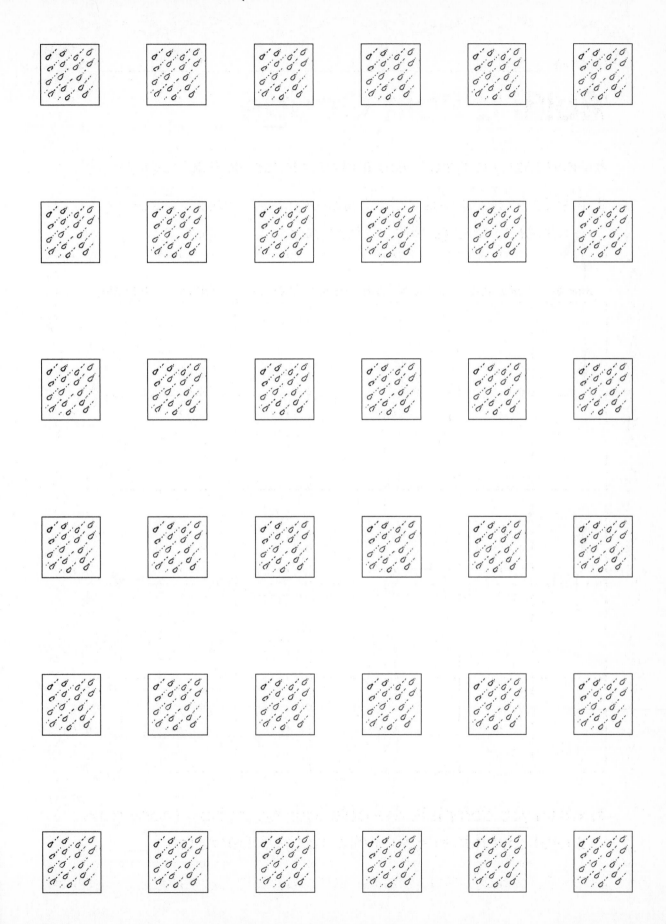

Name _____

Build a Rain Gauge

Directions: Measure the rain in your rain gauge. Color in this amount on the can. Be sure to record the date each time.

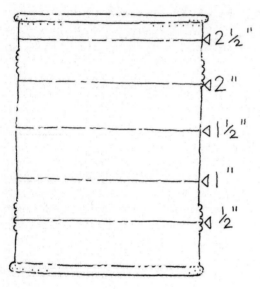

Date: _____

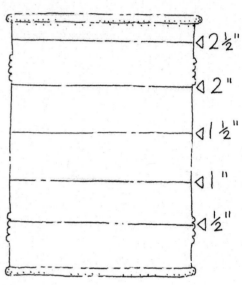

Date: _____

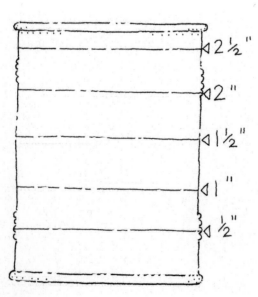

Date: _____

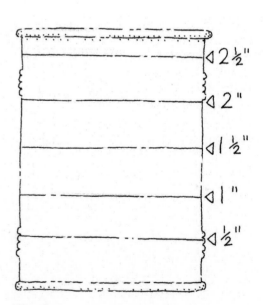

Date: _____

RESOURCES

FOR CHILDREN

The Cloud Book by Tomie dePaola (Scholastic, 1975). Describes the different kinds of clouds and the weather associated with them. Includes folk sayings about clouds and weather. Nonfiction.

Legend of the Bluebonnet by Tomie dePaola (Putnam, 1983). A young girl sacrifices a most treasured possession in order to bring rain to her people. Fiction.

One Monday Morning by Uri Shulevitz (Charles Scribner's Sons, 1967). A young boy is visited by a king, queen, prince, and the entire royal entourage while he sits daydreaming at a window on a rainy day.

Rain Rain Rivers by Uri Shulevitz (Farrar, Straus, Giroux, 1969). A girl watching a rainstorm travels to all the places that the rain touches, via her imagination. Fiction.

Water by Frank Asch (Gulliver Green, 1995). A simple description of water's forms and uses. Nonfiction.

The Water's Journey by Eleonore Schmid (North-South Books, 1995). Clear text and landscape paintings explain the water cycle for young readers. Nonfiction.

FOR TEACHERS

Tiny Life in a Puddle (Rookie Read-About Science) by Bobbi Early (Scholastic, 2006). Use the simple text and colorful photographs to help children learn about the types of organisms that can live in puddles. Nonfiction.

Usborne Science Activities: Science With Water by Helen Edom (Usborne, 2007). A collection of hands-on science activities that teach about characteristics and the states of water.

TECHNOLOGY CONNECTIONS

Ask Dr. Universe
Washington State University
(http://druniverse.wsu.edu/search.asp)
  Why? That's the question Dr. Universe tackles with this site that's chockfull of tough science questions (and down-to-earth answers). For instance, if you search by the topic *rain* you'll find dozens and dozens of interesting questions and answers. Or, invite students to come up with a few questions of their own and learn together with the help of Dr. Universe's reply. After the questions are posted, Dr. Universe's answers remain on the site for everyone else's edification.

Weston Woods: Rainy Day Stories (Scholastic, 2006). This DVD library features two stories: *Come On, Rain!* by Karen Hess and *Noah's Ark* by Jon J. Muth. Both stories are illustrated by Jerry Pinkney. Use the on-screen learning guides or download study guides from Weston Woods at http://teacher.scholastic.com/products/westonwoods/index.htm.

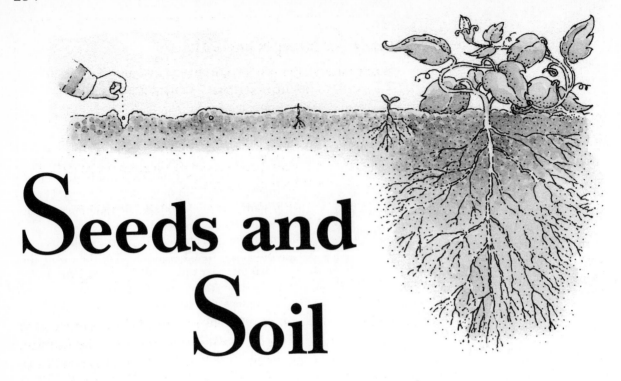

Seeds and Soil

As a natural follow-up to students' exploration of rain and the water cycle, your young scientists can now learn how those April showers help seeds grow. At the same time, students will get a chance to discover the other things that seeds need to grow.

 S c i e n c e   D i c t i o n a r y

germinate to start growing; the amount of time it takes a seed to germinate varies from plant to plant; some seeds may germinate in hours, while others may need weeks, months, or even years to germinate

seed the part of a plant that contains a tiny new plant; the new plant, located inside the seed, is called an *embryo*; there is also food inside the seed to nourish the embryo; these are called *cotyledons*; the seeds are surrounded and protected by the plant's fruit

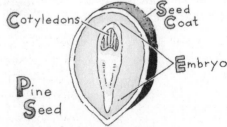

soil the top layer of the Earth where plants can grow; there are four basic types of soil: clay, silt, sand, and loam (a combination of clay, silt, and sand)

Science Concepts and Skills

Concepts: Students will learn that plants need air, water, and light to grow. They will also begin to recognize that plants have a life cycle that includes growing, reproducing, and dying.

Process Skills: observing, predicting, inferring, measuring, collecting and recording data, communicating, comparing, interpreting

Science on Display

Turn the bulletin board (or display space) in your science area into a garden where students' writing grows! Cover the bulletin board with brown craft paper. This will be the soil in which students can plant seed booklets they will be working on while studying seeds.

Add to your science area by displaying a collection of seed catalogs. Invite children to browse through these colorful catalogs, looking at the great variety of plants they can start from seed. Then let kids start their own big seed catalog. Make a catalog by stacking together 27 large sheets of construction paper and using several O-rings to bind them together. Write a title, like Our Big Seed Catalog, on the cover. Write a letter, from *A* to *Z*, on the top right corner of each page (or make use of that Ellison machine in the media center). As students visit the science area, invite them to cut out pictures and names of plants they like, then glue the picture and name to the appropriate pages.

Another fun way to use the catalogs is to make a copy of a generic looking order form. Use in conjunction with math lessons to practice money and other math-related concepts as children pretend to order from the catalogs.

SAFETY NOTE

If you bring in or order seeds for students to handle, please make sure they have not been treated. (Look for this information on seed packets at stores or ask when ordering from a catalog.) Pea seeds, for example, are often dusted with a pinkish colored chemical, and should not be handled by children. Seeds of Change is one company that sells only organic seeds; (888) 762-7333 or www.seedsofchange.com.

ACTIVITY 1 ~~~~~~

Seeds and Where to Find Them

Students look inside a variety of fruits to discover the seeds.

Note: Before starting this activity, write the name of each fruit you have on the left side of the chart paper. Make two more columns, the first for predicted number of seeds, and the second for the actual number of seeds.

Materials

* a variety of fruits, such as cherry tomatoes, apples, oranges, peppers, kiwi (provide one fruit per small group of students)
* knife (for teacher use)
* paper plates
* paper towels
* craft sticks and toothpicks
* chart paper

1   Show students each of the fruits. Remind them that a fruit is the place that holds and protects the seeds of a plant (see Science Dictionary, page 254). Ask each group to predict which of the fruits will have the most seeds. As they give their prediction, ask students to explain their reasoning.

2   Give each group a piece of fruit on a paper plate. Again, ask them to predict the number of seeds that will be in this piece of fruit and record this number on the chart.

3   Cut open the fruit for each group. Tell students that they can use craft sticks or toothpicks to help pull seeds out of the fruit.

4   Have students count the number of seeds in the fruit and record this number on the chart. Next to the name of each fruit, have students in each group draw a picture of the fruit and the seeds.

5   Bring students together to discuss the chart. Which fruit had the most seeds? Did anyone predict that this fruit would have the most seeds? Which fruit had the fewest seeds? Do all (name one of the fruits used) have the same number of seeds? How could we find out? (See Curriculum Connections, Count and Compare, page 263, for more.) Save the seeds from this activity for use with Shape Stories on page 263.

ACTIVITY 2 ~~~~~~

Inside a Seed

Students explore the inside of seeds to find out where new plants, called embryos, come from.

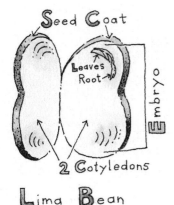

Materials (for each student)

* 2 lima beans (one soaked overnight, one not)
* hand lens
* paper towel
* Lima Bean Book reproducibles (see pages 265 and 266)
* jar

Note: Before the activity, soak enough lima beans so that every student will have one the next day. (Throw in a few extras just in case.) Consider charting related science words for easy reference (see Science Dictionary, page 254).

1 Give each student a lima bean that has not been soaked. How does it feel? What does it look like?

2 Now give each student one of the soaked lima beans. Explain that these are just like the first beans you handed out, but that these beans have been soaking in water overnight. Ask them to compare the two lima beans. How are they different? How are they the same?

3 Show students how to peel off the seed coat of the soaked lima bean. What do they think the seed's coat is for? (Hint: Think coat! It protects the seed until growing conditions are good for the seed.)

4 Next, show students how to open the seed. (It should split open easily.) Explain that inside this seed is a tiny new plant. See if they can locate this new plant. Refer students to the science word chart to find the word for this new plant (embryo). Walk around the room as the students examine their seeds, helping them locate the embryos.

5 Explain that to help the new plant get started, the bean has food-storage areas (cotyledons). What part of the inside of the seed do they think provides the food to the tiny, new plant?

Listen to their ideas, then help them locate the cotyledons (see illustration, previous page).

6 Let students begin their Lima Bean Books. On page 1 they will be drawing and labeling the insides of their lima bean seeds (an outline is provided). On page 2, they trace the dry beans, then place them in a jar of water. You can use the same jar you soaked the first batch of beans in. Just empty it out, collect the dry beans, and add water. This will get the seeds (and the students) ready for the next activity.

ACTIVITY 3

Soak and Sprout

Students discover the changes a seed makes as it grows—and make connections to changes as they grow, too.

Materials

- * jar of lima beans from Activity 2
- * lima beans that have not been soaked
- * resealable plastic sandwich bag (one per student)
- * masking tape
- * paper towels
- * water
- * Lima Bean Book reproducible from Activity 2
- * Soak and Sprout Science Journal page (see page 267)

1 Begin the activity by having students observe the lima beans they placed in water the day before. Ask them to describe the differences they observe. How have the beans changed? What has happened to the water in the jar? (Guide the students to infer that the dried limas soaked up the water. This is why the beans have swelled, causing the seed coats to begin to peel off.) Let students complete page 2 of their journals.

2 For this next part, let students work in pairs. Give each pair two bags, two pieces of masking tape, and two paper towels. Have partners write their names on masking tape and stick the tape to the bags. Next, they should fold the paper towels so they fit inside the bags.

3 Hand out six lima beans per pair (three soaked, three dry). Have students wet the paper towel in one bag, place three soaked limas inside, and seal the bag. Next, have students place the dry beans in the remaining bag (dry towel) and seal. Have students use masking tape to label the bags: Water and No Water.

4 Have students place their bags in a sunny location.

5 Ask students to predict what will happen to the seeds in each bag. How will they know when the seeds are growing? Write their definitions of growing (actually, *germination*) on a piece of chart paper. Explain that for this activity they will need to agree on one definition as a class. Help them decide which definition they will use to determine when their seeds have actually started growing. Write this definition on a chart and display in the science area.

6 Students can complete page 3 of their Lima Bean Books now. They should also check on their seeds daily, recording on their Science Journal page whether or not the seeds in each bag have started growing. Students can use pages 4, 5, and 6 of their Lima Bean Books to record their observations.

7 After the seeds germinate, guide students in a discussion: How do the seeds with moisture compare with the seeds without moisture? From this experiment, what do seeds need to grow? (Moisture.) What else will they need to continue to grow into healthy plants? (Soil and sunlight.) Now is a good time to make connections to what kids need to grow.

Extend the experiment by testing other variables (one at a time), such as light and temperature. Follow up with Everyone Eats Seeds (see Curriculum Connection, page 263).

BOOK BREAK
Lead into a class planting activity by sharing *The Big Seed* by Ellen Howard, a story about a big seed that teaches an important lesson about being just the right size, with engaging watercolors by Lillian Hoban. Your students will be just as curious as the story's Bess to see what grows from the big seed she plants.

ACTIVITY 4 ~~~~~~~~~~~~~~~~~~~~~~~~~~~~~~~~~~~

Sampling Soil

Students will be amazed at how much more there is to dirt than meets the eye.

Materials

* ❋ soil samples (see Note)
* ❋ alum (see Note)
* ❋ newspaper to cover the work areas
* ❋ pitchers of water
* ❋ 2 pint-size glass jars and lids that fit, two paper plates, a tray to set the jars on, a teaspoon, hand lens (for each small group of students)

Note: Before the activity, collect at least two different soil samples. The best way to do this is to dig down at least 6 inches. To get samples that will look different, collect from differ-ent kinds of places, like a farm field and a dry, roadside area or somewhere close to a beach. It would be fun to include a sample from the school yard, if possible. Alum can be found in the spice section of grocery stores. It's used as a separat-ing agent in this experiment. You only need a little bit—so you'll have plenty for a few years to come. It is okay for students to handle alum, just remind them not to put their fingers in their mouths after touching it and to wash their hands after the activity.

1 Divide the class into groups and ask them to cover their work areas with newspaper. Ask: What is soil? Listen to and discuss responses before going on to the next step.

2 Give each group two soil samples, one on a paper plate labeled 1 and the other on a paper plate labeled 2. Students can use pictures and words to record observations: What does the soil look like? Smell like? Feel like? How are the samples the same? Different?

3 Place a pitcher (measuring cups work well, too) of water at each table. Have students pour water to the line marked on the jars.

4 Once they have put water in the jars, students should add five teaspoons of soil sample 1 and add a pinch of alum to jar number 1. They then put five teaspoons of soil sample 2 and a pinch of alum in jar number 2.

5 Have students tighten the lids on the jars and take turns shaking the jars for about 30 seconds. After all students take a turn, the jars should be placed on the trays and left undisturbed. As students observe the soil and water mixtures, ask: What is happening inside the jars? (The soil will begin to separate into fairly distinct layers.) Let students describe and record in their science journals observations of different layers. Are the layers in both jars the same? (If you are using samples from different soil types, you should see some differences in the depth of the layers.)

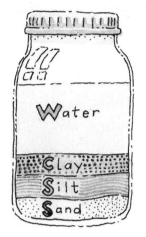

6 Explain that soil is made up of various materials. Some of these materials were once living things (like plants and bugs) that died and decomposed (broke down). This is the layer that is floating at the very top of the jar. The layers at the bottom of the jar are formed from nonliving materials (such as clay, silt, and sand). Clay will be the top layer, silt the middle, and sand the bottom.

7 The samples will continue to settle a little more overnight. After taking another look at them the following day, you can drain off the water and spread the soil on newspaper to dry. Children will enjoy watching the soil that was layered return to its mixed-up ways.

ACTIVITY 5

Grow a Mini-Garden

Tiny planters hold big surprises in this planting activity that connects home and school.

Materials

Note: Invite students to help collect the materials for this activity by asking them to bring in egg cartons and clean eggshell halves. Plan on several eggshell halves per student.

* 1 egg carton per group
* eggshells (halves)
* soil
* sunflower seeds
* water
* plastic wrap
* newspaper

1 Cover a work surface with newspaper and make planting stations with materials for groups of three or four students.

2 Have students gently initial their eggshells, then fill them two-thirds full of soil, plant a seed in each about a quarter inch deep, lightly water, and carefully place their eggshells in the cartons. Cover the cartons with plastic wrap.

3 Have students place their egg cartons in a dark spot and check daily for signs of sprouting plants. They should be sure to keep the soil moist, too. Ask students to record and date daily observations.

4 When the seeds sprout, have students move the cartons to a sunny windowsill and continue to observe.

5 When it's time to transplant, plant eggshell and all in a school garden (or in another approved spot). Ask: What do you think will happen to the eggshell? (It will decompose.) Let each student take an eggshell garden home, too, along with suggestions for transplanting.

Celebrate soil by writing a collaborative poem. Then eat some Dirt Cake. Following are recipes for both.

Poem: Across the top of a piece of chart paper, use black or brown marker to write: What is soil? Below this question, write: Soil is…. Invite students to fill in some words and phrases that describe soil. You can help them along by asking them to think about this theme's soil activities or other experiences they've had with soil. List their ideas on the chart paper, adding children's names after their contributions. To complete the poem, add a little water to your soil samples, just enough to make it stick to students' hands. Let each child press one hand into the mud paint and press it somewhere on the chart.

Dirt Cake

Ingredients:

* ✳ one 16-ounce package chocolate sandwich cookies
* ✳ 2 cups cold milk
* ✳ one 4-ounce box instant chocolate pudding mix
* ✳ one 8-ounce container whipped topping (or the equivalent of whipped cream)

Place cookies in a resealable plastic bag and crush. Pour milk into a bowl, add pudding mix. Beat for two minutes, then let stand five minutes. Stir in the whipped topping and most of the crushed cookies. Place spoonfuls of dirt cake in small cups, sprinkle with cookie crumbs, and serve.

Curriculum Connections

LANGUAGE ARTS
Shape Stories

Use the seeds from Activity 1 for this project. Give each student a piece of white paper. They should fold it in half and draw a picture of one of the fruits on one side of the paper. Next, have them cut out the fruit shape, cutting through both layers of paper. Use one or two staples to hold the two pages together. The top page can be colored to look just like the fruit. Inside, on the second page, students should glue several of the fruits' seeds. (Let them dry first.) They can also write a descriptive sentence on this inside page about the fruit. For example: A kiwi is a round and fuzzy fruit.

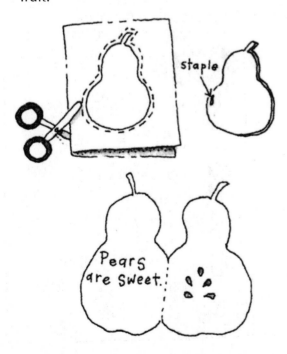

staple

Pears are sweet.

SOCIAL STUDIES
Everyone Eats Seeds

Bring in a bag of dried lima beans. Find out how many students have eaten lima beans before. Ask students if they know of other kinds of beans. Then ask how they've eaten these beans. Explain that beans are a plentiful and popular food source throughout the world.

Cook the lima beans in a pan using a hot plate. Encourage everyone to try at least one lima bean. Along with the limas, serve other edible seeds like peanuts, sesame, sunflower, and garbanzo. (Remember to always check for food allergies first.) Let students give their opinions of the lima beans and other edible seeds on pages 7 and 8 of their Lima Bean Books.

MATH
Count and Compare

The last question from Activity 1 is a fun one to pursue as a math lesson (see step 5). Select just one of the fruits and have each group count the seeds in a piece of this fruit. For example, let each small group count the number of seeds in an apple. Using this information, students can graph and compare the number of seeds found in the individual apples.

MATH
Beans in a Bag

Use a bag of dried lima beans (or other dried seeds) to have students practice skills like estimating, counting by ones, twos, or tens, and measuring. Students can:

* estimate how many beans they think are in the bag,

* empty and count the number of beans in the bag,

* find out how many cups of beans are in the bag,

* find out how much all of the beans weigh and compare this weight with the weight written on the bag,

* estimate and then calculate how to divide the beans so that each student has the same number of beans, and

* mix several kinds of beans or other kinds of seeds together in a bowl, then sort and count the number of each kind of seed.

Follow up by using assorted beans to make mosaics. For a twist, have students press their beans into slabs of clay. Unlike gluing the seeds on paper, this method enables students to change their designs as often as they like.

DRAMA
Guided Garden Imagery

After children have had a chance to sprout real seeds and watch them begin to grow, ask them to tell you the steps in the planting/growing process. Record their ideas on a large piece of chart paper. Refer to the chart as a springboard for a guided imagery session. Have children close their eyes and imagine they are little seeds being planted in the warm, brown soil. Include lots of sensory details and images in your description (warm brown soil; fresh spring rain; creeping, crawling worms; etc.). Use your words to coax the little seeds up through the soil until they sprout and grow tall enough to be picked or harvested.

5

Draw a picture to show
what the growing seeds
look like. Compare this
picture to your drawing on
page 3.

4

Which seeds sprouted first?

_____ water

_____ no water

It took _____ days for
my seeds to start sprouting.

Draw a picture of your face
to show how you feel about
the taste of cooked lima
beans.

LIMA BEAN BOOK

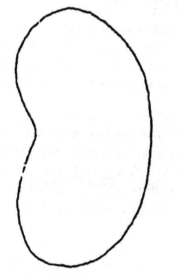

Draw the parts you found
inside the bean.

8

1

3

6

Draw a picture of what you
think the seeds will look like
when they begin to grow.

Draw a picture of
something seeds need
to grow.

Trace around the seed
here.

Draw a picture of each
seed you taste. Label each.

Now soak the seed
overnight. Draw a picture
to show how it looks.

2

7

Name _____

Soak and Sprout

Seed Name _____

Use this seed chart to keep track of when your seeds start to grow.
Each day, write Yes or No to tell if the seeds are growing or not.

	Water	**No Water**
Day 1		
Day 2		
Day 3		
Day 4		
Day 5		
Day 6		
Day 7		
Day 8		
Day 9		
Day 10		
Day 11		
Day 12		
Day 13		
Day 14		
Day 15		

RESOURCES

FOR CHILDREN

The Big Seed by Ellen Howard (Simon & Schuster, 1993). Bess is the smallest child in her class and is always being shoved out of the way. When it's time to plant seeds, she picks one big seed—from a package that pictures flowers that are small, like her—and watches with hope as it grows. Lillian Hoban's charming watercolors add to this story about being just the right size. Nonfiction.

The Gardener by Sarah Stewart (Farrar, Straus & Giroux, 1997). Carefully rendered text and illustrations tell of a girl's efforts to share her optimism with her uncle. This is a touching story that will enchant gardeners of any age. A Caldecott Honor Award winner. Fiction.

The Reason for a Flower by Ruth Heller (Grosset and Dunlap, 1983). Written in rhyme with colorful illustrations, this book introduces concepts related to seeds and plant life cycles. Fiction.

Our Community Garden by Barbara Pollack (Beyond Words, 2004). A young girl and her friends work collaboratively to raise vegetables . . . and end up celebrating diversity and the joys of gardening.

The Tiny Seed by Eric Carle (Picture Book Studio, 1987). Many seeds are released from a single plant and begin their journey. Which seed will survive to germinate and grow into a new plant? Fiction.

FOR TEACHERS

Nature in a Nutshell for Kids by Jean Potter (Jossey-Bass, 1995). Includes directions for 100 hands-on science activities that help children learn about the natural word in which we live.

The Giving Tree by Shel Silverstein (HarperCollins, 1964). Use this classic and contemplative story to prompt discussions about giving and stewardship. Fiction.

TECHNOLOGY CONNECTIONS

Singing in Our Garden by the Banana Slug Band (Let's Get Growing; [800] 408-1868). This tape features songs like "Dirt Made My Lunch," "Decomposition," and Ecology." There is also a songbook to go along with the tape. For a nominal fee you can download MP3s of individual songs (e.g., "Water Cycle Boogie" and "Give Plants a Chance"). Visit: www.amazon.com/Singing-In-Our-Garden/dp/B000R01OX0/ref=sr_1_1?ie=UTF8&s=dmusic&qid=1201719074&sr=1-1

Plant Power
National Geographic Explorer
(http://magma.nationalgeographic.com/ngexplorer/0604/games/game_intro.html)
Reinforce what students are learning about the role plants play in the lives of animals and people with this online game.

SOURCES OF SEEDS

W. Atlee Burpee & Co., 300 Park Avenue, Warminster, PA 18974, (800) 333-5808; www.burpee.com.

Seed Savers Exchange, 3094 North Winn Road, Decorah, IA 52101, (563) 382-5990; www.seedsavers.org.

Seeds of Change, PO Box 152, Spicer, MN, 56288, (888) 762-7333; www.seedsofchange.com.

Native Seeds/SEARCH, 526 North Fourth Avenue, Tucson, AZ 85705, (866) 622-5561; www.nativeseeds.org.

CHAPTER 11

May

Animals at Home

Sun Power

Highlights *of the* Month

Mark these dates, events, and activities on your calendar to help plan and supplement upcoming activities for this month's themes.

✻ May's full moon is called the Flower Moon.

✻ Be Kind to Animals Week is the first week of May.

✻ Hold a pet food drive for a local animal shelter.

✻ Mother's Day: What are names for mother animals? (Beaver, sow; reindeer, doe; sheep, ewe.)

✻ Memorial Day: Talk about tips for sun safety.

Plan Ahead

Start collecting pet care books for Theme 1, Activity 1. Check with veterinarians and local pet shelters.

Begin arranging a visit from an animal expert.

Activity 4 in Theme 1 features a classroom tadpole habitat. If you don't have an aquarium, you might want to send a note home to see if any families have one they're not using.

Your students will be able to catch some rainbows during this month's second theme, Sun Power. Collect pocket-size mirrors for Activity 2: Catch a Rainbow. Prisms are also great for catching and making rainbows. Sources include Delta Education, (800) 258-1302, www.delta-education.com; and Edmund Scientific, (800) 728-6999, http://scientificsonline.com.

SCIENCE AT HOME

Date _____

This month we are starting two new science themes.

1. Animals at Home

Always a favorite, this month we're taking a closer look at animals. If you have a pet at home, talk about the ways your family helps meet that animal's needs. Or think about other animals around your neighborhood, such as birds and bugs. Where do they live?

2. Sun Power

This month we celebrate the sun, observing how it appears to move across the sky (and learning more about what is really happening), as well as investigating how this star warms the Earth. Each child in the class will be keeping a weather calendar, noting sunny days. You can help your child complete the calendar by noting weekend weather together.

Wish List

Do you have materials you can donate for our science explorations? For this month's activities, we need:

_____

_____

_____

Reminders _____

_____

_____

Animals at Home

Bears and bugs. Whales and wolves. If you ask your students to name the things they most like to learn about, you'll find that animals top their lists. As students set off on a classroom safari with this month's activities, they'll meet up with their favorite animals and begin to understand their needs and how different habitats meet those needs.

Science Concepts and Skills

Concepts: As a result of these activities, students will recognize that the world has many different animals and that each of these animals lives in an environment that meets its needs.

Process Skills: observing, predicting, communicating, comparing, collecting and recording data, classifying, interpreting

Science Dictionary

adaptation a characteristic that has developed in an animal (or a plant) that helps it to survive

amphibian a cold-blooded animal that has a backbone and spends part of its life on land and part in water; frogs are amphibians

animal any living creature that can move about by itself, has sense organs, and does not produce its own food

bird a warm-blooded animal that has a backbone, two legs, feathers, and wings

habitat the natural home of an animal (or plant), where it finds food, water, and space to survive

insect a small animal that has a hard covering (exoskeleton), six legs, and three body parts

mammal a warm-blooded animal that has a backbone, is covered with hair, and can nurse its young

reptile a cold-blooded animal with a backbone and scales; reptiles either have four legs or slide along on their bellies

Science on Display

Transform the science area into an interactive mural that students create. Begin by covering the walls with craft paper. Display the title: Who Am I? Gather plenty of books about animals and where they live, along with magazines containing pictures of animals for inspiration and ideas. Invite students to browse the books and magazines for pictures of favorite animals. Ask them to use the pictures as reference to help draw their own pictures of these animals (checking with you first to avoid duplication). Because they are going to be creating animal riddles, explain that students need to keep their animal identities secret. Students can use manila folders as screens while they work.

Provide assorted materials for students' pictures, including markers, colored pencils, crayons, paints, fabric scraps, yarn, etc. Encourage children to draw their animals in their habitats. Next, have them write riddles about their animals, including information about where they live and what they eat. For example: I am green. I eat flies and I live in a pond. Who am I?

When they are finished with both pictures and riddles, give each child two pieces of colored construction paper that have been stapled together along the top. Show students how to glue the picture to the bottom sheet and the riddle to the top, so the riddle covers the picture. Riddles are now ready to add to the mural. Students can visit the display and try to guess which animal is hiding behind each riddle.

ACTIVITY 1 ~~~~~~

Our Pets

Young children are just beginning to understand the ways animals depend on their environment. At this age, when they think of animals, they often think of pets or animals in a zoo. This makes pets an appropriate introduction to a lesson on how habitats help meet animals' needs. Students can then apply what they know to an investigation of animals they are less familiar with—broadening their understanding of habitats as they explore and learn.

This is a perfect opportunity to revisit the concept of habitats developed in Chapter 3: Discover Butterflies (see page 32.) Remind students of the butterfly homes they built. Ask: What did your butterflies need to live? Follow up by asking children to describe ways people help meet the needs of animals such as dogs or cats.

Materials

* chart paper
* reproducible Our Pet Survey (see page 281)

BOOK BREAK
Introduce children to the needs of animals and how people sometimes help provide those needs by sharing a book about pets, such as *The House of a Million Pets* by Ann Hodgman (see Resources, page 283). Explain that pets are animals that we care for by giving them food and shelter. Ask children to describe their own pets' habitats.

1 Begin this activity by talking with students about pets. Questions to focus the discussion include: What is a pet? What are some examples of pets? What kind of care does a pet need? Help students to recognize the parts of a pet's habitat: place (house, yard), food, and water.

2 Divide the class into groups for a school survey. (They can use the survey form included on page 281 or create their own.) Have each group survey a different segment of the school population: people who work in the main office or in the cafeteria; teachers (by grade); etc. What kinds of pets do people have? How do they care for them? (Encourage students to get specific information on shelter and food.) What special needs do pets have? How are these needs met?

3 Bring students together and compile and graph information. Graphs the information will generate include: Kinds of Pets (and number of each), Kinds of Food (dry/wet or by favorite brand), Indoor/Outdoor Shelters.

ACTIVITY 2 ～～～～～～～～～～～～～～～～～～～～

Who Lives Here?

In Activity 1, students learn how people provide habitats for pets. Pets are easy to care for in our homes. But not all animals would be. Most other animals have their own special habitats, places that provide the kind of food and shelter they need. In this activity, students look at the needs of these animals, and discover how different habitats meet those needs.

Materials

* book-making materials (paper, pens, pencils, markers, etc.)
* scissors
* O-rings or other bookbinding materials

Note: This activity is a good opportunity to introduce basic research skills. As students select animals to investigate, help them narrow their search by providing assorted reference materials, such as Golden Book *encyclopedias, nonfiction books about animals, information they request from local animal experts, and online reference tools (see Resources, page 283).*

1 Brainstorm animals that are close to students' home, such as various bugs, birds, small mammals, deer, rabbits, mice, and squirrels. If students live near a zoo, they might want to add zoo animals to the list. (Then follow up the activity with a visit to the zoo, if possible.)

2 Divide the class into pairs and have each pair select an animal. Explain that students will be researching their animals' habitats. You might want to guide their selections to avoid duplication. Help them focus their research by listing key information they need to find out:

* What does this animal eat?
* What kind of shelter does this animal need?
* Where does this animal make its home?
* How does its habitat provide for the animal's needs?

3 Have children gather information, using index cards to organize their notes.

BOOK BREAK
As your students
work on their
pages, they will
enjoy listening to
*The Salamander
Room* by Anne
Mazer (see
Resources, page
283). Many children
will identify with
the young boy in
this story who
brings home a
salamander. What
changes will the
boy need to make
in his room to
meet the
salamander's
needs?

Here's a tip for your young researchers: Have them color-code their index cards by coloring a strip across the top—a different color for each topic. For example, green for food, blue for shelter, red for special needs. Students will have fun using this technique and will have an easier time organizing information on their book pages.

4 When they are ready, ask each team to use their notes to create a page about the animal's habitat for a class flap book. See illustrated steps for one way to construct the pages.

Be sure that students write the information about their animals' habitats on the outside of the page (without naming the animals) and draw and label a picture of the animal in its habitat on the paper under the flap.

5 Bind students' pages into a book. Display the book at the science area for students to read. Set up a schedule for students to take the book home and share with families.

ACTIVITY 3

Square by Square

After sharing the book *One Small Square: Backyard* by Donald M. Silver (Freeman, 1993), discuss the idea of "one small square" being a home to all kinds of creatures. Ask students: What animals do you think you'd meet in one small square of your backyard (or school play area)? Follow up with a trip outside, and explore the earth one square at a time.

Materials

* yardstick or meterstick
* twigs or string
* shovel
* magnifiers
* Science Journals
* field books

1 Start by having students use twigs or string to mark off a square of earth, about a yard long on each side.

2 Have students take turns digging down into the square to a depth of about 12 to 18 inches. Remind students to be gentle to minimize the disturbance to living creatures. Set any grass aside (to replace later).

3 As they work, encourage students to record detailed observations using both pictures and words: What animals live here? What are they doing? What are they eating? (Do nibbled leaves indicate plant eaters? Are they nearby?) What sounds can you hear? What plants do you see? What is the soil like? (Rocky, sandy, etc.)

4 Have students use magnifiers to take a close look at some soil, keeping an eye out for fungus (mushrooms, molds, etc.), small creatures (mites, ants, isopods), and small green plants. Discuss the role soil plays in the lives of living things. (Soil provides habitats for little creatures, minerals and nutrients for plants). How is soil important in our lives?

5 As they work, have children map what they see, using field books to help identify plants and animals and draw them.

6 Revisit the square at the same time on another day and at different times. Compare observations. Remind students to record the date and time of each visit.

7 Be sure to have students replace the soil and replant the grass when finished.

ACTIVITY 4

A Tadpole Nursery

Note: If you live in an urban area and will not be able to find tadpoles or frog eggs for your nursery, consider picking up guppies at a pet store or building a bug box instead. You can follow the directions in Chapter 3, on page 34, to build a butterfly home like the one pictured here, or try this:

* *Place clay around the entire inside bottom edge of a clean tuna can.*

* *Roll a piece of metal mesh screen (about 6 by 12 inches) into a tube shape and secure with several twist ties. Press the screen tube into the clay.*

* *Use the second tuna can as a lid for your bug box.*

Magnifier bug boxes are available from science supply companies such as Delta Education, (800) 258-1302, www.delta-education.com; and Edmund Scientific, (800) 728-6999, scientificsonline.com.

It is not uncommon this time of year for students to show up in the classroom with a jarful of frog eggs or tadpoles. And their natural fascination multiplies if they can observe the eggs hatching into tadpoles. Here are some suggestions for creating a classroom habitat for amphibians. Depending on the time of year and the amphibian species, students may even get to see the tadpoles fully transform into the adult stage, as they gain valuable experience in providing for the needs of animals.

Materials

* an aquarium
* pond water
* one or two rocks (large enough so that part of the rock sits above water)
* small container of pond mud

SETTING UP

1 Have students use a thermometer to scout out a location for the aquarium—someplace that can be kept around room temperature (about 62° to 72°F) and is out of direct sunlight. Depending on the kind of thermometer you have, keep it somewhere in, on, or near the tank to check the temperature.

2 Fill the aquarium one third to one half full of pond water. Add mud and rocks. (The mud helps provide nutrients to the water for the tadpoles. It will settle to the bottom.)

3 Add eggs or tadpoles to the aquarium. A couple dozen eggs should be just about right.

4 After the eggs hatch (or if you already have tadpoles), you will need to supply food. This is best done by adding more pond water (with a little pond muck thrown in).

THINGS TO DO AT THE AQUARIUM

BOOK BREAK

Revisit the concept of metamorphosis with *From Tadpole to Frog* by Wendy Pfeffer. Remind students of the changes they saw in their butterflies (see Chapter 3, page 32). If possible, look back together at students' earlier journal entries. How long did it take their caterpillars to turn into butterflies? How long do they think it takes tadpoles to turn into frogs? After reading the story, compare the life cycles of these two creatures.

1 Ask students if they have ever seen a frog. What kinds of things did they see in the frog's habitat? (Students who haven't seen frogs can use information from Wendy Pfeffer's *From Tadpole to Frog* (see Book Break, this page).

2 Keep several hand lenses near the aquarium. Invite students to take a close look at developing eggs and tadpoles, and to record changes they see in their science journals.

3 When the tadpoles have grown legs and lost their tails, they are adult frogs and will spend time out of the water (on the rocks). Encourage students to use field guides to identify their frogs. (It is possible that what you thought were frog eggs and tadpoles may turn out to be toads or newts!)

4 You may wish to keep the frogs for a couple of days, so be prepared to feed them mealworms or flies. After a couple of days, let students decide where to release the frogs.

5 If the school year ends before the tadpoles become adult frogs, try to bring in a live frog so the students can observe the differences between the tadpole part of the life cycle and the adult stage. If you can't get a live frog, use color photographs. Discuss how the life cycle of the frog compares to that of a butterfly. Then, like you did with the butterflies, release your wildlife into its natural habitat.

COMMUNITY HELPERS

Animal Experts

As students learn about different animals and their needs, they are sure to have lots of questions. This would be a good time to invite several visitors to the classroom to share their expertise in caring for different animals. Good choices include a humane society worker, a veterinarian, or a farmer. Also invite pet owners, including your students and their parents. Let these guests know ahead of time that your class is learning about the needs of animals. Another good idea is to provide guests with a list of student questions before they arrive in your classroom. Take photographs of each visitor. After the visit, have students dictate a story about the visit and what they learned. Compile these visits into a class book or album.

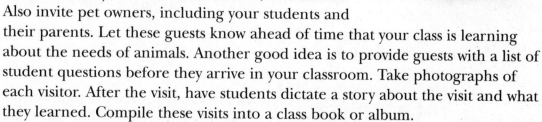

Curriculum Connections

LANGUAGE ARTS
Jump, Wiggle, Jiggle

Read "Jump or Jiggle" on page 282 aloud, inviting children to act out the words that tell how each animal moves. Then have pairs from Activity 2 write a line about the animal they researched (working with another pair to make them rhyme) using "Jump or Jiggle" as a model. Have children illustrate their parts, then collate pages into a class book of animal movements.

LANGUAGE ARTS
Interactive Animal Dictionary

Make an interactive animal dictionary that will help students learn about animals and reinforce reference skills, too. Make copies of a page divided into three parts, as shown. Have each student choose an animal to research. (You can have them check with you to avoid duplication or write names of animals on slips of paper and let students choose at random.) Have each child write the name of the animal across the top, draw a picture of the animal in the bottom left, and describe the animal in the bottom right.

Cut off the top third of each child's paper, mix up the order, and staple across the top. Put the bottom sections together and staple along the left side. Let students play with the book in pairs, trying to match the bottom section with the top section.

MATH
Look Again

Follow up on Activity 3 by inviting students to take another look at the habitats they discovered in one small square of earth. Working in pairs or small groups, have students create picture graphs of their findings. You might offer a structure for this (for example, graphing mammals, birds, amphibians, insects, fungi, plants, rocks, etc.) or leave it up to students to decide on a plan.

Our Pet Survey

THEME:
Animals
at Home

Group Members _____

_____

Name of Owner	Type of Pet	Type of Food	Where the Pet Lives

Jump or Jiggle

Frogs jump
Caterpillars hump

Worms wiggle
Bugs jiggle

Rabbits hop
Horses clop

Snakes slide
Sea gulls glide

Mice creep
Deer leap

Puppies bounce
Kittens pounce

Lions stalk—
But—
I walk!

—Evelyn Beyer

RESOURCES

FOR CHILDREN

And So They Build by Bert Kitchen (Candlewick Press, 1993). Discover the fascinating nests and homes different animals construct. Nonfiction.

From Tadpole to Frog by Wendy Pfeffer (Let's-Read-and-Find-Out Science/HarperCollins, 1994). A pond wakes up when the winter ice melts, giving young readers a look at metamorphosis. Back pages profile five different kinds of frogs. A map shows where bullfrogs live in the United States. Nonfiction.

The Great Kapok Tree by Lynne Cherry (Harcourt Brace Jovanovich, 1990). As a tree-cutting laborer sleeps under the kapok tree, animals from the rain forest visit him and tell him of the need to preserve the trees. Fiction.

The House of a Million Pets by Ann Hodgman (Holt, 2007). This memoir delights readers with entertaining anecdotes about raising and caring for ordinary and extraordinary pets. Fiction.

One Small Square: Backyard and *One Small Square: Pond* by Donald M. Silver (Freeman, 1993 and 1995). Like others in the acclaimed *One Small Square* series, these books introduce children to the richness of life in different habitats.

The Salamander Room by Anne Mazer (Knopf, 1991). A young boy brings a salamander home, then begins thinking about the changes that would need to happen in his own room to meet the needs of the salamander. Fiction.

FOR TEACHERS

mammalabilia by Douglas Florian (Voyager, 2004). A collection of playful animal poems accompanied by the poet's own illustrations. Share these poems aloud.

Story Stretchers for the Primary Grades by Shirley C. Raines and Robert J. Canady (Gryphon House, 1992). Several chapters highlight books and activities to help students learn more about animals and their habitats.

TECHNOLOGY CONNECTIONS

Xpeditions
National Geographic
(www.nationalgeographic.com/xpeditions/lessons/gk2.html)
> The lessons on this site are searchable by grade level as well as by the geography standard you're trying to address. Among other topics, you'll find dozens of activities on animals and where they live.

e.encyclopedia: Animal (Dorling Kindersley, 2005). This resource is the result of a collaborative effort between Dorling Kindersley and Google. It combines online learning with the breadth of an encyclopedia. Want to know more about a particular animal? Begin your research with the book and then visit the Web site that supports it (and keeps the URLs current). Students will find cross-referencing throughout the text, spectacular photographs, and oodles of information.

Sun Power

It is responsible for lighting and heating the Earth, the appearance of day and night, the seasons, the wind, the food we eat, even rainbows! It's easy to see why people for centuries have celebrated the sun. Your students will probably have their own reasons for celebrating the sun, namely warm weather to play outside! Take advantage of these sunny days to introduce your students to the powers of the sun.

Science Concepts and Skills

Concepts: Students will observe that the sun appears to move across the sky in the same way every day. They will also observe that the sun provides the light and heat necessary to warm the Earth.

Process Skills: observing, inferring, predicting, measuring, collecting and recording data, comparing, classifying, interpreting

S c i e n c e   D i c t i o n a r y

heat a form of energy that makes something feel warm or hot

light energy that allows us to see

rainbow a band of colors created by the sun's light passing through water; the colors of a rainbow are always in this order: red, orange, yellow, green, blue, indigo, violet

sun the star that is closest to Earth; it is a medium-sized star; the sun provides our planet with heat and light

Science on Display

Cut out a large sun from yellow craft paper. Outline the sun with orange marker. Ask students to think of words that describe the sun, listing them on the sun shape. Display the sun in the science area in a spot where students can easily read or add to the words.

Now cut out rays of yellow and orange paper. Ask students to name some things they can do because of the sun. (For example: "I can go swimming on sunny days" and "The sun helps dry our wet clothes.") Write a few of their ideas on the rays (one per ray) and attach them to the sun display. Place extra rays at the display and invite students to add to the sun as they discover new ways the sun works for them.

Set up a calendar for the month at the science area where students will record sunny days. They can write in the dates and take turns observing the weather each day and drawing a picture of the sun on the days it is shining.

Students revisit the concept of weather this month as they track sunny days and record their observations. Use the May Science Journal page (see page 292) to have students record the number of sunny days this month. This page is similar to the reproducible journal page for April, when students tracked rainy days. For each sunny day, have students cut out a sun and paste it on the calendar in the appropriate space. Questions on the calendar page invite students to analyze the data.

ACTIVITY 1 ～～～～～～～～～～～～～～～～

Sunlight and Heat

This experiment gives you an opportunity to revisit the concept of evaporation and how the sun aids in the evaporation process.

PART 1

Materials

* thermometers (for each student or pair)
* Sunlight and Heat: Part 1 Science Journal page (see page 294)

1   Take students outside on a sunny day, equipped with reproducible charts and pencils. Ask everyone to find a sunny place to sit. After several minutes ask: Can you feel the sun? How does it feel? (Warm on skin and clothing.)

2   Hand out thermometers. Ask students to read the temperatures on their thermometers and record this information on their charts (under 0 Minutes in Sun).

3   Ask students to set their thermometers in their sunny spots, wait five minutes, then read and record the temperature again (under 5 Minutes in Sun). While they are waiting, students can record predictions and scout out a shady spot.

4   Gather at the shady spot. Again, have students set down their thermometers and wait five minutes before reading and recording the temperature (under 5 Minutes in Shade). While waiting, ask them how they think the shady spot temperatures will compare with the sunny spot temperatures (higher, lower, no change). They can record these predictions on the chart under Prediction: 5 Minutes in Shade.

5   Discuss students' data. What can they learn from their charts? Where were the temperatures the warmest? Coolest? Why were the temperatures different? How did the results compare with their predictions?

PART 2

Materials

* thermometers
* cups of cold water
* Sunlight and Heat: Part 2 Science Journal page (see page 295)

1 Have students review their temperature charts from Part 1. Ask them to predict and record what they think will happen if they set a cup of cold water in a sunny spot.

2 Give each student or pair of students a thermometer and a cup of cold water. Have them measure the temperature of the cold water and record this temperature on the worksheet.

3 Have students place the cups in a sunny location, leaving their thermometers in the cups. What do they think the temperature will be in 30 minutes? Again they should record predictions, check the thermometer after a half hour, and record the temperature on the worksheet.

4 Gather students together to discuss their observations. What happened to the cup of cold water? Besides measuring the temperature, were there other ways they could tell the temperature of the water had changed? (By touching it.)

5 A fun way to finish up this activity is to have students make sun tea. Fill a large, clean jar with water. Add herbal tea bags. (Most boxes will recommend a number of bags per amount of water. Try strawberry!) Have students describe what they see happening as the water warms in the sun.

Note: As students wait for their tea to brew, ask: What do you think would happen to a cup of water left in a sunny spot? They may remember from Chapter 10 that the water will eventually disappear. Would water left in a shady spot disappear, too? Place one cup of water in a sunny spot and one cup in a spot that does not receive direct sunlight. Draw lines on both cups indicating the water level. Let students check on the cups every few days and record observations on chart paper. They will discover that the cup in the sunnier location evaporates more quickly, thanks to the sun's heat!

ACTIVITY 2 〰〰〰〰〰〰〰〰〰〰〰〰〰〰〰〰〰〰〰

Catch a Rainbow

Capture the sun's light to find and investigate rainbows.

〰〰〰〰〰〰〰〰〰〰〰〰〰〰〰〰〰〰〰〰〰

Materials

* ❋ glass of water (large enough to hold a small mirror)
* ❋ small mirror
* ❋ piece of white paper
* ❋ prism (optional)

〰〰〰〰〰〰〰〰〰〰〰〰〰〰〰〰〰〰〰〰〰

Note: You'll need to do this activity on a clear, sunny day.

1 Ask students to share stories about rainbows they've seen (in real life or books). What does a rainbow look like? What colors do we see in rainbows?

2 Place the mirror at an angle in the glass of water. Turn the glass so that the mirror is facing the sun. Hold the piece of white paper in front of the glass so that students can better see the colors produced as the sun's light bounces off of the mirror and passes back through the water.

3 Have students identify the colors they see. Explain that these colors always occur in the same sequence in rainbows. An easy way to remember the sequence is to introduce students to ROY G BIV (red, orange, yellow, green, blue, indigo, violet).

4 Explain how a rainbow in the sky is produced in the same way: As the sun's light passes through raindrops, the light is broken into colors that we see as a rainbow.

5 If you have a prism, set it out as well, so students can see the resulting rainbow.

6 Let students make rainbows of their own using watercolor paints. (If you have any rainwater saved from Chapter 10, use this instead of tap water.)

BOOK BREAK
Before beginning Activity 3, invite students to share *All the Colors of the Rainbow* by Allan Fowler. (See Resources, page 296.) This story is rich in images and will inspire your students' own language as they discuss their observations in the following activity.

ACTIVITY 3 ～～～～～～～～～～～～～～～～～～～～～～～～～～～

Does the Sun Move?

Students observe the apparent movement of the sun during the school day.

Note: Before this activity, determine which way is north if you are standing in the school yard. As with Activity 2, it's best if you do this activity on a clear day.

Materials

* chart paper
* yellow or orange marker
* black marker

CAUTION

Remind students that they are not to look directly at the sun, as this can harm their eyes.

1 Take students outside early in the school day. Have them stand facing north with their arms out to their sides. Which of their arms is pointing toward the sun? This is east. Explain that the sun rises in the east every day.

2 Return to the classroom and, on chart paper, draw a picture of a person standing. (You can do this step outside, too, if you prefer.) Have students help you determine where they should add the sun to this chart. Draw the sun on the chart in the proper location. Write the time of day under the sun and label this side of the chart "east."

3 Repeat steps 1 and 2 several times throughout the course of the school day. Each time, have students determine where the sun is in relation to their own bodies (for example, at noon the sun will be directly overhead). Record their observations of the sun's location on the chart, indicating the time of day each time. Explain that, by the end of the day, their arms will be pointing west, because the sun sets in the west every day.

Note: Young children may believe that the sun moves across the sky each day. The next two activities (3 and 4) will help them begin to understand that it is Earth's movement that gives us night and day.

4 Encourage students to go home and make the following observations over a period of a few days:

* When they get up in the morning, on which side of their house is the sun shining?

* When they are getting ready to go to bed, on which side of their house is the sun shining?

Help students recognize that the pattern is always the same. Encourage children to notice a similar pattern with the moon. (Like the sun, the moon rises in the east and sets in the west.)

ACTIVITY 4 ∼∼∼∼∼∼∼∼∼∼∼∼∼∼∼∼∼∼∼∼∼∼∼∼∼∼∼∼∼∼∼

Day and Night

From the time they can talk, children wonder about day and night. Where does the sun go? Why do we have dark? This activity helps children to answer some of their questions and to better understand this part of their daily lives.

∼∼

Materials

   * lamp or flashlight
   * *What Makes Day and Night* by Franklyn Branley (see Resources, page 296)

∼∼

BOOK BREAK
Read *Why the Sun and the Moon Live in the Sky* by Elphinstone Dayrell. (See Resources, page 296.) This retelling of an African legend describes how the sun and the moon once lived on Earth, until water pays a visit and forces them out with floods. Where do they go? The sky, naturally.

1 Ask: Why do we have day and night? Listen carefully to students' responses. (Write down their answers so that all of you can later examine any changes in their understanding.)

2 Begin reading the book aloud. When you get to the experiment on pages 22 and 23, let students do the activity themselves:

   * Begin by having one student be the sun (the light source) and another the Earth.
   * Turn on the lamp or flashlight and have the sun hold it. Have Earth stand, left side facing the sun. Explain that this is like sunrise, when the sun comes up in the morning.
   * Ask Earth to slowly turn until he or she is completely facing the sun. This is the middle of the day.
   * Now have Earth make another quarter turn, so that his or her right arm is pointing toward the sun. This is sunset.
   * Finally, ask Earth to make another quarter turn until his or her back is toward the sun. This is nighttime.

3 Let each student have an opportunity to act out this routine.

4 Finish reading the book. Guide students in making connections between Activity 3, where the sun seems to move across the sky, and this activity, where the Earth actually turns to create day and night.

Curriculum Connections

LANGUAGE ARTS
Day and Night

Have students brainstorm a list of things they do and see during the day and the night. Use two separate pieces of chart paper to list their ideas. Let students use the list as a reference to make a day-and-night book.

First, give each student two pieces of white paper, cut to about 6-inch squares. On one piece, students illustrate and describe something that they do or see during the day. On the second piece, they illustrate and describe something that they do or see at night. Have students center and glue their daytime pictures to yellow construction paper and their night pictures to black construction paper. Students can add sun designs to the yellow border and sticky stars to the black border. Glue yellow and black sheets back-to-back, then stack all pages so that yellow is facing up. Bind with O-rings.

ART
Sun and Sandpaper Pictures

Students can use old crayons for this sunny art project. Cut up sheets of sandpaper into four equal pieces. Have students use the crayons to color pictures of the sun or other designs on the sandpaper.

Remind them to press hard with the crayons. (The heavier the crayon application, the better the results.) Set pictures in a sunny spot and watch what happens. After a while, the heat from the sun will begin to melt the crayon wax. When pictures are heated up and the colors are sticky, have students press plain white paper over the top of the sandpaper pictures and gently rub without moving the paper. When students peel off the paper, they'll have prints of their sun designs. Display in the room with a sign that announces your students' sun art.

ART
Sun Tambourines

Provide each child with two white paper plates and some dried beans. Have each child place a few dried beans on one plate, cover with the other, then staple around the rim. Pass out yellow crepe-paper streamers and have children staple them around the rim, then paint the plates yellow. When the plates are dry, children can glue on glitter accents, if desired. Students can use their sun tambourines to keep time to sunny-sounding music selections (especially appreciated on cloudy days).

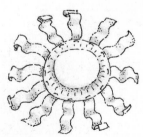

Name _____

May

Write in the dates on this calendar for May.

How many sunny days do you think there will be this month?

Write your prediction here. _____

Sunday	Monday	Tuesday	Wednesday	Thursday	Friday	Saturday

Each sunny day, cut out a sun and glue it to that day. How many days were sunny in May? _____

How does this compare with your prediction?

_____

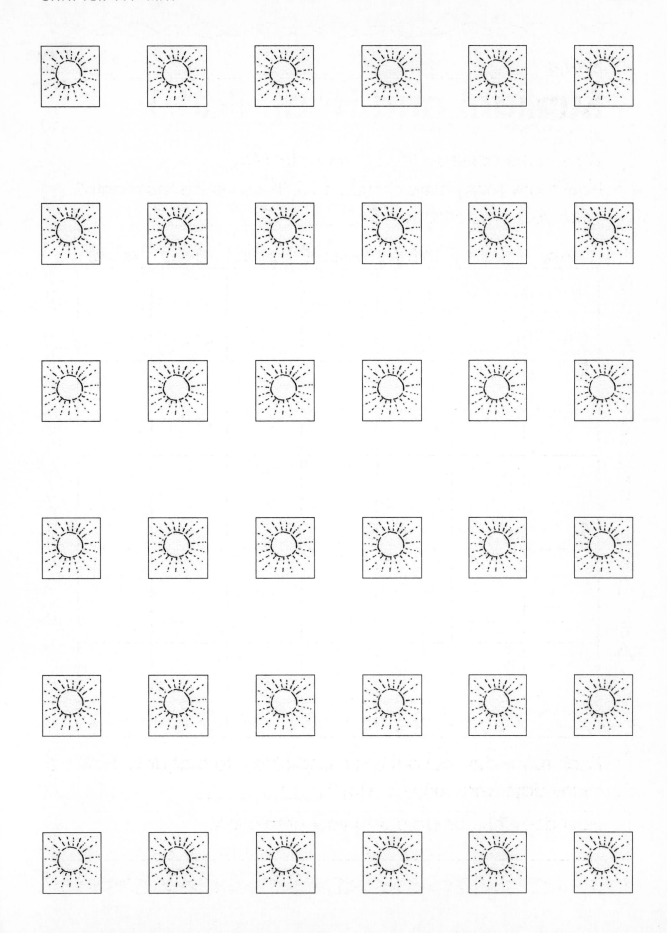

Name _____

THEME:
Sun
Power

Sunlight and Heat: Part 1

DATA COLLECTION CHART			
	0 Minutes in Sun	5 Minutes in Sun	5 Minutes in Shade
My Prediction			
Actual Temp.			

Where were the temperatures the warmest?_____

Where were the temperatures the coolest?_____

Why were the temperatures different? _____

_____

_____

_____

How did your results compare with your predictions?_____

_____

_____

_____

Name_____

Sunlight and Heat: Part 2

Make a prediction. The temperature of the water in the sunny
spot will be: the same _____   higher _____   lower _____

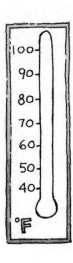

**Before you place the
cup in the sun: Color
in the thermometer
to show the
temperature of
the water.**

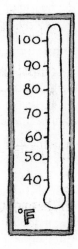

**After 30 minutes in
the sun: Color in the
thermometer to show
the temperature
of the water.**

Write a sentence about what happened to the water in
the sun.

_____

_____

_____

_____

On the back of this paper, draw a picture that shows you
doing a favorite sunny-day activity.

RESOURCES

FOR CHILDREN

All the Colors of the Rainbow (Rookie Read-About Science) by Allan Fowler (Grolier, 1999). A book that helps answer some of the many science questions children have about rainbows. Nonfiction.

The Sun: Our Nearest Star by Franklyn Branley (HarperCollins, 1988). The importance of the sun to our everyday existence is described. Nonfiction.

Sun Up, Sun Down by Gail Gibbons (Harcourt Brace Jovanovich, 1983). Just about everything a child needs to know about the sun is here. Nonfiction.

What Makes Day and Night by Franklyn Branley (HarperCollins, 1986). An excellent explanation for young children as to why we have day and night. Nonfiction.

Why the Sun and the Moon Live in the Sky by Elphinstone Dayrell (Houghton Mifflin, 1987). This retelling of an African legend describes how the sun and the moon once lived on Earth, but were forced by visiting water's floods to move to the sky. A Caldecott Honor book. Fiction.

FOR TEACHERS

How Come by Kathy Wollard (Workman, 1993). If you're looking for a handy resource to help you find answers to your students' questions, you'll appreciate this book. It has easy-to-understand (and entertaining) answers to questions about everyday, science-related phenomena.

Stars by Herbert Zim (Golden Press, 1985). A simple, pocket-size field guide to the stars, including the sun.

TECHNOLOGY CONNECTIONS

Welcome to the Universe (Virtual Exhibit)
Museum of Science, Boston, MA
(www.mos.org/educators/student_resources/virtual_exhibits)

Want to see what the moon looked like the day you were born? That's just one of the exciting things you can do when you visit this site that offers a compendium of links for learning about the cosmos.

Exploratorium
(www.exploratorium.edu/educate/index.html)

Visit Tools for Teaching—offered through Exploratorium, a museum of science, art, and human perception based in San Francisco. Since 1993 this Web site has been providing exciting online opportunities for visitors to explore diverse science topics. Resources include access to Exploratorium's digital library (check out the eclipse photos!), science experiment how-to's, Webcasts, online exhibits, and much more.

GLOSSARY

adaptation a characteristic that has developed in an animal (or plant) that helps it to survive

amphibian a cold-blooded animal that has a backbone and spends part of its life on land and part in water; frogs are amphibians

animal any living creature that can move about by itself, has sense organs, and does not produce its own food

bear a large mammal; three kinds of bears live in North America: the black bear, the grizzly bear, and the polar bear; all go into a winter sleep; black and grizzly bears enter their period of winter sleep when food is scarce, usually during winter months; but polar bears can enter into winter sleep at any time of the year if food is scarce

Beaufort scale a measure of how strong the wind is blowing; wind speed is often estimated using this scale

bird a warm-blooded animal that has a backbone, feathers, wings, two legs, and breathes through lungs; there are more than 9,000 species of birds in the world

butterfly the adult stage of this colorful, winged insect

caterpillar the larval or wormlike stage of a butterfly or moth

chrysalis the hard shell covering the pupa

clouds billions of tiny water drops or ice crystals; as water vapor rises into the atmosphere, it cools; as it cools it condenses and turns into water drops or ice crystals; the droplets or the ice crystals combine with particles of dust or dirt to form a cloud; the shape, size, and color of a cloud can help us forecast the weather

condensation the process by which water vapor cools and turns into drops of water

conifer trees, such as evergreens, that have needles and cones

constellation a pattern of stars that forms an imaginary picture; there are

88 recognized constellations, but only a few of these can be seen year-round; constellations that can be viewed all year are called *circumpolar* constellations, because they are found in the area of the night sky located around the poles of the Earth; Ursa Major (contains the Big Dipper) and Ursa Minor (contains the Little Dipper) are circumpolar constellations in the Northern Hemisphere

crater a bowl-shaped dent or hole made when something like a meteoroid crashes into a surface

deciduous trees that shed all of their leaves during autumn; leaves on these trees are usually broadleaf, unlike the needle-like leaves found on conifers (evergreens); oaks, maples, and birches are examples of deciduous trees

den a cave or shelter for an animal; bears go to dens for the winter, where they sleep until spring comes again

dormancy (or winter sleep) the way some animals cope with winter by "sleeping" for part of the winter; a dormant bear's body temperature drops a little below normal (from about 100°F to 88°F) and its heart rate drops to almost 8 beats per minute (from 50 to 80 beats per minute when active); during winter sleep a bear lives entirely off its stored body fat

drag the air resistance that happens to aircraft as they move forward; opposite of thrust

evaporation the process by which water (a liquid) turns into water vapor (a gas); heat speeds up evaporation because as water molecules warm up they move faster, and evaporate more quickly

freezing when it is cold enough for ice to form

frost frozen water vapor

fruit the part of the plant that forms around the seeds; fruits are usually wet and fleshy (like peaches and berries) or dry and hard (like walnuts and pea pods); there are some fruits that people often think of as vegetables (like tomatoes)

germinate to start growing; the amount of time it takes a seed to germinate varies from plant to plant; some seeds may germinate in hours, while others may need weeks, months, even years to germinate

gravity a downward pulling force

habitat the natural home of an animal (or plant) where it finds food, water, and space to survive

heart a muscular organ that pumps blood through the body

heart rate number of beats per minute; in adults the heart contracts or pumps blood about 70 times each minute; for children ages six to eight the average beats per minute is 65 to 130 (resting)

heat a form of energy that makes something feel warm or hot

hibernation a deep sleep that animals go into during winter; true hibernators (such as bats, chipmunks, and many rodents) experience a drop in body temperature that is just above freezing; the breathing rates of animals that hibernate slow down; if disturbed, true hibernators take several hours to rouse, whereas bears remain relatively alert and can get up right away if they need to

ice water that has become solid; pure water freezes at 32°F

insect a small animal that has a hard covering (exoskeleton), six legs, and three body parts

larva the second stage of metamorphosis, when the insect is wormlike and wingless

leaf the part of the plant where food for the plant is made

magnet an object made from iron and ore that can push or pull objects made of iron or steel

lift a force that helps keep flying things aloft, or in the air

light energy that allows us to see

mammal a warm-blooded animal that has a backbone, is covered with hair, and can nurse its young

metamorphosis the changes that happen during a lifetime

migration the movement of some animals from one place to another to find food and shelter

moon a huge ball of rock; the closest planetary body to our planet

moon phases new, waxing crescent, first quarter, waxing gibbous, full moon, waning gibbous, last quarter, waning crescent (every 28 days the moon passes through all its phases); the phase or appearance of the moon depends on how much of the sunlit half of the moon we are able to see from Earth; if you look closely at the moon during the various phases (excluding full moon), you will probably see the part of the moon that is in Earth's shadow

nutrition the kinds of foods we need to stay healthy, including proteins, carbohydrates, fats, vitamins, minerals, and some fiber; examples of these nutrients are found in the food pyramid

opaque something that you can't see through, like a notebook

penguin a mostly black-and-white bird that lives near the oceans in the Southern Hemisphere; there are 18 species of penguins

photosynthesis the way plants use sunlight to make food

precipitation the solid (snow, hail, frost) and liquid (rain) states of water that fall from the sky

pulse the way arteries throb when the heart contracts

pupa the third stage of metamorphosis, when the larva is changing into the adult insect inside a hard shell or cocoon; also called a chrysalis

push and pull forces that cause motion

rainbow a band of colors created by the sun's light passing through water; the colors of a rainbow are always in this order: red, orange, yellow, green, blue, indigo, violet

rain gauge the instrument used to measure rainfall

relief the changes or ups and downs in a surface

reptile a cold-blooded animal with a backbone and scales; reptiles either have four legs or slide along on their bellies

seed the part of a plant that contains a tiny new plant; the new plant, located inside the seed, is called an *embryo*; there is also food inside the seed to nourish the embryo; these are called *cotyledons*; the seeds are surrounded and protected by the plant's fruit

shadow a dark shape that is made when an object blocks out the light

shooting stars these are not stars at all; they are *meteors,* or glowing chunks of rock moving through space at great speed; a "shooting star" may be spotted on any night, but there are times of the year when there are meteor showers and many meteors per hour can be seen; the most productive meteor shower of the year happens to fall during the first days of January (see Highlights of the Month, page 146)

snow tiny six-sided ice crystals; each crystal is different, but every crystal is hexagonal (six-sided)

soil the top layer of the Earth where plants can grow; there are four basic types of soil: clay, silt, sand, and loam

star a ball of gas that can be seen in the night sky as a small point of light; stars come in different sizes and colors; the star nearest to our planet is the sun; stars differ from the planets and our moon in that they give off their own light (Planets and the moon shine because they reflect light from the sun.)

storm a very strong wind that usually includes rain, snow, or hail and sometimes thunder and lightning

sun the star that is closest to Earth; it is a medium-sized star; the sun provides our planet with heat and light

temperature a measure of how hot or cold something is; we measure temperature with a thermometer

thermometer an instrument for measuring how hot or cold something is; when the liquid inside a thermometer is heated, the liquid expands and moves up the tube; when the liquid cools, it contracts and moves down the tube

thrust the force that pushes an aircraft forward

translucent something that you can see through, but not clearly, like a piece of wax paper

transparent something you can see through clearly, like window glass

water cycle   the movement of water from clouds to the Earth and back to the clouds again; the rain falling today is the made up of the same water that fell on Earth as rain millions of years ago

weather   a description of the conditions outside, including temperature, precipitation, and wind

wind   moving air; as air is warmed by the sun, it rises, and colder, denser air moves in to replace it; the direction and strength of the wind is influenced by geographical features like mountains, deserts, and bodies of water; the direction of the wind, determined by where the wind is blowing from, often affects our weather

wind vane   instrument used to show wind direction

winter   the time of year when, in the Northern Hemisphere, the Earth's axis is pointing away from the sun; as a result, the sun's rays are hitting this part of the Earth at more of an angle and are scattered over a larger area, so they do not heat the Earth as much as the more direct rays of summer